New Perspectives on Conflict and Ireland in the Nineteenth Century

The Society for the Study of Nineteenth-Century Ireland

SSNCI

The Society for the Study of Nineteenth-Century Ireland

The purpose of the Society is to promote research into nineteenth-century Ireland, and membership is open to scholars both from Ireland and other countries. The Society welcomes members from a wide range of disciplines: literature, history, economics, geography, sociology, anthropology, theology, women's studies, fine arts, etc. It thus seeks to foster an inter-disciplinary approach to nineteenth-century Irish studies.

Series editors: Ciaran O'Neill & Olwen Purdue

New Perspectives on Conflict and Ireland in the Nineteenth Century

EDITED BY

PAUL HUDDIE, CATHAL BILLINGS &
ARLENE CRAMPSIE

LIVERPOOL UNIVERSITY PRESS

First published 2025 by
Liverpool University Press
4 Cambridge Street
Liverpool
L69 7ZU

British Library Cataloguing-in-Publication data
A British Library CIP record is available

ISBN 978-1-83624-389-2
eISBN (PDF) 978-1-83624-407-3
eISBN (ePub) 978-1-83624-378-6

The manufacturer's authorised representative in the EU for product safety is:
Easy Access System Europe, Mustamäe tee 50, 10621 Tallinn, Estonia
https://easproject.com (gpsr.requests@easproject.com)

Typeset by Carnegie Book Production, Lancaster
Printed and bound by CPI Group (UK) Ltd, Croydon CR0 4YY

Contents

Warfare

Figures

Contributors

Cathal Billings is a lecturer in Modern Irish at University College Dublin, where he is Director of the de Bhaldraithe Centre for Irish Language Scholarship and Academic Director of the MA in Irish Writing and Communications. He is a graduate of UCD (BA, 2006; MA, 2007; PhD, 2014) and is interested primarily in the social and political history of the Irish language revival, Irish sports history and translation. He is currently writing a monograph on the impact of the Boer War on the Irish language revival, and has recently published articles on the same topic in *Australasian Journal of Irish studies, Éigse: A Journal of Irish studies* and *Comhar Taighde*.

William Butler is Head of Modern Collections at The National Archives, UK, with responsibility for promoting its military records. He previously worked as an Outreach Officer at the University of Kent, where he also completed his PhD. He has published work on nineteenth- and twentieth-century Irish history, and the history of the British army, including *The Irish amateur military tradition in the British Army, 1854–1992* (MUP, 2016); *The disparity of sacrifice; Irish recruitment to the British Armed Forces, 1914–1918* (LUP, 2023); and, most recently, co-authored a study of the National Archives records in *Captives: prisoners of war and internees 1939–1945* (History Press, 2024).

Julien Clénet is a graduate of UCD where he currently lectures in the Sociology of Sport. His research focuses on recreation and leisure in nineteenth-century Dublin. He has published articles on Irish soccer and is currently completing a monograph on the emergence and development of modern sport in Dublin.

Arlene Crampsie is a lecturer in Historical Geography at UCD. She is a graduate of Trinity College Dublin (BA, 2003; PhD, 2008). Her research interests lie at the intersection of political, socio-cultural and environmental geographies highlighting the evolution of everyday lives and landscapes through archival and oral history methodologies. She is a Director and Committee

Member of the Oral History Network of Ireland and a committee member of the Geographical Society of Ireland.

Timothy D. Hoyt is a Professor of Strategy and Policy at the US Naval War College, where he holds the John Nicholas Brown Chair of Counterterrorism. He received a PhD in international relations and strategic studies from Johns Hopkins University's School of Advanced International Studies. He is working on a book on the strategy of the Irish republican movement during the Irish Revolution and has made multiple presentations to Irish audiences during the Decade of Centenaries.

Paul Huddie is a historical researcher interested in war and society, principally within the British Empire in the long nineteenth century. His specialisms include the Crimean War, Royal Navy reserve services and British military charities. He is a graduate of UCD (BA, 2008; MA 2009) and Queen's University Belfast (PhD, 2014) and is the author of *The Crimean War and Irish society* (2015). He is the founder and coordinator of both the International Network for Crimean War Studies and the Military Welfare History Network.

William Jenkins is an associate professor in the Department of History at York University, Toronto, where he teaches courses on the histories of modern Ireland and North American immigration. He is the author of the award-winning *Between raid and rebellion: the Irish in Buffalo and Toronto, 1867–1916* (2013) and the editor of the forthcoming *Canada and the Great Irish Famine*, to be published by McGill-Queen's University Press. He is currently writing a book on Irish famine and post-famine immigrants in Toronto through their interrelationships with poverty, crime and street culture. He has served since 2021 as president of the Canadian Association for Irish Studies / L'association Canadienne d'Études Irlandaises.

Ciarán McCabe is a lecturer in modern Irish history at Queen's University Belfast. Among his publications are *Begging, charity and religion in pre-Famine Ireland* (2018) and *Dublin and the Great Irish Famine* (jointly edited with Emily Mark-FitzGerald and Ciarán Reilly), as well as chapters on charity and poverty in the *Oxford history of British and Irish Catholicism* (2023) and Bloomsbury's *Cultural history of poverty* (forthcoming, 2025). Ciarán is a fellow of the Royal Historical Society and serves as secretary of the Economic and Social History Society of Ireland.

Michelle McGoff-McCann is a professional historian and independent researcher. She holds a PhD in history from Queen's University Belfast and is the author of *Melancholy madness: a coroner's casebook* (2003), *The Irish coroner: death, murder and politics in Co. Monaghan, 1846–78* (2023) and other published chapters and articles. She specialises in writing and speaking on nineteenth-century Irish history. Michelle is currently working on several publications with the Irish Manuscripts Commission and a monograph on the Bath Estate, County Monaghan.

Liam Mac Mathúna is Emeritus Professor of Irish at UCD. Among his recent publications are *Douglas Hyde: my American journey* (co-ed., 2019), *The Ó Neachtain window on Gaelic Dublin, 1700–1750* (2021), *Douglas Hyde: Irish ideology and international impact* (co-ed. M. Nic an Bhaird, 2023), and the chapter 'Irish–English bilingualism', in *The Oxford handbook of Irish English* (ed. R. Hickey, 2024). Editor of *Éigse: A Journal of Irish Studies* (NUI), he is currently engaged in research on the Ó Neachtain circle in eighteenth-century Dublin, and the life and work of Douglas Hyde (in collaboration with Dr Máire Nic an Bhaird) as part of a study of the impact of modernity on Irish language communities.

Patrick Maume is a graduate of University College Cork and Queen's University Belfast who works as a researcher for the Royal Irish Academy's *Dictionary of Irish biography*. He is a longstanding member of the Society for the Study of Nineteenth-Century Ireland (SSNCI) who has published extensively on the political and cultural history of nineteenth-century Ireland with special reference to newspapers and print culture, religion, nationalism and unionism. His recent publications include (co-edited with Daire Hogan) *The reminiscences of Ignatius O'Brien, Baron Shandon, Lord Chancellor of Ireland* (Dublin, 2021) and 'After Castle Rackrent: The Wardlaws (1896) and Literary Responses to Maria Edgeworth's Castle Rackrent', in Heather Laird and Jay R. Roszman (eds), *Dwelling(s) in nineteenth-century Ireland* (Liverpool, 2023).

Kathryn Milligan is an art historian specialising in nineteenth- and twentieth-century Irish art, and Assistant Librarian at the Edward Murphy Library, National College of Art & Design. Kathryn's first monograph, *Painting Dublin, 1886–1949: visualising a changing city*, was published by Manchester University Press in 2020. Recent and forthcoming publications include chapters on W. B. Yeats and Dublin Art Institutions and the history of exhibitions in Dublin during the late nineteenth and early twentieth centuries.

Máire Nic an Bhaird is Associate Professor at Maynooth University, specialises in censorship of Irish language literature, the life and the work of Ireland's first president, Douglas Hyde, children's literature, and science–society nexus education. Awarded the 2022 Maynooth Teaching Award, she leads the €2M

Horizon Europe BioBeo project, creating tailored education programmes that are disseminating the bioeconomy concept throughout Europe. Máire also collaborates on the €8M Horizon 2020 AgroCycle project, translating circular economy concepts for primary school curricula. With numerous publications, she actively engages in H2020 research bids and shares her expertise on national and international media.

Gerry O'Keeffe is an imperial historian and independent researcher. Having spent more than thirty years in the global technology industry, he was awarded a doctorate in history in 2022 through Maynooth University. His research explores the military and social histories of Irish soldiers serving in the British East India Company's Indian armies in the middle third of the nineteenth century and sheds new light on Ireland's nuanced and unstable relationship with the British Empire during the nineteenth century. Gerry delivers numerous archaeological field walks, history lectures and tutorials, heritage presentations and tours annually.

Kerron Ó Luain is a Research Fellow in Acadamh na hOllscolaíochta Gaeilge, University of Galway, where he is conducting research on Irish language services within the Public Service on behalf of The Department of the Gaeltacht. His forthcoming book *Cath idir an Pobal agus an Murder Machine: Stair Ghluaiseacht na Gaelscolaíochta c. 1973–2023* analyses the development of the gaelscoil movement over the past half-century through the lenses of class and decolonisation. He is currently working on a book focusing on the radical potentialities of the Irish language for Cork University Press's *Síreacht: longings for another Ireland* series.

Introduction

Paul Huddie, Cathal Billings and Arlene Crampsie

Overview

When it comes to the narrative of conflict and nineteenth-century Ireland, nowhere is its connection and embedded nature more clearly illustrated than in two of the core textbooks on the period from the past generation, namely D.G. Boyce's *Nineteenth century Ireland: a search for stability* and K. Theodore Hoppen's *Ireland since 1800: conflict and conformity*.[1] Boyce, in the opening lines of his work, notes that the century was bookended 'with a rebellion followed by a civil war',[2] while in between, for Hoppen, 'conflict of all kinds – among neighbours, within families, between social groups, between nationalists and unionists, between rulers and ruled – form[ed] a kind of rolling bass to much of what happened in the years since 1800'.[3] And so it has been for decades that the history of Ireland in the nineteenth century, both at home and abroad, has been one of conflict.[4] Scores of books and hundreds of articles and chapters have been written on multiple types of conflicts and areas of discord and contention.

Yet despite this broad and multi-disciplinary historiography, not one book has been written focusing solely on this diverse theme. Much has been written on rebellions and uprisings, on subversive groups and organisations, on inter-faith and intercommunity rancour and violence, on the volatile political landscape, on legal high-profile court cases, and on Irishmen's involvement in the armies of Britain and multiple foreign powers around the world. Various

1 K.T. Hoppen, *Ireland since 1800: conflict and conformity* (London, 1999); D.G. Boyce, *Nineteenth century Ireland: the search for stability* (Dublin, 2005).

2 Boyce, *Nineteenth century Ireland*, p. 1.

3 Hoppen, *Ireland since 1800*, p. i.

4 For example, William Jenkins, *Between raid and rebellion; the Irish in Buffalo and Toronto, 1867–1916* (Montreal and London, 2013); D.M. MacRaild, *Faith, fraternity and fighting: the Orange Order and Irish migrants in Northern England, c. 1850–1920* (Liverpool, 2005).

publications have examined the significance of form, mode and genre, for example, in representing and negotiating conflict, considering how conflict is portrayed in fiction, art, music and drama and how different forms of conflict permeated, influenced and were influenced by popular culture, such as literature and ballads.[5] Indeed, areas such as these, as Barr, Buckley and O'Cinneide have shown, featured recurring and sometimes virulent 'cultural conflict'; at certain times, '[t]o read in Ireland, to read while being Irish, was to enter into contested cultural exchanges'.[6] This is in addition to lesser-researched and under-discussed personal, or inner conflicts as well as familial and intergenerational conflicts. As Roy Foster notes, the revolutionary generation that came of age in late nineteenth-century Ireland 'became alienated not only from British rule but from the values and ambitions of their parents', with the political radicalisation of Irish society reflecting a generational shift as 'the fracture between old and new broke along lines of age as well as of ideology'.[7]

Conflict permeated the realm of culture in nineteenth-century Ireland too, as seen in the areas of language, literature and sport during the Irish Revival in particular. For example, while festivals and great national campaigns to promote Irishness in all facets of life may have been a unifying force among Gaelic Leaguers, its members simultaneously engaged one another in vigorous and public debate on topics such as teaching methods and the use of colloquial or classical Irish, orthography and font.[8] The creation of a modern literature in Irish not only brought Gaels into conflict with their Anglo-Irish counterparts over the 'national' credentials of their works,[9] but it also provoked strife amongst themselves as progressives sought to emulate their continental peers, while traditionalists stood firm that Ireland's literature should reflect her

5 For example, R.A. Barr, Sarah-Anne Buckley and Muireann O'Cinneide (eds), *Literacy, language and reading in nineteenth-century Ireland* (Liverpool, 2019); N.A. Kelly, *Imaging the great Irish famine: representing dispossession in visual culture* (London, 2020).

6 Barr, Buckley & O'Cinneide, *Literacy, language and reading*, p. 11.

7 R.F. Foster, *Vivid faces: the revolutionary generation in Ireland 1890–1923* (London, 2015), pp xxii, 1–4 and chap. 1.

8 On teaching methods, see for example Máire McCafferty, 'You cannot teach the children of Ireland Irish until the teachers have got Irish themselves': na Coláistí Samhraidh agus modhanna múinte na Gaeilge, 1904–1922' in *Comhar Taighde*, viii (2022), DOI: 10.18669/ct.2022.02; on debates on the use of colloquial Irish in literature, see Liam Mac Mathúna, '*Séadna* agus *Abhráin grádh Chuige Connacht*: caint na ndaoine, an meon Gaelach agus an nua-aoiseacht' in *Léann*, iii (2014), pp 53–79; for debates on Gaelic font, see Brian Ó Conchubhair, 'The Gaelic font controversy: the Gaelic League's (post-colonial) crux' in *Irish University Review*, xxxiii, no. 1 (2003), pp 46–63.

9 Regina Uí Chollatáin, *An Claidheamh Soluis agus Fáinne an Lae* (Dublin, 2004), pp 69–74; P.J. Mathews, *Revival: the Abbey Theatre, Sinn Féin, the Gaelic League and the co-operative movement* (Cork, 2003), pp 57–60; Philip O'Leary, *The prose literature of the Gaelic revival, 1881–1921: ideology and innovation* (University Park, PA, 1994), chap. 5.

ancient manuscript heritage.[10] Furthermore, as T.G. McMahon has shown,[11] different factions of revivalists embraced contrasting identities, held wildly varying attitudes towards the practical use and promotion of the language and, more significantly, espoused and promoted political ideals contrary to the founding principles of the organisation of which they were part.[12]

Similar tensions between cultural and political forms of nationalism and activism were also present in the sporting realm, as has been shown by the considerable body of work that has examined the emergence of the Gaelic Athletic Association, its intersection with nationalist politics and its efforts to utilise sport both as a vehicle for expressing national identity and challenging British imperial culture in Ireland.[13] However, as a number of social and local histories of Irish sport have shown, the process by which specific politico-cultural identities came to be attached to particular games was, by the turn of the twentieth century, far from complete. Rather, one's decision to go 'native' or 'foreign' on the playing field often depended less on political ideology and more on socio-economic status, with class constituting the primary factor in determining the constituency of Irish games in late nineteenth-century Ireland.[14]

Further still, other researchers have engaged with conflict in the realm of law, which overlaps with so many other areas, such as policing, crime, politics, diplomacy, religion, business, workers' rights, gender issues, incarceration, imperialism and conflict in the courts.[15] Publications in the legal field range

10 O'Leary, *The prose literature of the Gaelic Revival*, esp. chaps 1 and 2.

11 T.G. McMahon, *Grand opportunity: the Gaelic revival and Irish society 1893–1910* (Syracuse, 2008).

12 See for example Cathal Billings, 'Cogadh na mBórach agus an pholaitíocht forbartha náisiúnach i gConradh na Gaeilge' in *Éigse: a Journal of Irish Studies*, xli, no. 1 (2021), pp 212–35; Regina Uí Chollatáin, 'Ó Chéitinn go Conradh: the revivalists and the 1916 Rising' in *Studies in Arts and Humanities*, ii, no. 1 (2016), pp 52–66; B.P. Murphy, 'J.J. O'Kelly, the *Catholic Bulletin* and contemporary Irish cultural historians' in *Archivium Hibernicum*, xliv (1989), pp 71–88.

13 See esp. W.F. Mandle, *The Gaelic Athletic Association and Irish nationalist politics* (Dublin, 1987). See also: David Hassan and Andrew McGuire, 'The GAA and revolutionary Irish politics in late nineteenth- and early twentieth-century Ireland' in *Sport in Society*, xix, no. 1 (2016), pp 51–61; Mike Cronin, *Sport and nationalism in Ireland: Gaelic games, soccer and Irish identity since 1884* (Dublin, 1999).

14 This was similarly true of sport in Victorian England: see Mike Huggins, *The Victorians and sport* (London, 2004), p. 19. For insight into the socio-economic profiles of Irish sports, see for example Conor Curran, *The development of sport in Donegal 1880–1935* (Cork, 2015); Liam O'Callaghan, *Rugby in Munster: a social and cultural history* (Cork, 2011), esp. chaps 3 and 5; and Tom Hunt, *Sport and society in Victorian Ireland: the case of Westmeath* (Cork, 2007), esp. chap. 4.

15 Examples of this include Elaine Farrell, *Women, crime and punishment in Ireland: life in the nineteenth-century convict prison* (Cambridge, 2020) and Kyle Hughes and D.M. McRaild (eds), *Crime, violence and the Irish in the nineteenth century* (Liverpool, 2017).

from the personal level to the political, with the former comprising family conflict (marriage breakdown, domestic abuse), civil conflict (disputes over property, wills, land, commercial cases), employer–employee conflict and criminal conflict (petty or localised violence, feuds, gangs, intimidation). Amongst the latter are the contested issues of land agitation and tithes, which often led to agrarian and sectarian violence and conflict.[16] Beyond the courts, conflict and the administration of 'justice' (or 'rough justice') has also been the focus of historians who have looked at secret societies and local and parliamentary elections.[17]

Most evidently though, conflict was manifest and personified daily through the multifarious Crown Forces in Ireland: the British army, the Royal Navy, the Militia, the Coastguard, the Royal Naval Coast Volunteers, the Royal Naval Reserve and the police forces. For several historians and historical commentators, as far back as the sixteenth century, Ireland was a place of perpetual conflict: 'a land of war in which peace occasionally and fitfully breaks out'.[18] This (perceived) condition necessitated the presence of a large military garrison from the eighteenth century until 1921.[19] On the one hand, many Irish people actively opposed and subverted the work of these forces, particularly as the nineteenth century progressed and 'Irish people became more synonymous with efforts to subvert … and reform the empire'.[20] On the other hand, cooperation, engagement and interaction with these forces was also deeply embedded in Irish society, not least of all through recruitment. Thus, 'from the beginnings of the British Empire in the sixteenth century, Irishmen played a prominent role in helping to conquer and to govern both Ireland and the various parts of the globe to which British power and influence extended'.[21] But there were also many who sat somewhere in the middle, between service and resistance, a fact noted by Jill Bender in relation to the significant number of the Irish-born soldiers who identified as Irish nationalists but who helped suppress the Indian mutiny of 1857–9.[22]

16 See case studies by D.S. Lucey, *Land, popular politics and agrarian violence in Ireland: the case of County Kerry, 1872–86* (Dublin, 2011) and Noreen Higgins, *Tipperary's tithe war 1830–1838: parish accounts of resistance against a church tax* (Tipperary, 2002).
17 For example, Kyle Hughes & D.M. MacRaild, *Ribbon societies in nineteenth-century Ireland and its diaspora: the persistence of tradition* (Liverpool, 2018) and K.T. Hoppen, *Elections, politics and society in Ireland 1832–1885* (Oxford, 1984).
18 Thomas Bartlett & Keith Jeffrey, *A military history of Ireland* (Cambridge, 1996), p. 6.
19 Ibid.
20 Barry Crosbie, 'Ireland and the empire in the nineteenth century' in James Kelly (ed.), *The Cambridge history of Ireland Vol. III 1730–1880* (Cambridge, 2018), p. 620.
21 Ibid., p. 627.
22 Jill Bender, 'Mutiny or freedom fight? The 1857 Indian Mutiny and the Irish press' in S.J. Potter (ed.), *Newspapers and empire in Ireland and Britain: reporting the British Empire, c. 1857–1921* (Dublin, 2004), p. 102. Irish-born soldiers constituted 42 per cent of the

This diverse and complex theme of *conflict and Ireland in the nineteenth century* is the focus of this volume. It is the product of the annual conference of the Society for the Study of Nineteenth-Century Ireland (SSNCI), which was held at University College Dublin in June 2022. That event brought together forty-eight researchers from across Ireland, Europe and North America, representing a range of disciplinary backgrounds and international and transnational perspectives. Over the course of two days, they presented papers providing new perspectives and approaches to the study of the history of conflict relative to Ireland and Irish people throughout the world in the long nineteenth century. Eleven of those papers are presented here and grouped together under three broad themes: 'Religious Conflict', 'Conflict in Society' and 'Warfare'.

Religious Conflict

The nineteenth century was a period of transformation and transition for religious bodies in Ireland. The formal ending of the penal laws through emancipation and the disestablishment of the Church of Ireland altered the balance of power between the churches, while the widening of the franchise towards the end of the century politically weakened the long-held dominance of the mainly Protestant Anglo-Irish Ascendancy. As Joseph Ruane notes, this was also a period of church and religious renewal that led to growing religious mobilisation across the island.[23] This mobilisation was further reinforced by grassroots organisations, including the Orange Order, the Catholic Association and the Ancient Order of Hibernians among others, whose more political focus fed growing tensions. While many of the inter- and intra- denominational conflicts that emerged in this period are already well documented, the chapters by William Jenkins, Ciarán McCabe and Patrick Maume offer diverse and novel perspectives on their respective case studies.

The first chapter in this volume by Jenkins explores the place of group-based social conflict in the lives of immigrants in Ontario, Canada, between 1820 and 1880. Taking 'the Irish' – Protestants (primarily from Ulster) and Catholic (primarily from Munster) – as a case study, he discusses a series of 'trouble-spots' involving predominantly male groups in Canada's primary growth region in the nineteenth century. Although many social conflicts

regular army and 50 per cent of the East India Company's army in 1857. See Kevin Kenny, 'The Irish in the empire' in idem (ed.), *Ireland and the British Empire* (Oxford, 2004), pp 104–5.

23 Joseph Ruane, 'Long conflict and how it ends: Protestants and Catholics in Europe and Ireland' in *Irish Political Studies*, xxxvi, no. 1 (2021), pp 109–31.

did not involve the Irish, it was inevitable that they, as the most prominent immigrant group in the region at the time, were at the centre of many confrontations concerning land, labour, religion, collective identity and the shape of community values. Taking a multi-directional viewpoint, Jenkins highlights that such conflicts did not always pit Irish Catholics against bourgeois Protestant elites, but also against French-Canadians, unscrupulous bosses and contractors, soldiers and policemen, and, on occasion, other Irish Catholics, often for reasons of regional background. Jenkins's Ontario case study provides not only an excellent example of conflict relative to the Irish diaspora in the nineteenth century, but also a useful comparison for present-day multiracial and multi-faith Canada, where immigration dynamics are a near-constant in public and political debates.

In Chapter 2, Ciarán McCabe examines the parish vestry as a site of growing interdenominational conflict in early nineteenth-century Ireland. A much understudied institution, the parish vestry constituted a public forum open to ratepayers in Church of Ireland parishes. Though originally restricted to Church of Ireland congregants, from the 1720s Roman Catholics and Presbyterians who paid the parish tax, or cess, were permitted to attend their local vestry and have their say on a variety of local issues, including parish spending, but not on matters relating to the church itself. The vestry thus provided civically engaged Catholics and (predominantly Presbyterian) Dissenters with an important opportunity to participate actively in the management of their community. McCabe's analysis illustrates how these meetings became a battleground where Catholics and Protestants vied for political power, and how seemingly insignificant issues of local governance functioned as a lightning rod for underlying sectarian tension and conflict within the community.

The timing of these incidents is significant, of course. The 1830s was a decade of growing Catholic confidence, as O'Connell's campaign for emancipation had 'raised a people who were degraded and defeated', and fostered in them 'a new kind of involvement in politics'.[24] This manifested on a macro level in popular opposition to paying the tithe from 1830, but, as McCabe suggests, it was also reflected on a micro, or local, level in the parish vestry. With their privileged minority position under threat from Catholic democracy, some Church of Ireland members and Presbyterians chose to forget their confessional differences and sought to promote Protestant unity.[25] This desire was not shared by many grassroots Presbyterians, however, who rejected

24 P.M. Geoghegan, 'The influence of O'Connell, 1815–1850' in J. Kelly (ed.), *The Cambridge history of Ireland volume III: 1730–1880* (Cambridge, 2018), pp 126, 115.

25 J.H. Murphy, 'Introduction' in idem (ed.), *Evangelicals and Catholics in nineteenth-century Ireland* (Dublin, 2005), p. 9.

the Established Church as the institution of their landlords and of political conservatism.[26] Far more than petty squabbles in cramped parish halls over the funding of street cleaning or the payment of the organists' salaries, the conflicts McCabe presents are rather locally felt symptoms of a broader and ever-intensifying inter- and intra-religious power struggle that informed much of the story of conflict in nineteenth century Ireland.[27]

Finally, in Chapter 3, Patrick Maume presents the case study of John Duncan Craig, Church of Ireland clergyman, language student, preacher and Orangeman. He shows that attitudes associated with Irish society in the first half of the nineteenth century (also evident in McCabe's work) survived in certain quarters for decades afterwards, allowing later nineteenth-century conflicts to incorporate older loyalist narratives into their thoughts, outlooks, writing, preaching and political activities. They also display the fantasy and half-concealed despair of political and cultural intransigence that featured so prominently amongst many in the Anglo-Irish elite and Irish unionists in the latter decades and into the Edwardian period. Looking at Craig's writings and public speeches, Maume discusses how he related his continental interests (including serving as a Prussian Army chaplain in the Franco-Prussian War of 1870 and Protestant evangelism on the Riviera) to his Irish experiences, which he then assimilated into a wider narrative of conflict between Catholicism and Protestantism across Europe.

Conflict in Society

The essays contributed to this volume by Máire Nic an Bhaird and Liam Mac Mathúna, Kerron Ó Luain, Michelle McGoff-McCann and Julien Clénet are illustrative of the extent to which conflict suffused nineteenth-century Irish society, particularly in the realms of language, law and leisure. Writing in *The handbook of the Irish Revival*, Kiberd and Mathews advised their reader against thinking that the cultural Revival that blossomed in fin-de-siècle Ireland 'was a great communal moment of liberal and harmonious revelation' and rather highlighted the 'serious ideological differences' held by many who considered themselves Revivalists.[28] Similarly, Valente and Howe's more recent and unique appraisal of the Revival finds a 'complex system' rather than a 'unified

26 A.R. Holmes, 'Protestantism in the nineteenth century: revival and crisis' in Kelly (ed.), *The Cambridge history of Ireland volume III*, pp 339, 340.

27 Boyce, *Nineteenth century Ireland*, p. 328.

28 Declan Kiberd & P.J. Mathews, *Handbook of the Irish Revival: an anthology of Irish cultural and political writings 1891–1922* (Dublin, 2015), p. 26.

ideological endeavour', in which 'individual components or agents follow their own respective paths, toward their own respective aims'.[29]

Such complexity and conflict could also be identified within the constituent organisations of the cultural Revival, and this is especially true of the Gaelic League as its members debated the past, present and future of the Irish language. It is perhaps fitting, then, that the man who most came to symbolise the apolitical Gaelic League, its co-founder and first president, Douglas Hyde, should also be formed and defined by conflict. Further contributing to their own considerable body of work on Hyde's personal life, career and international influence,[30] Chapter 4, by Máire Nic an Bhaird and Liam Mac Mathúna, is rooted in an in-depth examination of the thirteen personal diaries kept by Hyde between 1874 and 1912. These ego-documents elucidate the many conflicts surrounding self-identity, familial relationships, religion, politics, culture and the Gaelic Revival that permeated Hyde's early home life, influenced his development as a scholar and informed his later public career.[31] Nic an Bhaird and Mac Mathúna examine in particular Hyde's use of various pseudonyms that reveal, albeit surreptitiously, his deeply held political beliefs and the lasting influence of those he learned Irish from as a boy in rural County Roscommon.

In his introduction to Douglas Hyde's collected essays and lectures, Ó Conaire observed how British colonial policy was largely successful in its aim to instigate cultural change in Ireland, as the population broadly became ignorant of their own language, history, music and literature. He argued, however, that '[a]n even more malign outcome was the inculcation of the seeds of shame and inferiority in the minds of Irish speakers for their own language'.[32] Kerron Ó Luain's contribution to this volume attempts to trace the history of a tool designed to sow those seeds of shame and inferiority in Irish speakers: the *bata scóir*, or tally stick. Writing of the *bata scóir*, Hyde himself described how 'fathers and mothers ... tied sticks round the necks of the children to keep them from talking Irish, and every time they spoke a word a notch was cut in the stick, and when they went to school next morning

29 Joseph Valente & Marjorie Howes, 'Introduction: a complex revival' in idem (eds), *The Irish Revival: a complex vision* (Syracuse, 2023), pp 2–3.

30 See for example: Liam Mac Mathúna & Máire Nic an Bhaird (eds), *Douglas Hyde: Irish ideology and international impact* (Dublin, 2023); and Máire Nic an Bhaird, Liam Mac Mathúna, Brian Ó Conchubhair, Niall Comer & Cuan Ó Seireadáin, *Douglas Hyde: my American journey* (Dublin, 2019).

31 For further insights into Hyde's early life, and the various conflicts therein, see G.W. Dunleavey & J.E. Dunleavey, *Douglas Hyde: a maker of modern Ireland* (Oakland, 1991); on Hyde and politics, see Earnán de Blaghd, 'Hyde in conflict' in Seán Ó Tuama (ed.), *The Gaelic League idea* (Cork, 1972), pp 31–40.

32 Breandán Ó Conaire (ed.), *Language, lore and lyrics: essays and lectures by Douglas Hyde* (Dublin, 1986), p. 20.

they were beaten in proportion to the number of notches'.[33] Such a scenario is illustrative of the way in which the decline of the Irish language in the public sphere, which began in earnest in the sixteenth century and continued apace during the penal-law era, was followed by the rapid and almost total eclipse of Irish as the language of the hearth and home during the nineteenth century.[34] The *bata scóir* allegedly played an important role in this process, yet contemporary, first-hand accounts – either by victim or perpetrator – of its use are hard to come by and its prevalence as a tool of cultural oppression was contested during the nineteenth century itself. Using archival and press sources, Ó Luain therefore examines when, how and where the *bata scóir* was used and posits explanations for its decline during the nineteenth century. In doing so, he contributes essential new insights into the history of an object that has loomed large in narratives of the decline and revival of Irish, although it has attracted a surprising lack of scholarly attention.

The Great Irish Famine of 1845–52 was 'a subsistence crisis and social calamity without parallel in nineteenth-century Europe'.[35] In addition to the estimated one million deaths over the famine period itself, it 'precipitated a virtual tidal wave of emigration' leading some four million people to leave Ireland from 1845 to 1865.[36] A multitude of topics relative to this catastrophe have been engaged with by scholars over the past half-century, including landlord–tenant relations, the decline of the Irish language and the Catholic devotional revolution.[37] While topics like workhouses, soup kitchens, public works schemes and coffin ships are well known, others remain largely untouched, such as the work of county coroners during this period, the basis of Chapter 6, by Michelle McGoff-McCann.

Using a cross-section of newspapers, official government reports and correspondence between local and administrative officials, she illuminates

33 Douglas Hyde, 'Drafts of essays and lectures by Douglas Hyde; mainly relating to Irish language and literature and their revival' (N.L.I., Douglas Hyde Papers, MS 17,756, pp 26–7).

34 Gearóid Ó Tuathaigh, *I mbéal an bháis: the Great Famine and the language shift in nineteenth-century Ireland* (Hamden CT., 2015); N.M. Wolf, *An Irish-speaking island: state, religion, community, and the linguistic landscape in Ireland*, 1770–1870 (Madison, WI, 2014), p. 13; Joep Leersen, *Hidden Ireland: public sphere* (Syracuse, 2006), p. 33; Seán de Fréine, *The great silence* (Dublin, 1965), p. 131.

35 Ó Tuathaigh, *I mbéal an bháis*, p. 7.

36 Ibid.

37 Ibid., pp 7–8; Cormac Ó Gráda, *Ireland before and after the Famine* (2nd ed., Manchester, 1993); J.S. Donnelly, Jr, 'Production, prices, and exports, 1846–51' in W.E. Vaughan (ed.), *A new history of Ireland, union*, i, 1801–70 (Oxford, 2010), pp 286–93; idem, *Landlord and tenant in nineteenth-century Ireland* (Dublin, 1973), p. 81; Emmet Larkin, 'The devotional revolution in Ireland, 1850–1875' in *American Historical Review*, lxxvii, no. 3 (1972), pp 648–50.

the widespread conflict surrounding inquests (public inquiries into sudden or suspicious death). McGoff-McCann not only illustrates how coroners captured the circumstances surrounding excess deaths owing to starvation and disease, but also how some were refused payment for their services and threatened with abolition by MPs and county grand juries displeased by their findings. In highlighting the destitute circumstances of the poorest in society, the coroners' inquests shed an unwelcome spotlight on the contributory role played by government legislation and mismanagement by local elites, of which the coroner was very often a member. McGoff-McCann's chapter highlights the contemporary debates around coroners' utility in investigating deaths during the Famine, and their value for the local elites who were legally obliged to pay for their services. It further reveals the challenges faced by coroners who were brought centre stage in social and political conflict during the humanitarian crisis.

Conflict has also been a recurring theme throughout the history of sport and leisure in Ireland, an academic area that has seen rapid growth, especially in the past thirty years. As noted by Lane and Murphy, much of this scholarship has understandably focused on the modern sporting 'revolution' of the final decades of the nineteenth century.[38] This imbalance in the historiography has lately been addressed in studies that have examined the evolution of Irish sport in the broader context of leisure and set it against social, cultural, political and economic change since the seventeenth century.[39] The rapid onset of industrialisation during the nineteenth century in particular drove major societal change, resulting in a more complex stratification of society and the emergence of an aspirational middle class who came to dominate education, politics and the press. They soon brought their influence to bear on the world of recreation too, seeking to mould it according to their own tastes and morals. Their prime targets were the informal, unregulated, sometimes violent, alcohol-fuelled and gambling-led pastimes of the impoverished masses,[40] which traditionally took place in public spaces. These were out of harmony with a middle-class desire for 'rational recreation' and with the new modes of behaviour expected of citizens in the public sphere.[41] As James Kelly notes, 'the respectable had powerful allies', and these social standards were endorsed by municipal authorities and

38 Leeann Lane & William Murphy, 'Introduction' in idem (eds), *Leisure and the Irish in the nineteenth century* (Liverpool, 2016), pp 2–3.

39 See esp. James Kelly, *Sport in Ireland 1600–1840* (Dublin, 2014) and Paul Rouse, *Sport and Ireland: a history* (Oxford, 2015).

40 Rouse, *Sport and Ireland*, chap. 2; James Kelly, 'Sport and recreation in the eighteenth and nineteenth centuries' in idem (ed.), *The Cambridge history of Ireland vol. III*, pp 489–90, 502, 508.

41 Peter Bailey, *Leisure and social class in Victorian England: rational recreation and the contest for control, 1830–1885* (London, 1978).

enforced by a more effective police force, who 'compelled … "recreations" … and traditional field sports to modify in order to survive, and traditional fairs and patterns to cease or to change'.[42]

In Chapter 7, Julien Clénet traces the dynamics of this social and sporting conflict as it played out in Dublin City during the nineteenth century. He traces how the delegitimisation of traditional pastimes was reinforced by the creation of public parks, playgrounds and dedicated sporting grounds throughout Dublin's suburbs, as the city urbanised. These highly regulated spaces reflected the aesthetic tastes, moral values and socio-economic aspirations of their proprietors and catered for the bureaucratised and commercialised recreations of the middle-class. However, as Clénet shows, their efforts to stamp out traditional recreations were met with only moderate success, and the conflict between the middle and working classes over what constituted legitimate places to play continued throughout the late nineteenth century and beyond. This research represents a novel and important contribution to the history of Irish sport and leisure, complementing the work of Vanessa Rutherford on playground culture in nineteenth-century Dublin,[43] for example, as well as that of Hunt, Curran and Bracken in their studies of the social, cultural, political and economic forces that shaped local sporting cultures in nineteenth century Ireland.[44] Clénet's study also adds a new chapter to the historiography of the social and spatial development of Dublin, which has largely overlooked the importance of leisure and sporting culture in shaping the city and the lives of its citizens.[45]

Warfare

For centuries Ireland was home to a large and visible military garrison, owing to recurring periods of conflict and to perceived threats, both internal and external. Additionally, the presence of the British army and Royal Navy in and around Ireland permeated society and was both felt and seen in the country's politics, at social events, in local economies and through a multitude of popular cultural outlets. Moreover, as Bartlett and Jeffrey have argued, the presence of the British army and the auxiliary forces in Ireland, including the Royal Irish Constabulary, in the nineteenth century clearly shows the

42 Kelly, *Sport and recreation*, p. 489.

43 Vanessa Rutherford, 'Muscles and morals: children's playground culture in Ireland 1836–1918' in Lane & Murphy, *Leisure and the Irish*, pp 61–79.

44 Curran, *The development of sport in Donegal*; Hunt, *Sport and society*; Patrick Bracken, *'Foreign and fantastic field sports': cricket in county Tipperary* (Thurles, 2004).

45 Mary Daly, *Dublin, the deposed capital: a social and economic history, 1860–1914* (Cork, 1985); David Dickson, *Dublin: the making of a capital city* (Dublin, 2014).

interwoven nature of civil and military power: 'In short, it is incontestable that armed men in uniform were, to a degree unthinkable in England, everywhere in Ireland in the period 1600 to 1900 and after.'[46] Sometimes, that military presence was reassuring; often, it was intimidating. At all times, however, it served as a reminder that conflict was never far away and it inevitably reached its apex in times of war and unrest. Together, William Butler, Gerry O'Keeffe, Kathryn Milligan and Tim Hoyt show the diverse ways in which war and warfare were manifest in nineteenth-century Ireland: through the presence of the British army in Ireland's countryside and urban areas; through the portrayal of the army or of high-profile individuals within the army in the press or artistic works; and through the persistent but elusive presence and threat of militant nationalists.

During the latter half of the nineteenth century, the locally recruited Irish militia formed a significant part of the military fabric in the country, especially during periods of international conflict and invasion scares, such as the French Revolutionary and Napoleonic Wars and the Crimean War.[47] Consisting largely of the labouring classes, officered by the local landed gentry, it played a significant part of British defence planning, dealing primarily with conflict at home. This manifested in several ways, but principally in tensions and occasionally outright hostility between regiments and civilians in the localities where they were based during periods of embodiment, or annual training. There was also conflict and suspicion between the authorities and the individuals that formed the nucleus of the force, fuelled by accusations that the members would rise up against British rule if provided with the opportunity. William Butler's contribution, in Chapter 8, examines this form of conflict, taking examples from across the latter half of the nineteenth century. He also places these tensions into a wider context exploring how the public in Ireland and Great Britain viewed the Irish militia. The militia in Ireland clearly held a prominent role in society. Occasionally, this worked in its favour; it usually proved to be a catalyst for conflict, and a detriment.

While Butler's contribution provides a macro-level case study of Ireland's amateur military tradition, in Chapter 9 Gerry O'Keeffe brings the focus down to the individual with his analysis of the (in)famous Victorian war hero Field Marshal Viscount Hugh Gough. Gough presents a useful case study of the over-representation of Irishmen within the British army from the 1790s until the end of the nineteenth century: Catholics in the rank-and-file and

46 Bartlett & Jeffrey, *A military history of Ireland*, p. 8.

47 See William Butler, *The Irish amateur military tradition in the British army, 1854–1992* (Manchester, 2016), various pages; Paul Huddie, *The Crimean War and Irish society* (Liverpool, 2015), pp 184–8; I.F. Nelson, *The Irish militia, 1793–1802: Ireland's forgotten army* (Dublin, 2007).

Church of Ireland Protestants in the officer corps. As O'Keeffe demonstrates, being part of this social elite (in Ireland) and a war hero, did not protect such men from becoming the targets of aggressive and potentially career-ending campaigns by sections of the British press and individuals in parliament.

Serving as commander-in-chief in India between 1843 and 1849, Gough was hailed in Britain and Ireland as an archetype Victorian military hero, winning glorious victories against the empire's enemies in exotic India. However, he was also excoriated in the British press for his perceived 'Tipperary tactics', and the irrational temperament to which his Irish blood supposedly predisposed him. O'Keeffe's chapter sheds light on the nuanced attitudes to the participation of Irishmen in empire emanating from the British print and political establishments and the independent moderate Irish nationalist press at the height of the Great Famine. Using a collection of centrist Irish nationalist newspapers, which sprang to Gough's defence, coupled with English titles like *The Times*, the *Standard* and the *Sun*, O'Keeffe offers a more sympathetic appraisal of the Irish general's predicament in India at this time. He also explores how the polemical discourse centred on Gough, and the Great Famine context within which it played out, exposed the mid-nineteenth-century fault lines and inequalities that beset Britain's imperial centre.

Chapter 10, by Kathryn Milligan, represents the sole engagement with the visual arts in this volume and thus provides a refreshing example of how conflict was consumed by the public in nineteenth-century Ireland. Speaking directly to the seminal work of J.W.M. Hichberger, Milligan's chapter focuses on the medium of military painting.[48] According to early nineteenth-century art critic William Michael Rossetti, this was an artistic genre that did not exist in England and for which there existed little appetite, as he believed the English to be a wholly un-militaristic nation. However, as Hichberger rightly noted, this was wholly untrue. Not only did artists from all parts of the United Kingdom paint, display and tour with their military and war compositions, the public also eagerly sought and engaged with those compositions. Milligan's chapter speaks directly to this, focusing on a single commercial venue in Dublin City that specialised in the exhibition and sale of engravings, art supplies and other luxury paper goods and one-painting exhibitions. Specifically, she both recounts and contextualises the exhibition of a dozen war-related pieces by Mr Thomas Cranfield at his Dublin premises between the 1840s and the 1880s. In doing so, she presents us with a case study of how conflict (war) was presented to the public in Ireland, but also how they engaged with and consumed it. She illustrates how the commercialism of Britain's imperial military exploits stood in opposition to the more established

48 J.W.M. Hichberger, *Images of the army: the military in British art, 1815–1914* (Manchester, 1988).

fine art venues, such as the Royal Hibernian Academy, and regularly in political or aesthetic opposition to those attempting to find a more distinctly 'Irish' mode of visual art. Focusing on Dublin and the business of Cranfield, her chapter explores how two nineteenth-century conflicts were represented through the gallery's displays: the Peninsular and Waterloo campaigns during the Napoleonic Wars (1807–14 and 1815, respectively) and the Crimean War (1853–56). She illustrates the ways the ever-present nature of British military action, and the Irish soldiers who participated in these conflicts, tied these artworks to contemporary Irish life, bringing, even in an imagined and mediated way, the sights of the battlefields to the exhibition rooms of Dublin.

The final chapter of this volume, by Tim Hoyt, focuses on the Irish Republican Brotherhood (IRB) and Clan na Gael. The history of the IRB, it could be said, is by now a well-trodden topic, as is evident from works by Marta Ramon, Owen McGee, Matthew Kelly and R.V. Comerford, among others.[49] However, as a scholar of (counter)terrorism and irregular warfare, Hoyt approaches this aspect of Irish nineteenth-century political history from a unique and global perspective. His chapter comprises a survey analysis of the IRB in the late nineteenth century, through which he explains the organisation's resilience over its sixty-five-year lifespan. During this time, the IRB experienced, endured and survived most, if not all, of the processes that typically prove fatal to terrorist groups throughout history and the world. Hoyt discusses the challenges, weaknesses, opportunities and necessities that turned a covert military organisation into an elite revolutionary cabal operating on both sides of the physical force/constitutional divide in Irish nationalism. He suggests that it was the IRB's ability to adapt to internal and external challenges and changing political conditions that ensured its survival through the nineteenth century and its re-emergence as a force in the Irish revolutionary period. This ability, he shows, was evident in the IRB's evolving methods that reflected the different 'waves' of terrorism and irregular warfare that emerged on a global stage during the late nineteenth and early twentieth centuries.

49 Marta Ramón, *A provisional dictator: James Stephens and the Fenian movement* (Dublin, 2007); Owen McGee, *The IRB: the Irish Republican Brotherhood, from the Land League to Sinn Féin* (Dublin, 2005); M.J. Kelly, *The Fenian ideal and Irish nationalism, 1882–1916* (Woodenbridge, 2006); R.V. Comerford, *The Fenians in context: Irish politics and society, 1848–82* (Dublin, 1998).

Conclusion

Thanks to the endorsement and support of the SSNCI committee, sponsorship by several schools in UCD's Colleges of Arts and Humanities and College of Social Sciences and Law, and the efforts of the conference organisers and contributors, the 2022 SSNCI conference was a unique opportunity to bring together researchers from diverse academic disciplines and to use the theme of conflict as a lens through which to examine and interpret the long nineteenth century.

As diverse as they are, the eleven chapters in this volume represent only a fraction of the excellent and invaluable contributions made by dozens of scholars at the 2022 SSNCI conference. We are grateful to all of those who participated and made our conference a success. We hope that this volume's dedicated and focused analysis will serve to encourage others to continue to provide new perspectives on and approaches to the study of conflict relative to Ireland and Irish people in the nineteenth century.

Religious Conflict

1

'Strange and Belligerent Factions': Irish Immigrants and Social Conflict in Nineteenth-Century Ontario

William Jenkins

Introduction

This chapter explores the place of group-based social conflict in the lives of Irish immigrants in Ontario, Canada, between 1820 and 1880.[1] The Irish were the most significant group emigrating to what was the developing western region of this British North American colony between the 1820s and mid-1850s, consistently outnumbering arrivals from England and Scotland.[2] Ulster was the most prominent Irish source of emigrants in the 1820s and 1830s, most of them Protestant land-seekers, artisans ands labourers, but over time the immigrant stream became increasingly Catholic and oriented towards other parts of the island, particularly Munster. By the 1840s, it was also drawing largely from the ranks of the unskilled before Canada became tragically inundated by tens of thousands of refugees from the Great Irish Famine in the summer of 1847.[3] As pre-famine Irish arrivals sought out

1 Although 'the social' is often intertwined with economic, cultural and political concerns, space does not permit the inclusion of formal political/electoral conflicts here. The role of Irish Orangemen in violently upholding Tory political traditions in Canada has, however, been illustrated by authors such as Carol Wilton, *Popular politics and political culture in Upper Canada, 1800–1850* (Montreal, 2000) and Peter Way, 'Street politics: Orangemen, Tories, and the provincial election of 1841' in *British Journal of Canadian Studies*, vi, no. 2 (1991), pp 275–303.

2 D.A. Wilson, *The Irish in Canada* (Ottawa, 1989), p. 9; J.K. Johnson, *In duty bound: men, women, and the state in Upper Canada, 1793–1841* (Montreal, 2014), p. 222.

3 C.J. Houston & W.J. Smyth, *Irish emigration and Canadian settlement* (Toronto, 1990) and R.J. Grace, 'Irish immigration and settlement in a Catholic city: Quebec, 1842–61' in *Canadian Historical Review*, lxxxiv, no. 2 (2003), pp 217–51.

opportunities in a range of urban and non-urban settings, their demographic presence was one reason they could not be ignored. Their capacity for engaging in conflict on a communal scale was another.

As Canadian historians have long recognised, the fledgling colony was anything but a 'peaceable kingdom' and localities that witnessed visceral episodes of social conflict involving the Irish were part of a wider pattern evident in both British North America and the United States in the early to mid-nineteenth century.[4] Bloody showdowns featuring Irish-born 'Plug-Uglies', 'Roche Guards' and other collectives in the tenement-laden districts of New York, such as Five Points, represented but one urban extremity.[5] In the period of sustained Irish immigration from the 1820s to the mid-1840s, however, when more than 400,000 arrived in British North America, conflicts tended to occur in three largely non-urban contexts: (1) land clearance and settlement by pioneer farmer-landowners; (2) the evolving wilderness or resource frontier; and (3) the ever-shifting construction frontier associated with public works projects, principally canal building.[6] In all three, as in Manhattan and other urban places, Irish factions were lumped under various group monickers, many but not all of them self-ascribed.

The chapter draws on recent and older scholarship to discuss the contexts of social conflicts involving the Irish in a series of localities within the territory of what was Upper Canada (1791–1841), then Canada West (1841–67), and now the Canadian province of Ontario.[7] Scholars have shown poor and working-class Irish male immigrants to be mostly at the centre of these violent and often bloody affairs, several involving the loss of life.[8] Contrary to what many contemporary commentators believed, such instances of conflict were not the simple transplanting of Old World sectarian hatreds or 'feuding' traditions to a New World setting. Many were bound up within wider struggles among immigrants to secure land, jobs and shelter in the transition

4 M.S. Cross, '"The laws are like cobwebs": popular resistance to authority in mid-nineteenth-century British North America' in *Dalhousie Law Review*, viii, no. 3 (1984), pp 103–24; S.W. See, 'Nineteenth-century collective violence: towards a North American context' in *Labour – Le Travail*, xxxix (1997), pp 13–38.

5 Tyler Anbinder, *Five Points* (New York, 2002), pp 27–37 and 269–96. Herbert Asbury, *The gangs of New York: an informal history of the New York underworld* (New York, 1927), reels off a host of nineteenth-century gangs and their supposed exploits, though its reliability is questionable; see pp 5–26, 206–11, and 234–54.

6 Wilson, *Irish in Canada*, p. 5.

7 The Province of Canada (1841–67) comprised Canada West and Canada East, the latter now the province of Quebec. The confederation that brought the Dominion of Canada into being in July 1867 comprised the former British North American colonies of Canada, Nova Scotia and New Brunswick.

8 Ruth Bleasdale, *Rough work: labourers on the public works of British North America and Canada, 1841–1882* (Toronto, 2018).

towards a capitalist economy, pitting the Irish against other groups as well as each other. In the process of putting down roots and/or maintaining livelihoods, place mattered. As the chapter shows, older scholarly insights from fields such as labour history and historical geography have been supplemented by recent contributions from social and gender historians informed by transnational approaches. The semi-frequent reporting of conflict-related episodes within an expanding colonial press perpetuated negative stereotypes of the 'wild' Irish character that revolved around a primitive brutality, often alcohol-fuelled, a stereotype that affected poor and working-class Catholics in particular. Despite the compassion shown to famished and diseased migrants (also mostly Catholic) in 1847, these unflattering representations remained in circulation, informed by the realities of post-famine urban Irish settlement and fostering indifferent if not hostile feelings about the enduring Irish presence when Ontario moved into the boom-and-bust economy of the industrial age.

The story begins in September 1868 in Toronto, a city that had by then become known as 'the Belfast of Canada'. This label reflected the presence of not only a roughly even split between Protestants and Catholics of Irish birth and ancestry, but also the prominence of the exclusively Protestant Orange Order fraternity in public life and local politics.[9] The city's fifty-five thousand or so inhabitants were already possessed of a social memory of intermittent strife between largely working-class members of both subgroups stretching back almost two decades. Indeed, this memory was not limited to their city, for such sectarian flare-ups had occurred at multiple locations throughout the colony since the 1820s, and there were many who wondered if these recurring 'Orange' and 'Green' rivalries would ever end. But in directing our initial attention to Toronto's police court in 1868, I want to first indicate ways in which connections between factional conflict and Irishness could be drawn that not only foregrounded locality rather than religion but also demonstrated an imaginative, if not mythical, quality.

Stanleyites and Dummeronians

On 11 September 1868, Toronto's newest daily, the *Telegraph*, published its 'city police' column. Its paragraphs detailed some of the previous day's activities in the downtown police court and in contrast to the stories it published in relation to higher courts dealing with serious crimes, the newspaper had evidently decided that accounts of petty offences belonged somewhere between gossipy entertainment and the straightforward accounts found in

9 W.J. Smyth, *Toronto, the Belfast of Canada: the Orange Order and the shaping of municipal culture* (Toronto, 2015).

more highbrow dailies such as the *Globe*. The column's opening paragraph reveals that 'Stanleyites and Dummeronians congregated in front of the *Palais de Justice*' where they 'eyed each other defiantly and fiercely. The feud between the rival factions, for some time suppressed, now threatens to break out with some redoubled and terrific fury, owing to a rencontre which happened yesterday between Tim Crawley and a Stanleyite youth.'[10] After having had his toe accidentally trodden on by Crawley, the youth reportedly exclaimed: 'Take yer dirthy brogans aff ov me fut, ye ugly looking divil', to which Crawley responded: 'Och thin ye might better go alay now and keep eyer shirt on Alanna .... Sure a man must put his feet somewhere and ye're tinder toes cover a dale of space that might be better occupied, I'm afther thinkin.' According to the court journalist, this 'little occurrence, slight as it was, was sufficient to fan the smouldering embers of hostility into a flame. The Dummeronians insist on being separated from the Stanleyites and the latter express their entire concurrence with this idea, which apart from their common devotion to the cause of freedom is about the only thing the factions agree on.' The journalist then referred to a petition submitted to Toronto's Chief of Police, 'praying that a partition may be put up dividing the vestibule into two portions, one for each of the parties'.

Telegraph readers unaware of Toronto's demography or social geography would have nonetheless speculated that wherever these Stanleyite and Dummeronian factions resided in the city, they were likely to be places with concentrations of Irish households, based on the speech of Crawley and the unnamed youth. Readers may have been familiar with such representations of Irish speech from literature or trips to the theatre and surmised that a certain group of Irish, likely Catholics, were once again causing trouble, albeit more a case of playful threats than a confrontation with shillelagh sticks or firearms. They may have concluded that it was just part of their character, that all-pervasive Victorian watchword.

Continuing to the next paragraph describing events inside the court, the reader was directed to the heading of 'drunk and disorderly' and the first case concerning 'John Whalen, a Stanleyite, 47 years old, short bullet-headed, pock marked, seedy and demoralized', who apparently whispered to the *Telegraph* reporter, 'Don't now fur the live av ye shpell me name wrong. Tis Whalen – W-h-a-l-e-n, not Whelan – that name av the shpalpeen that murthered McGee and nothin to me at all sure. Ye'll mind now, won't ye?' No doubt a linguist of what has been termed Hiberno-English (and more recently Irish English) would take an interest in such accounts, if they were to believe the journalist's

10 *Daily Telegraph*, 11 Sept. 1868. Original emphasis. 'Brogans' and 'Alanna' are Irish English expressions for 'shoes' and 'my child' respectively.

story at all.[11] For our purposes, it not only repeatedly mentions a 'Stanleyite' but also notes the assassination of Irish Canadian politician Thomas D'Arcy McGee the previous April and the subsequent arrest of Patrick James Whelan, an alleged member of the revolutionary Fenian Brotherhood, a body of men dedicated to establishing an Irish republic.[12] Through the so-called 'Fenian alarm', and the raids on the Canada–United States border in the summer of 1866, Canadians had another reference point for Irish troublemaking and factionalism, this time in the geopolitical sphere. Such factionalism occurred with the 1865 division of North American Fenianism into wings led by John O'Mahony and William Roberts, each possessed with different revolutionary tactics. The previous mention of Stanleyites' and Dummeronians' 'common devotion to the cause of freedom' is likely an ironic reference to their perceived Fenian sympathies. And given John Whalen's dirty shoes and overall shabbiness, the reader may also have drawn connections to now-familiar depictions of the poorest of the city as 'the great unwashed'. Whalen, unable to pay the $3 dollar fine for his drunkenness, was sent to jail for a month, a sentence for a public order offence not untypical for the period.

Who were these apparently fierce-eyed Stanleyites and Dummeronians? The labels referred to two Toronto streets, Dummer Street in the west end, and Stanley Street, close to the downtown. Both had sizeable numbers of working-class Irish Catholic immigrant households, growing steadily since the famine-era immigrations. Indeed, Stanley Street's notoriety and Irish character predated the famine.[13] Known as March Street before 1850, it is a mere two city blocks in length, and tavern names listed in city directories between 1846 and 1851 included the Cavan Arms Inn, the Erin Go Bragh Tavern and the Queen's County Sportsman's Inn.[14] As minor as both Stanley and Dummer streets were in length, both possessed a negative hold in

11 C.P. Amador-Moreno, *An introduction to Irish English* (London, 2010); T.P. Dolan (comp. and ed.), *A dictionary of Hiberno-English: the Irish use of English* (3rd ed., Dublin, 2020); and Aidan Doyle, 'Language and literacy in the eighteenth and nineteenth centuries' in James Kelly (ed.), *The Cambridge history of Ireland vol. III: 1730–1880* (Cambridge, 2018), pp 353–79.

12 D.A. Wilson, 'Was Patrick James Whelan a Fenian and did he assassinate Thomas D'Arcy McGee?' in idem (ed.), *Irish nationalism in Canada* (Montreal, 2009), pp 52–82. Whelan was found guilty and hanged on 11 February 1869. For insights on the social atmosphere in Toronto around the time of the 'Fenian alarm', see D.A. Wilson, *Canadian spy story: Irish revolutionaries and the secret police* (Montreal, 2022), pp 38–100.

13 William Jenkins, 'Poverty and place: documenting and representing Toronto's Catholic Irish, 1845–1890' in P.J. Duffy & William Nolan (eds), *At the anvil: essays in honour of William J. Smyth* (Dublin, 2012), pp 477–511.

14 *Brown's Toronto city and home district directory 1846–47* (Toronto, 1846), pp 23, 32 (pages relate to A–Z directory section); *Rowsell's City of Toronto and county of York directory for 1850–1* (Toronto, 1850), p. 105 (page relates to A–Z directory section). Stanley Street is presently known as Lombard Street.

the imagination of morally minded Torontonians in a way that no other residential streets did, if one considers repeated references to them in the city's dailies in the 1860s. Reporting on Toronto's larceny statistics in 1870, Police Chief William S. Prince drew attention to

> the young denizens of Stanley and Dummer Streets, many of whom have been charged at the Police Court with larceny, or suspicion of larceny, but being mere children were discharged by the Magistrate, from the fact of their [*sic*] being no place for their confinement, but the Gaol; and to have sent them there to associate with hardened criminals, would not have bettered their moral condition.[15]

Though they may not have spoken English quite like John Whalen, this cohort of Canadian-raised Stanleyites and Dummeronians was continuing what the likes of Chief Prince would have considered a familiar history of casual law-breaking, on an occasionally gang-like scale, from residents of these streets. The Irish were overrepresented in the city's jails and on its police register rolls before the summer of 'Black 47', and this pattern persisted into the late 1860s, as illustrated by the periodic publication of statistics of the nationalities and occupations of offenders.[16] As the *Daily Leader* put it in relation to Stanley Street in 1865: 'It is well known that the denizens of this celebrated locality have a great weakness for three things – whisky, fiddling, and fighting' – again, without naming the street as Irish, references to alcohol, fiddle-playing and fighting as recreational pursuits of equal validity were unmistakable, and the use of 'celebrated' was ironic.[17] If Toronto had an equivalent of New York's Five Points, where scenes of conflict were as common as scenes of conviviality, this was it. The description of John Whalen's speech pattern, bodily appearance and behaviour marked him as a certain type of irredeemable Catholic Irish immigrant – beholden to alcohol and caring nothing for Victorian middle-class expectations of self-improvement. His being identified as a resident of Stanley Street did not surprise local readers.

Although this and many other newspaper accounts point to colourful exchanges in Toronto's police courtroom in the late 1860s, the idea that there

15 City of Toronto Archives, *Minutes of proceedings of the council of the corporation of the city of Toronto, 1870* (Toronto, 1871); Appendix 3, Report of the Chief Constable; S.E. Houston, 'Victorian origins of juvenile delinquency: a Canadian experience' in *History of Education Quarterly*, xii, no. 3 (1972), pp 254–80.

16 Brian Clarke, *Piety and nationalism: lay voluntary associations and the creation of an Irish-Catholic community in Toronto, 1850–1895* (Montreal, 1993), pp 25–30. This overrepresentation was evident in the Upper Canadian era as well; see Johnson, *In duty bound*, pp 185–7.

17 *Daily Leader*, 6 Feb. 1865.

were two organised factions of working-class Irish from different parts of the city engaged in a hostile feud with each other was an exaggeration. Nor is there evidence that the Irish from Stanley Street prided themselves on being labelled 'Stanleyites' or that those from Dummer Street embraced the self-image of 'Dummeronians', though feuds between individuals and families on these streets did occur. Territorial labels were seemingly the invention of court journalists, but as the police chief indicated, the activities of roaming gangs of youngsters from such streets were the real problem. In this respect, Toronto mirrored contemporary concerns within Canadian and American cities about the formidable ranks of rootless 'arabs' and 'urchins'.[18]

The Toronto press's coverage of crime through such short but illustrative stories reinforced, or at least added a semi-fictional layer to, prevailing perceptions of working-class Irish character, and that of Irish Catholics especially, as one that was prone to factionalism, feuding and defiance of authority in general, not to mention being strongly territorial and clannish. It also pointed to the prominence of alcohol, and whisky in particular, in this web of relations. The stage Irish-like portrayals of Tim Crawley, John Whalen and the Stanleyite youth illustrate this.[19] Toronto's literate elites and middle classes may have gained reassurance that their lives and habits were superior to those of dissolute immigrants, but there were other outlets besides newspapers for them to access the above ideas about Irish character and Irish English speech. There were, for example, best-selling books such as that of Englishwoman Susannah Moodie's finessed account of her family's early years in Canada or in the works of County Leitrim-born and later Toronto-based poet and satirist James McCarroll, whose fictional character Terry Finnegan resided in a place called 'Stanly Sthreet'.[20] There were also transatlantic publishing circuits that brought to North America popular works such as *Handy Andy* by the Irish satirist, painter and songwriter Samuel Lover. In the otherwise

18 T.J. Gilfoyle, 'Street-rats and gutter-snipes: child pickpockets and street culture in New York City, 1850–1900' in *Journal of Social History*, xxxvii, no. 4 (2004), pp 853–82. Gilfoyle's data sample from the New York district attorney (1859–76) revealed the Irish to be the most prominent foreign-born child pickpockets, though some of the American-born offenders probably had one or both parents born in Ireland; see p. 859 and p. 876, note 20.

19 See 'stage-irishman' in Robert Welch (ed.), *The concise Oxford companion to Irish literature* (Oxford, 2000), e-version, DOI:10.1093/acref/9780192800800.001.0001. For an early analysis, see G.C. Duggan, *The stage Irishman: a history of the Irish play and stage characters from the earliest times* (Dublin, 1937).

20 Susannah Moodie, *Roughing it in the bush* (Toronto, 1871, originally published 1852). Two characters with Irish English speech are John Monaghan (pp 174–92) and Malachi Croak (pp 335–7); Michael Peterman, *Delicious mirth: the life and times of James McCarroll* (Montreal, 2018) and 'From Terry Finnegan to Terry Fenian: the truncated literary career of James McCarroll' in D.A. Wilson (ed.), *Irish nationalism in Canada* (Montreal, 2009), pp 140–59.

harrowing year of 1847, Lover performed an 'Irish Evening' entitled 'Sprigs of Shillelah [*sic*]' at Toronto's Old City Hall as part of a two-year sojourn touring the continent.[21] And finally, there was travel writing by English visitors to pre-famine Ireland that discussed faction fighting traditions, such as Mr and Mrs S.C. Hall's *Ireland: its scenery, character, and history* that was available to Toronto readers in the 1850s.[22]

Ballygiblins and Blazers

In their classic study of Irish immigration and settlement in nineteenth-century Canada, Cecil J. Houston and William J. Smyth identified three main zones of pioneer settlement: first, along the Rideau Canal axis linking Ottawa and Kingston in eastern Ontario; second, in the Peterborough area of central Ontario north of Port Hope, and third, in a series of townships running northwest from Toronto towards Georgian Bay.[23] Conflicts that erupted in these zones, bringing groups such as the 'Ballygiblins' and 'Blazers' to the public's attention, concerned mainly religion and social class. While immigrations of land-seeking Protestants (funded from within family/kin networks) were prominent in the 1820s, a scheme sponsored by the British exchequer transported groups of poor and mostly Catholic families from selected parishes in Munster (mainly north County Cork) to Upper Canada under the supervision of Canadian politician Peter Robinson. This experimented with the idea that the removal of 'surplus populations' from the United Kingdom could benefit British colonial development, and it won approval from landlords in a region of Munster that had high population densities and had recently experienced the Captain Rock agrarian outrages. The 1823 migration of 571 persons was directed to the Bathurst District west of Ottawa (then known as Bytown) while the 1825 migration of 2,050 individuals headed for the northern portion of the Newcastle District in the vicinity of Peterborough.[24]

The immigrants to the Bathurst District, whose deadly engagement in May 1824 gave rise to their being known as the 'Ballygiblins', are the subjects

21 *Globe* (Toronto), 7 Jul. 1847. See also M.A. Walton, 'Samuel Lover R.H.A. (1797–1868)' in *Dublin Historical Record*, xxxii, no. 2 (1979), p. 63.

22 W.H. Williams, *Tourism, landscape and the Irish character: British travel writers in pre-famine Ireland* (Madison, 2008), pp 76–8; for the Halls' book notices, see *Globe*, 20 Oct. 1853, 9 Jan. 1854 and 7 Jul. 1857.

23 Houston & Smyth, *Irish emigration*, p. 207.

24 Ibid., p. 205. See also Alan Brunger, 'Geographical propinquity among pre-famine Irish settlers in Upper Canada' in *Journal of Historical Geography*, viii, no. 3 (1982), pp 265–82, and John J. Mannion, *Irish settlements in eastern Canada: a study of cultural transfer and adaptation* (Toronto, 1974), pp 15–54.

of a recent study by Laura Smith.[25] The group name refers to a locality in County Cork, though it is not known if the group identified with it since not all originated in that part of the county; another theory is that it was the name given to the emigrant depot for a temporary period after arrival. As Smith explains, the emigrants arrived in a part of Upper Canada not long settled, but with Protestants from England, Scotland and Ireland already present. An Orange lodge had been established, setting the tone for a developing local society where pioneer farmers were still negotiating the economic uncertainties and physical challenges of frontier living. The legal system was also in its infancy and was still weakly administered and susceptible to local partisan pressure.

Histories of ideas about gender, in this case 'settler manhood', inform Smith's study of the Ballygiblins' encounter. Would these arriving Catholic men live up to defined ideals of colonial manhood with all the self-reliance that such required, not to mention being loyal to the Crown? How would they be perceived upon arrival? For Smith, the reception given to the Munster newcomers 'was conditioned both by the legacy of the 'old world' in real and expected patterns of violence' and by 'the immediate context of British emigration policy and the process by which that policy was applied, interpreted, and experienced'.[26] The optimism within imperial policy about the better lives awaiting sufficiently capable 'surplus' peoples abroad clashed with on-the-ground visions of community development, and the two-day riot that took place in and around a local tavern in the aftermath of a militia muster, leaving one person dead, was 'as much about a local community expressing its opposition to new arrivals in their midst as it was about anti-social behaviour on the part of those immigrants'.[27] The negative views of established Protestants were informed by 'a stereotype of the Irish Catholic peasant as dangerous, lawless, and to a certain extent helpless' that was 'easily accessible in the colonial press' before the riot occurred as well as in its description, the papers in this case being the *Kingston Chronicle* and the *Montreal Herald*.[28] Press accounts drew comparisons between the 'Ballygiblins' and 'secret Irish factions' active in Munster over the previous decade and more.[29] The Protestant Irish settlers, probably informed by precedents of

25 Laura Smith, 'The Ballygiblins: British emigration policy, Irish violence, and immigrant reception in Upper Canada' in *Ontario History*, cviii, no. 1 (2016), pp 1–23.

26 Smith, 'The Ballygiblins', p. 3.

27 Ibid.

28 Ibid., p. 6.

29 Ibid. Besides the Captain Rock disturbances, communities in east Munster had also experienced the conflict between the Caravats and Shanavests. For an introduction to secret societies and violence in this period, see K.T. Hoppen, *Ireland since 1800: conflict and conformity* (2nd ed., Harlow, 1989), pp 48–56.

sectarian tension in the parts of Ireland they left and by contemporary Orange desires to shape the religious make-up of the district, were also jealous of the government-assisted newcomers obtaining local resources and judged the latter's skills and suitability for settler life accordingly. Smith concludes that the transatlantic circulation of 'varying perceptions and prejudices against Irish Catholic peasants' condemned the latter to an unfavourable reception in an Upper Canadian context where 'notions and expectations of who and what made a deserving settler', including 'concepts of loyalty, religion, deservedness, and manhood' were in evolution.[30]

About 150 miles west from the Bathurst District, other Munster settlers laid down roots in the Newcastle District. Their experience was different in that they moved into largely uninhabited tracts in the northern part of the district where their goals to settle in proximity to each other were achievable.[31] Further to the south, in Cavan township, groups of Protestant settlers originating in south and west Ulster as well as other parts of Ireland had been doing likewise for at least five years, and once again the Orange institution (lodge number 40 was organised in 1830, the same year as the Grand Orange Lodge of British North America) was a key institutional support in a community where multiple Anglican, Presbyterian and Methodist congregations would be founded.[32] No Catholic church would ever be built in Cavan, however, much as Catholic families from the townships to the north and east took interest in expanding their settlements into the township. The main reason for this was a group of mostly young men, many of them Orangemen, calling themselves the 'Cavan Blazers', who believed in defending Protestant claims to place. While the origins of this name are unknown, a number of accounts relate an episode whereby the attempts of the local postmaster to not only sell land to Catholics but also convert to Catholicism himself were resisted by the Blazers to the point of them burning down log cabins built in advance for the would-be settlers.[33] A story in the *Toronto Examiner* in 1849 referred to similar 'blazer' activities extending further west to Cartwright township 'where no Roman Catholic subject of Her Majesty is allowed to live'.[34] The

30 Smith, 'The Ballygiblins', p. 23.

31 Brunger, 'Geographical propinquity', pp 272–4.

32 Houston & Smyth, *Irish emigration*, p. 205; see also C.J. Houston & W.J. Smyth, *The sash Canada wore: a historical geography of the Orange Order in Canada* (Toronto, 1980), pp 30–1. Quentin Brown (ed.), *This green and pleasant land: chronicles of Cavan township* (Millbrook, 1990), indicates Irish regional and county (Cavan, Monaghan and Fermanagh) origins and connections on pp 1, 8, 14 and 31.

33 S.B. Leetooze, *Irish, Orange, and proud: a brief history of Cavan township* (Bowmanville, 1999), pp 11, 12, 59–60; Brown, *Green and pleasant land*, p. 35; and William Smith, *The pioneers of old Ontario* (Toronto, 1923), pp 320–4.

34 *Toronto Examiner* (henceforth cited as *TE*), 18 Jul. 1849. See also the thoughts of Denis Feely of Cobourg in Wilson, *Canadian spy story*, pp 95–6.

depiction of Protestant intimidation towards Catholics was not a simple one, however, since the *Examiner* reproduced in the previous year a letter by Nassau Gowan, son of Ogle, the driving force of Canadian Orangeism, who described the intimidation of his Methodist congregation to the east in Percy township by local Catholics who 'swore that the Protestants should never have a School-house or Chapel in that part of Percy'.[35] Finally, in Peel County west of Toronto, where Orangeism also gained a foothold, Houston and Smyth relate how attempts by Catholics to settle 'were challenged by a gang called the Town Line Blazers'.[36]

These examples indicate the desire of Protestants and Catholics alike to establish New World roots among families who resembled them (if they were not kin-related) in their religion and values and their reactions to the potential or actual disruption of such visions. Brunger has shown how Munster settlers in Newcastle sought the comfort of living near each other on the basis of family and parish of origin.[37] Further to the south, Protestant immigrants originating in Ulster counties such as Cavan and Monaghan had experienced life in places where they were demographic minorities. They were now hoping for a fresh start in Upper Canadian localities with names, honouring their Irish origins but doing so as a local if not a regional demographic majority. While the mix of denominational institutions and the presence or absence of Orange lodges suggested the religious flavour of various settlements, attempts to enforce territorial distinctions could be subtle, as in a placename geography that included 'Orange Corners' and an 'Orange Line', or they could be more forceful, as exemplified by the shadowy 'blazers'.[38] As was the case in Toronto, the town of Peterborough would in subsequent decades become a zone for Orange and Green confrontations during the annual commemorations to St Patrick (March 17) and the Orange icon of King William III (on July 12).[39]

35 *TE*, 19 Jul. 1848.

36 Houston & Smyth, *The sash Canada wore*, p. 31. The Town Line Blazers operated in the vicinity of Streetsville in what was then the township of Toronto.

37 Brunger, 'Geographical propinquity', pp 274–80.

38 C.J. Houston & W.J. Smyth, 'Community development and institutional supports: life on the agricultural frontier of Adjala and Mono townships' in Brian Clarke & Mark McGowan (eds), *Catholics at the gathering place: historical essays on the archdiocese of Toronto, 1841–1991* (Toronto, 1993), p. 13.

39 Brown, *Green and pleasant land*, p. 37 and Wilson, *Canadian spy story*, p. 80 refer to the St Patrick's Day incident of 1863 when 400 or so Orangemen sought to violently disrupt proceedings.

Shiners, Corkonians and Connaughtmen

While there were competing conceptions of settler manhood within pioneer farming communities, Irish Catholic men were more likely to define the sense of manhood ascribed to transient wage-labouring lumbermen and canal builders (canallers), given that thousands of them were involved in these industries in Canada between the 1820s and 1840s. Returning to the Ottawa region, both Protestant and Catholic Irish immigrants participated in the building of the Rideau Canal (1826–32).[40] Canalling life was particularly hard on newcomers – picks and shovels were the norm on a project directed by the British military; work availability and wages varied by year, season and skill level; labourers worked fourteen to sixteen hours a day six days a week; under- and non-payment of wages occurred on occasion; disease (ague/'swamp fever') was rampant, the Irish did not bring sufficiently warm clothes for the winter, and the cost of living in workcamps took 'most of the earnings of a common labourer', leaving the latter perilously close to destitution.[41] Conflicts erupted periodically under such trying conditions. In 1829, hungry workers raided nearby farms for food, while a battle between Orange and Green factions in December of that year involving more than four hundred men was 'likely precipitated by a struggle for jobs'.[42] The Irish experience on the Rideau Canal would have striking parallels on later construction projects.

Another by-product of the Rideau was the settlement of Irish Catholics in a section of Bytown's Lower Town named Corktown. This was a place that suffered badly during the 1832 cholera epidemic where in-group values of solidarity and mutuality tightened in resistance to attempts by the British military to police the locality.[43] If Corktown was a pre-famine reference point for a 'wild Irish' gathering place in the eyes of established Canadians, Toronto's Stanley Street would serve as a post-famine equivalent. Following the completion of the canal in the summer of 1832 and the outflow of labourers that resulted, Corktown was a likely source of recruitment for the Shiners, a group of mainly Irish lumbermen and raftsmen who emerged as an organised force in the Ottawa Valley's timber industry by the mid-1830s.[44]

While the origin of their name is obscure, there is no doubt about the ferocity of the Shiners' battles with French-Canadians for job and wage supremacy along the Ottawa River. Although they may not have been an

40 William Wylie, 'Poverty, distress, and disease: labour and the construction of the Rideau canal' in *Labour – Le Travail*, vi (1983), pp 7–29.

41 Wylie, 'Poverty, distress, and disease', p. 15.

42 Ibid., p. 26.

43 Ibid., p. 23.

44 Jane McGaughey, *Violent loyalties: manliness, migration, and the Irish in the Canadas, 1798–1841* (Liverpool, 2020), p. 157.

exclusively Catholic Irish group, Shiners indicted at various times had names such as Hennessy, Ryan, Hoolahan, Power, Whalen, Macaulay, Burke, O'Brien and Leamy, and the leader was an Irish immigrant raised in Liverpool who had changed his name from Peter Vallely to Peter Aylen and made his money as a wealthy timber merchant in the district after more than a decade in the trade.[45] While the Shiners' prime opponents in the forest were French-Canadians, the latter's counterparts in Bytown were the Anglo-Protestant elites of largely Scottish origin who held these Irish in disdain, regardless of the wealth amassed by Aylen and his associates through their frontier exploits. There was little police power in Bytown twenty years before it became the capital of Canada as Ottawa, and the nearest jail was forty miles away in Perth. But no amount of jail time deterred Aylen or his men as they swaggered their way around Bytown each spring. Michael Cross considers the actions of Aylen as 'explainable only by one of two causes: a genuine desire to aid his Irish countrymen; or a drive for personal power'.[46] Aylen gave his followers not only jobs but housing and lavish entertainments that, as Cross puts it, 'often combined the dual pleasures of debauchery and insult to the respectable community'.[47] His motives were far from unselfish. Members of the 'respectable' layer of society were prepared to tolerate a certain level of violence but once they were being targeted directly, the forces of social order, buoyed by having defeated the cause of radical reform in the Upper Canada rebellion of 1837, swung into action and arrested Aylen once again, ultimately heralding the decline in the Shiners' presence and notoriety.

In her recent *Violent Loyalties*, McGaughey contributes a gender-based perspective on the lives of these Irishmen between the forest frontier and Bytown.[48] Informed by insights on masculinity by historians of gender such as Tosh, McGaughey argues that in the Ottawa Valley forests, where 'the "wild Irish" and the wilderness became one and the same ... continued demonstrations of performed masculinity' were par for the course while the lumbermen endured a collective but also isolating existence bereft of the potentially taming influence of women.[49] As she speculates, 'the lines between homoeroticism, homosociality and homosexuality could become blurred' in such environments.[50] With no respectability to lose, no supportive church institution and consigned to the role of perpetual outsiders feared by townsfolk, journalists in turn embellished the image of Irish brutality.

45 M.S. Cross, 'The shiners' war: social violence in the Ottawa valley in the 1830s' in *Canadian Historical Review* liv, no. 1 (1973), pp 14, 15, 21–2.

46 Ibid., p. 3.

47 Ibid., p. 4.

48 McGaughey, *Violent loyalties*, pp 133–66.

49 Ibid., p. 145.

50 Ibid., p. 149.

There was a sharp downturn in immigration from Ireland around the time of the rebellions in Canada in 1837 and 1838, though the numbers of Irish arrivals would rise again in the early 1840s as canal projects opened up on the St Lawrence River and on the Welland Canal in the Niagara Peninsula. Although historians have noted the importance of remittances in financing pre-famine migrations from Ireland, many newcomers nonetheless found themselves in port cities such as Quebec or Montreal with few funds remaining, seeking wage labour opportunities. Indeed, the Irish were at the centre of both the rise of the wage labourer on a large scale in Canada and the integration of the Canadian economy through their role in the construction of transportation infrastructure. For H.C. Pentland, the canal builders of the 1840s 'stood between pre-capitalist and capitalist labour'.[51] Ruth Bleasdale estimates there to have been a peak of ten thousand labourers on such projects in Canada during the decade, most of them Irish.[52] Much like the Shiners and the Rideau canallers before them, the transiency of these men, often but not always without families, marked them as a 'dangerous class', who were difficult to control. They moved between conditions of being waged and wageless, finding it almost impossible to save money for a more secure future.[53]

In an era where the potentially riotous protest was the precursor to the organised labour strike, the scope for a unified class consciousness developing among canallers was disrupted by conflict spurred by regional Irish factionalism whereby each side made efforts to protect its material interests in circumstances of grinding subsistence. In *Common Labour*, Peter Way explains how two principal Irish factions, the 'Corkonians' and the 'Connaughtmen', sought to monopolise construction contracts by driving away the other party; in good times, this strategy could increase wages; in more precarious times, it served to shore up scarce jobs within a large labour pool.[54] With each faction living and working in close proximity from the start, violence and intimidation were used to achieve work and material advantages amidst an evolving 'settlement

51 H.C. Pentland, 'The Lachine strike of 1843' in *Canadian Historical Review*, xxix, no. 3 (1948), p. 256. See also H.C. Pentland, 'The development of a capitalist labour market in Canada' in *Canadian Journal of Economics and Political Science*, xxv, no. 4 (1959), pp 450–61, and Bryan Palmer, 'Labour protest and organization in nineteenth-century Canada' in *Labour – le Travail*, xx (1987), pp 61–83.

52 Ruth Bleasdale, 'Class conflict on the canals of Upper Canada in the 1840s' in *Labour – le Travail*, vii (1981), p. 12.

53 On the transitions between waged and wageless employment within the wider process of proletarianisation: see Bryan Palmer & Gaetan Heroux, 'Cracking the stone: the long history of capitalist crisis and Toronto's dispossessed, 1830–1930' in *Labour – le Travail*, lxix (2012), pp 9–62.

54 Peter Way, *Common labour: workers & the digging of North American canals, 1780–1860* (Cambridge, 1993), p. 197.

pattern of different groups collecting in tribal villages along extended lines of public works'.[55]

The canal conflicts that erupted in Canada between 1842 and 1845 stood out on not only a regional but also a North American scale.[56] A story headed 'Riotous proceedings of the Irish' appeared in the *St Catharines Journal* on 7 July 1842, describing a 'shameful and most unnatural feud' between the Corkonians and Connaughtmen on the Welland Canal, spurred not by wage issues but by an earlier riot on the St Lawrence Canal in which 'the Connaughts' triumphed.[57] After an altercation with a road-building crew at Sixteen Mile Creek, the latter were said to be moving towards St Catharines with 'old fowling pieces, rusty muskets, pistols, and shillalies [*sic*]' and with rumours of Corkonian reinforcements arriving from across the American border, it was imperative to 'ascertain the movements of these strange and belligerent factions ... thirsting like savages for each others blood – horrible infatuation!'[58] In the aftermath of the 'Battle of Stone Bridge' involving five to six hundred men at Christmas 1843, 'secret society' influence in the form of oath taking was reported to be at hand by the Rev. William Patrick McDonagh, the canallers' priest, while one Edward McEvoy explained to a Niagara District magistrate that he was 'King of the Connaughtmen' who 'did not care a curse for any bloody "Tips" or Munsterman'.[59] Further to the east, Belfast-born Wilson Benson, working on a St Lawrence River steamboat in the spring of 1844, witnessed another full-scale riot between the same two factions on the Cornwall Canal, and wrote: 'My countrymen earned for themselves an unenviable notoriety, and produced an impression, especially among the rural population of Canada at that time, that the Irish, one and all, were "hard cases"'.[60] As we have seen, these labouring cohorts were not the first hard cases, though canal conflicts could take different turns, such as when the Irish closed ranks to face down contractors and the Board of Works to strike, as in January 1843.[61] There were also a number of confrontations with the region's Orangemen, most infamously at Slabtown near St Catharines in July 1849. To enforce conformity, Catholic labourers were said to be 'given the ultimatum to join in a show of force or leave the canal'; in the end, two labourers were killed and four wounded.[62]

55 Way, *Common labour*, p. 193.
56 Ibid., p. 204.
57 *St Catharines Journal*, 7 Jul. 1842.
58 Ibid.
59 Way, *Common labour*, p. 196; McEvoy is quoted in Bleasdale, *Rough work*, p. 171; see also Bleasdale, 'Class conflict', p. 28. 'Tip' is a reference to the Munster county of Tipperary.
60 Wilson Benson, *Life and adventures of Wilson Benson* (Toronto, 1876), p. 28.
61 Bleasdale, 'Class conflict', p. 26.
62 Bleasdale, *Rough work*, p. 179.

These disturbances on the Canadian canals plus the Rev. McDonagh's suspicions invite speculation about the transmission to Canada of aspects of Irish popular protest, not least the secret 'Ribbon' traditions that circulated within both rural and urban pre-famine Catholic Ireland. In their recent transnational investigation, Kyle Hughes and Donald MacRaild highlight several elements of these traditions besides their secrecy: their anti-Orangeism; their customary notions relating to employment and wages; their role as informal moral regulators, their parochialism and their general defiance of state authority.[63] In a Canadian context where the coordination of large labour forces was a novelty, there was space for what Hughes and MacRaild term Irish 'peasant-law' to become transformed into wage-labourers' social codes.[64] Rev. McDonagh was unable to infiltrate the secrecy in 1843, however, save for his naming them the 'Shamrock and Hibernian societies'.[65] The proto-trade unionism displayed by such groupings in Canada also hints at potential connections through the experiences and memories of workers involved in similar underground activity on the Royal and Grand canals in Ireland and/or group feuds such as those of the 'Billy Welters' and 'Billy Smiths' in Dublin in the late 1830s.[66] In depicting the Canadian faction fights as moments sparked by exploitation, Peter Way considers them 'rational labour strategies that both recapitulated traditional social conflict and undermined the achievement of a broader understanding of labour's collective interests'.[67]

Canada's colonial state responded to the frequency and ferocity of these conflicts. With reports of the canallers having accumulated guns, pikes, pitchforks and scythes to use for the next tussle, the Canadian legislature passed the Preservation of the Peace near Public Works Act in 1845 to disarm them and install a police presence until the projects' completion.[68] On a wider scale, public fears instilled by a 'dangerous class' combined with the momentum of popular temperance campaigns and increased intolerance for public drunkenness led to heftier fines and jail sentences for public order offenders, particularly in cities.[69] In the immediate aftermath of 'Black 47', however, Corkonians and Connaughtmen were again at each other's throats, this time at the works of the Great Western Railway Company in Hamilton

63 Kyle Hughes & D.M. MacRaild, *Ribbon societies in nineteenth-century Ireland and its diaspora: the persistence of tradition* (Liverpool, 2018), pp 1–30, 90–124, 169–77, 224–62 and 305–11.

64 Ibid., p. 55.

65 Bleasdale, 'Class conflict', p. 28.

66 Hughes & MacRaild, *Ribbon societies*, pp 136–43.

67 Peter Way, 'Evil humors and ardent spirits: The rough culture of canal construction laborers', in *Journal of American History*, lxxix, no. 4 (Mar. 1993), pp 1423–4.

68 Bleasdale, *Rough work*, p. 170.

69 See Johnson, *In duty bound*, pp 195–7.

in January 1848 where the men of the west 'broke sundry heads, after the most approved manner' in a disagreement about whether or not to strike for higher wages.[70] In July 1852, Irish Catholic navvies took on the Orangemen on Hamilton's streets in another deadly encounter.[71]

Young Irishmen and Young Britons

Although regional Irish factionalism may have moved into the arena of railway construction for a time, it seems to have largely disappeared by the time such projects began in earnest in Ontario in the first half of the 1850s. With more work available and less competition from rival groups, the rationale for such feuds declined.[72] The numbers of urbanised working-class Irish continued to grow in the wake of famine-era immigrations, and as labour became more organised, Irish immigrants joined their English, Scottish and Canadian-born counterparts in the many industrial strikes that hit Ontario in the 1850s. The most prominent 'Irish' conflicts that remained were those pitting Orange against Green, which returns us to the urban realm and Toronto's era as a purported Canadian Belfast for this final section.

By the time of the 1851 census, 11,305 Irish-born individuals formed 36.7 per cent of Toronto's population of 30,763.[73] Catholics numbered approximately eight thousand, most of them of Irish birth or ancestry. The city's infrastructure of Catholic churches, schools, voluntary associations and other institutions grew during the decade under the newly installed French-born bishop, Armand-François-Marie de Charbonnel. While stories tall and true of bygone Cork and Connaught feuds may have been recounted in taverns frequented by Irish Catholics, Toronto Orangeism consolidated its presence in public life. It had successfully defied a legislative attempt to ban its July processions between 1843 and 1851, and these parades were now the largest in the city. British flags and banners dominated main thoroughfares along with the sounds of fifes and drums with crowds taking in speeches hailing Britain's empire while underlining the order's role in the defence of Protestantism in British North America.[74] In this cold social climate for Catholics, the 1850s and 1860s also witnessed the politicisation of St Patrick's Day and the rise of the militant Hibernian Benevolent Society (HBS) as an

70 *Hamilton Spectator*, 16 Jan. 1848.
71 *Mirror* (Toronto), 16 Jul. 1852.
72 Bleasdale, *Rough work*, p. 173.
73 *Census of the Canadas, personal census, 1851–52, vol. 1* (Quebec, 1853), p. 30.
74 Brian Clarke, 'Religious riot as pastime: Orange Young Britons, parades, and public life in Victorian Toronto' in D.A. Wilson (ed.), *The Orange Order in Canada* (Dublin, 2007), pp 110–14.

organisation defending Irish Catholic interests in the wake of the stabbing death of a Catholic man in a riot following the 1858 parade.[75] It too echoed some of the Irish Ribbonite traditions noted above. The cultural activities of the HBS, which included the promotion of the Gaelic sports of football and hurling, also dampened Irish regional particularisms, not least among those of its members who subscribed (and took a secret oath) to the Fenian ideal of a separate and non-sectarian Irish republic.[76]

Although Canada's 'Fenian alarm' came and went, Toronto's era of sectarian strife did not subside. Brian Clarke identifies twenty-two significant outbreaks of religiously motivated collective violence in the city between 1870 and 1889, with sixteen occurring in the 1870s and eleven arising from Orange and Green parades. He also notes other instances of conflict arising from Orange invasions of Irish Catholic taverns and streets, including the 'celebrated' Stanley Street. Finally, he identifies four full-scale riots, two in connection with the Catholic Jubilee year in 1875 (some five to eight thousand people affected), and two in connection with the visit of the Fenian Jeremiah O'Donovan Rossa in 1878.[77] At the heart of most of these clashes, most of which occurred during an economic downturn, were two new organisations – the Orange Young Britons and the Young Irishmen's Catholic Benevolent Association.

The Young Briton and Young Irishmen organisations emerged in the late 1860s at a time when 'young men' became a distinct and much-discussed demographic. For Clarke, the rising cohort of young men needed outlets for organised leisure activities in an industrialising Toronto; they would find them in streets, taverns and dancehalls. The Young Britons had approximately six hundred members by the mid-1870s, and were run by young men without the guiding hand of older and now more status-conscious Orangemen. That they were 'Britons' indicated the Orange institution's success in attracting members of English and Scottish ancestry as much as their loyalty to the Crown. The Young Irishmen, on the other hand, represented a regrouping of Toronto Irish Nationalists and were given to similar social pursuits as the Young Britons. The absence of the crown on the former group's logo did nothing to dampen popular suspicions of disloyalty among Catholics at a time when a campaign for their increased political inclusion at the provincial level was underway.[78] In another nod to gender history, Ian Radforth locates the exploits of the

75 Michael Cottrell, 'St. Patrick's Day parades in nineteenth-century Toronto: a study of immigrant adjustment and elite control' in *Histoire Sociale – Social History*, xxv, no. 49 (1992), pp 57–73; Wilson, *Canadian spy story*, pp 58–73.

76 Dennis Ryan & Kevin Wamsley, 'A grand game of hurling and football: sport and Irish Nationalism in old Toronto' in *Canadian Journal of Irish Studies*, xxx, no. 1 (2004), pp 21–31.

77 Clarke, 'Religious riot as pastime', p. 114.

78 The image is reproduced in William Jenkins, *Between raid and rebellion: The Irish in Buffalo and Toronto, 1867–1916* (Montreal, 2013), p. 188.

two organisations within a larger youth culture in Toronto, noting that the youngest members of both groups 'learned about masculinity by watching males older than themselves'.[79] For Radforth, sectarian violence in Toronto 'persisted in part because of city authorities' toleration of Orange violence', even if not every large confrontation in Toronto had a sectarian context.[80] While the Jubilee Riots affected thousands, Radforth speculates that much of this number were 'thrill-seeking youths' who poured 'into the streets however troubled, or not, they were by the issues at stake'.[81] There were no deaths, but at least ten policemen were injured in the second riot, and Orange instigators 'accounted for over a third of the arrests made that day'.[82]

The exploits of 'Stanleyites' and 'Dummeronians' in Toronto's police court may have served as a point of amusement for the city's bourgeois class, but the Stanleyites' real enemies were the Young Britons and what passed for their predecessors in the 1850s and 1860s. Having resisted absorption into the larger Orange organisation, the Britons splintered on the issue in 1882 but with more peaceful times and more policing on Toronto's streets, the breakaways did not last much more than a decade.[83] While the era of open sectarian conflicts was ending in Toronto, the social and political inclusion of Catholics into the city's public life was a different matter altogether.[84] With Irish immigration to the city and to Ontario reduced to a trickle and the reduction of the working day for the skilled working class, conceptions of leisure focused increasingly on recreation and organised team sports such as lacrosse, rowing and baseball. And here, too, were teams with identifiable Catholic and Protestant support bases.[85]

Conclusion

This chapter has discussed a select series of 'trouble-spots' involving groups of mostly Irish-born men in what was Canada's primary growth region in the

79 Ian Radforth, 'Boys, young men, and disorder in Victorian Toronto' in Elizabeth Mancke, Jerry Bannister, Denis McKim & S.W. See (eds), *Violence, order, and unrest: a history of British North America, 1749–1876* (Toronto, 2019), p. 336.
80 Ibid., p. 341.
81 Ibid., p. 339.
82 Clarke, 'Religious riot as pastime', p. 118.
83 For changes in Toronto's policing, see Helen Boritch, 'Conflict, compromise, and administrative convenience: the police organization in nineteenth-century Toronto' in *Canadian Journal of Law and Society*, iii (1988), pp 141–74.
84 Smyth, *Toronto, the Belfast of Canada*, pp 114–51. For a more optimistic interpretation, see Mark McGowan, *The waning of the Green: Catholics, the Irish, and identity in Toronto, 1887–1922* (Montreal and Kingston, 1999).
85 Ryan & Wamsley, 'A grand game', pp 27–8.

nineteenth century. Communal social conflicts featuring such men on one or both sides during these decades also occurred in what was Lower Canada (the province of Quebec since 1867) and in other British North American colonies, notably New Brunswick. And there were of course other social conflicts that did not involve the Irish.[86] But as Canada took shape as an economic, social and geopolitical (imperial) entity, it is unsurprising that its most prominent immigrant group should have been at the centre of so many confrontations concerning land, labour, religion, collective identity and the shape of community values. As Scott See writes, 'enough people believed in the utility of crowds to make collective violence a common phenomenon in the nineteenth century'.[87] The communal conflicts reviewed here were multi-directional: if the Irish were not squaring off against French-Canadians, bourgeois Protestant elites, unscrupulous bosses and contractors or soldiers and policemen, they were doing so against each other largely for reasons of regional background and religion, fuelled by economic marginalisation and cheap whisky. Senses of social legitimacy underpinned these contests, however strange and irrational some appeared to observers at the time. A sense of irrationality and wildness, however, also coloured media portrayals of working-class Irish Catholic police courtroom crowds and their clannish affiliations with Toronto streets and neighbourhoods. While more can be said about these various cases in future scholarship, potential conflicts between the Irish and Canadian Indigenous peoples remain understudied, and the discussion of group conflict here foregrounded masculinity. Nonetheless, Ian Radforth's conception of 'quotidian violence', encompassing incidents 'that involved fewer people and appeared spontaneous', invites studies of how Irish immigrant women engaged in conflict situations involving violence.[88]

As the waves of Irish immigration subsided, communities matured in rural locations, and the major canal and railroad projects were completed, epicentres of social conflict became concentrated in urban places, with Toronto serving as the prime example here. Local monuments and plaques now narrate the past presence of the Shiners, canallers and Munster 'Ballygiblins', though Irish Canadian social memory remains dominated by the Great Famine migration of 1847.[89] In present-day multiracial and multi-faith Toronto, there

86 Cross, 'The laws are like cobwebs', and Scott W. See, *Riots in New Brunswick: Orange nativism and social violence in the 1840s* (Toronto, 1993).

87 See, 'Nineteenth-century collective violence', p. 25.

88 Radforth, 'Boys, young men and disorder', p. 342. On the dark side of Irish immigrant women's lives in Toronto, Boston, and New York, see Elaine Farrell & Leanne McCormick, *Bad Bridget: crime, mayhem and the lives of Irish emigrant women* (Dublin, 2023) and their project website: https://badbridget.wordpress.com/ (accessed 21 May 2023).

89 Mark McGowan, *Creating Canadian historical memory: the case of the famine migration of 1847* (Ottawa, 2006).

is little appetite for remembrance of the city's Orange imprint that for many summons memories of a dour and conservative social atmosphere and widely held assumptions of Protestant supremacy. Nevertheless, as rural settler communities in Ontario pass the point of their 175th (and soon their 200th) anniversaries and delve into their pioneer-era pasts, their Irish heritages may re-emerge to find their way into creative public histories. One intriguing example is *The Cavan Blazers*, a play written and produced in 1992 by Robert Winslow of Cavan township in which the Catholics and Blazers of the mid-nineteenth century exhibit 'conflicting collective memories, but they both see themselves as victims, of each other'.[90] Here, past local tensions arising from mutual distrust are offered for contemplation in the secular present and at a time when the dynamics and demography of immigration is a near-constant element within public and political debates in Canada. It also leads us to speculate on the future insights and productive lessons that may be generated through critical reflections on past conflicts in which Irish Canada was in some way implicated.

90 Albert Braz, 'United in oppression: religious strife and group identity in "The Cavan Blazers"' in *Literature & Theology*, xvi, no. 2 (2002), p. 160. The Cavan Blazers name also lives on as the name of the local hockey team.

2

Parish Vestries as Sites for Interdenominational Conflict in Ireland, 1820–45

Ciarán McCabe

Introduction

The meetings of Church of Ireland parish vestries constituted public forums for discussion of the most pressing issues affecting large proportions of Ireland's population in the pre-Famine decades. Vestry meetings were attended by members of the Established Church, as well as non-Anglicans,[1] and at times of heightened political, economic and social tensions, these assemblies could descend into heated disagreements and occasional violence, arising from the expression of a wide array of grievances. As such, parish vestries became sites for the public expression of increasingly sectarian tensions and conflict between Protestant and Catholic parishioners. This was particularly evident in urban centres, where members of the Church of Ireland constituted a higher proportion of the local population than in rural parishes, thus fostering more involvement in local affairs by Anglicans, while also lending itself to increasingly polarised relations between different communities. This chapter will explore this conflict in a period of polarisation through a case study of Easter vestries in two urban parishes (in Cork and Dublin cities). A general outline of the vestry system as it operated in early- to mid-nineteenth-century Ireland will precede an analysis of two particularly reflective exchanges of words at Easter vestry meetings in Holy Trinity (Christ Church) parish, Cork, in 1830 and in St Paul's parish, Dublin, in 1838.

1 I use the term 'Anglican' to denote members of the Church of Ireland, even though it was not commonly used by contemporaries; it is used here for convenience.

The vestry system in early- to mid-nineteenth-century Ireland

Parish vestries were gatherings of the ratepayers of Church of Ireland parishes, who met to oversee the administration of certain matters within the geographical parish area. While the vestry did possess powers pertaining to the Church of Ireland congregation, from the seventeenth century its remit was extended increasingly into the civil realm, and parishes held responsibility over street cleaning, policing (through their beadles and nightwatchmen), street lighting, firefighting and various welfare measures, such as providing coffins for poor parishioners, badging (and, thus, licensing) local 'deserving' street beggars and paying for the upkeep of local orphans – matters pertaining to all those living within the geographic boundaries of the parish (Anglican and non-Anglican). From 1819, in response to a particularly devastating typhus fever epidemic, parishes were empowered to elect unpaid officers of health who had the authority to direct that tenements, lanes and streets be cleaned, that nuisances be removed from the streets, and that beggars be apprehended or removed from the parish. These services were funded through the levying of a parish tax known as a cess, which was approved at the annual Easter vestry; at this meeting, the most important officers of the parish, the two churchwardens, were elected. The churchwardens were indispensable to the efficient running of the parish and among their duties was to represent the parish's interests in courts of law. Gallagher has pointed to legal requirements on churchwardens to reside within the parish ('because [a non-local churchwarden] cannot take notice of absences from church, nor disorders in it', according to an 1814 legal text) to suggest that these officers were more important figures in parochial administration than the (commonly non-resident) minister.[2] Churchwardens were almost invariably Church of Ireland members, yet there were attempts – ultimately unsuccessful – to elect Catholics to these positions in a number of Dublin parishes in the mid-1790s.[3] The annual statutory meetings were usually held in the small vestry room. Such rooms adjoined the main body of the church and, by the nineteenth century, typically proved too small in urban parishes to accommodate all those wishing to attend, thus adding to the atmosphere of clamour, discomfort and impatience that reared its head at contested vestry meetings in this period. John Crawford writes of the Easter vestry as serving as 'something of a forum for the expression of grievances'.[4]

2 M.C. Gallagher, 'Bishop Thomas Lewis O'Beirne and his church-building programme in the diocese of Meath 1798–1823' (PhD thesis, Maynooth University, 2009), p. 96.

3 Jacqueline Hill, *From patriots to unionists: Dublin civic politics and Irish Protestant patriotism, 1660–1840* (Oxford, 1997), pp 174–5, p. 175 n. 44.

4 John Crawford, *The Church of Ireland in Victorian Dublin* (Dublin, 2005), p. 153.

A 1726 statute, reaffirmed in 1826, empowered Catholics to attend vestry meetings but withheld from them the right to vote on church-related matters, such as expenditure on the upkeep of the church building, 'providing Things necessary for the celebration of Divine service' and the election of churchwardens.[5] By the nineteenth century, a system based on two separate vestries evolved in many parishes: an exclusive select vestry, wherein only Church of Ireland congregants could vote, and a general vestry, at which local non-Anglicans who lived within the parish boundaries and were liable to pay the parish cess could vote. The protocol was usually for, first, the select vestry to assemble and to vote on the election of churchwardens and to confirm budgeted expenditure on church-related matters; this vote was open only to members of the Church of Ireland. A second, general, vestry was then held – sometimes immediately after the select vestry, sometimes days or weeks later. At the general vestry, ratepayers of all denominations could attend and vote, with the items of expenditure under consideration ranging from the fire-engine keeper's salary to welfare measures for penurious parishioners.

For instance, in the Dublin parish of St Paul's, the Easter select vestry in 1830 was held on 12 April. Here, attendees were presented with the sums assessed 'for which Roman Catholics are by law excluded, or supposed to be excluded, from voting'. These items included £30 for the sextoness, £10 for 'Sacramental elements', £7 10s. for 'Painting exterior of church' and £10 for alterations and repairs to the church pews. The following day, the second, general vestry was convened, to consider the 'Sums assessed for which the Roman Catholic inhabitants are entitled to vote'. These items included a salary of £20 for the parish beadle, £30 for 'Coffins for the poor' and £10 for 'Repairing church-yard wall'.[6]

Other relevant legislation that affected Catholics, Dissenters and their role within the parish vestry system of local government included the 1819 Contagious Diseases Act, by which persons of all denominations could be appointed as unpaid officers of health, and, more significantly, the 1833 Church Temporalities Act, which is best remembered for reforms to the Church of Ireland archbishoprics, but was also significant in prohibiting the levying of cesses for Church of Ireland expenditure on non-conformists.

5 12 Geo. I, c.9 [Ire.] (8 Mar. 1726); 7 Geo. IV, c.72 (31 May 1826). The prohibition on Catholics on voting for the election of churchwardens was clarified in 25 Geo. III, c.58, s.3 [Ire.] (1785) and reaffirmed in 33 Geo. III, c.21, s.4 [Ire.] (1793).

6 'Dublin vestries. Returns of the several sums of money assessed in the several parishes in the city of Dublin, by vestries holden during Easter week, in the year 1830; distinguishing the purpose for which each sum was assessed; and also distinguishing the sums assessed by the vestries at which the Catholic inhabitants were by law excluded, or supposed to be excluded, from voting, from those at which the Catholic inhabitants were entitled to vote ..., p. 14, H.C. 1830 (523), xxxi, 312.

This 1833 act was hailed by the liberal, pro-nationalist *Freeman's Journal* as revolutionary in ending the 'obnoxious items of the vestry cess'.[7] Removing the parishes' power to levy compulsory cesses in nearly all cases constituted a marked shift in the role of parishes in Irish society, as well as removing from non-Anglicans a longstanding grievance centred on their requirement to pay for items not pertinent to them: the Church of Ireland archbishop of Dublin Richard Whately relayed the instance of a clergyman who paid for the communion bread and wine out of his own pocket, for fear of exciting the aggrieved feelings of local Catholics.[8] This overlooked element of the Church Temporalities Act was significant in legislating for, as Akenson argues, the disestablishment of the civil parish, decades before the disestablishment of the entire church.[9]

Cork, 1830

The Cork incident referred to at the beginning of this chapter occurred at the Easter vestry in the parish of Holy Trinity (Christ Church) in April 1830. Holy Trinity parish was located on the southern bank of the River Lee, lying to the east of the parishes of St Paul's and St Peter's. The parish was bordered by Patrick Street and the river to the north, encompassed the prominent thoroughfares of Grand Parade and the South Mall, and, in its eastern extremity, contained the city's custom house. Interestingly, in 1832, just two years after the incident about to be described, work commenced at the southern tip of the parish on what became Fr Mathew Memorial Church (or Holy Trinity Church), a Gothic revival Catholic church and Capuchin friary, named after the temperance crusader. The erection of this church was reflective of the growing confidence and assertion of Irish Catholicism, especially in the second quarter of the nineteenth century, when extensive church-building programmes in dioceses throughout the island embodied the emergence of the Roman church from the penal era. Whereas, previously, Catholic places of worship (chapels) were confined to side streets and back lanes – tolerated as long as they, and by definition Catholic worship, were

7 *Freeman's Journal* (henceforth cited as *FJ*), 8 Jul. 1833. For the act, see 3 & 4 Will. IV, c.37 (14 Aug. 1833); see also Edward Brynn, *The Church of Ireland in the age of Catholic Emancipation* (New York and London, 1982), pp 436–7.

8 Minutes of evidence taken before the select committee of the House of Lords appointed to inquire into the collection and payment of tithes in Ireland ..., p. 107, H.C. 1831–2 (271), xxii, 107.

9 D.H. Akenson, *The Church of Ireland: ecclesiastical reform and revolution, 1800–1885* (New Haven and London, 1971), pp 172–6.

kept out of public view in prominent locations[10] – from the 1820s onwards, Irish towns and cities were increasingly witness to the erection of substantial churches and cathedrals on prominent urban thoroughfares. For example, in Cork city, newly erected churches, such as St Mary's on Pope's Quay, were 'intended to raise the esteem accorded to and felt by the Catholics of Cork'.[11] The population of Holy Trinity parish was recorded in the 1831 census as totalling 9,567, of whom an estimated 30 per cent belonged, according to the 1834 'religious census', to the Established Church, with the remainder (except for a small number of Dissenters) being Catholics. Of the city's parishes, Holy Trinity had the highest proportion of Protestants in its population.[12]

On Easter Monday, 12 April 1830, the annual vestry of Holy Trinity parish was held at 12pm noon, chaired by the vicar, Rev. Charles Leslie.[13] Originally scheduled to be held in the vestry room attached to the parish church, the attendance was so large that alternative accommodation in the nearby schoolhouse was arranged at short notice. A general trend at Irish annual vestry meetings was that at times of conflict and intercommunity tension, these meetings were well attended, requiring the relocation of assemblies to larger spaces. The relatively large attendance at Easter meetings can be explained partly by parishioners' eagerness to air their grievances over matters of local government, as well as the appeal of public discord and conflict at vestry meetings as a form of spectacle and entertainment for urban communities. As was seen at Easter vestry meetings throughout the country,

10 This can be seen in John Rocque's 1756 survey of the city and suburbs of Dublin, where Catholic chapels (and Dissenting meeting houses) are identified as part of the cityscape, but in less prominent locations (typically back streets) than their Church of Ireland counterparts. See John Rocque, *An exact survey of the city and suburbs of Dublin; in which is express'd the ground plot of all publick buildings, dwelling houses, ware houses, stables, courts, yards &c* (London, 1756), available at Harvard Map Collection, Harvard University (https://curiosity.lib.harvard.edu/scanned-maps/catalog/44-990114744870203941, accessed 16 Oct. 2023).

11 Brendan Grimes, 'Funding a Roman Catholic church in nineteenth-century Ireland' in *Architectural History*, lii (2009), p. 48. See also Edward McParland, 'Chapel or church? The case of St Mary's, Pope's Quay, Cork' in Raymond Gillespie & R.F. Foster (eds), *Irish provincial cultures in the long eighteenth century: making the middle sort* (Dublin, 2012), pp 231–41. For the wider context, see Colin Barr, 'The re-energising of Catholicism, 1790–1880' in Kelly, *The Cambridge history of Ireland, volume III*, pp 280–304.

12 Population, Ireland. Census of the population, 1831. Comparative abstract of the population in Ireland, as taken in 1821 and 1831, p. 21, H.C. 1833 (23), xxxix, 23; First report of the Commissioners of Public Instruction, Ireland, pp 124c–125c, H.C. 1835 [C 45], xxxiii, 634–5; Ian d'Alton, *Protestant politics and society in Cork 1812–1844* (Cork, 1980), pp 33–4.

13 Details of the vestry meeting's proceedings are from *The Constitution; or, Cork Advertiser* (henceforth cited as *CA*), 13 Apr. 1830. The newspaper report identifies the vicar as Rev. Leslie; his forename can be identified from *Finny's Royal Cork Almanack, for 1830* (n.p. [Cork], n.d. [1830]), p. 37.

the source of conflict at the Holy Trinity gathering in 1830 was that of the levying of the parish cess and who was liable to pay this local tax. In this instance, intercommunal tensions descended into heated exchanges between Anglicans and non-Anglicans (both Catholics and Dissenters) as to the nature, and funding, of charity in the locality.

The most colourful exchange arose from the application to assess parishioners for the sum of £9 'for keeping the church clean', a proposal opposed by two Catholics (Messrs Reynolds and O'Brien) and a Presbyterian (Mr Osborne). O'Brien was reported as telling the meeting that 'it would be some satisfaction if he could see some of those gentlemen who voted his money so liberally putting their hands into their own pockets'. O'Brien's comment clearly irked some of the Anglicans present, with the sheriff, Nicholas Vincent, immediately responding:

> Mr. Sheriff VINCENT thought that when such an observation as that was made, he might be allowed to remark, for the purpose of bringing it to the recollection of Mr. O'Brien and other Roman Catholics, that the charities of Cork were supported in a far greater proportion by Protestants than by Roman Catholics, and that whenever they were called on they were never backward in 'putting their hands into their pockets.[14]

The tension and conflict in the crowded school room were palpable to the reader, especially upon comprehending the immediately succeeding contribution to the discussion: 'Mr. FITZGIBBON thought that that question had better not be discussed, as it might lead to another – how the Protestants became possessed of their property?'

Regrettably, the response within the room to this comment went unrecorded. The intervention of Vincent is striking both in its assertive dismissal of the Catholic complaint and in its strident defence of Cork Protestants' supposedly greater disposition to dole out charitable assistance than Catholics. Vincent's rush to defend his fellow Cork Protestants against this Catholic charge can be better understood by noting his prominent position as founding secretary of the Cork Brunswick Club. This club was part of a national movement of Protestant political mobilisation in the late 1820s that aimed at heading off the advance of Daniel O'Connell's Catholic Emancipation campaign.[15] The Brunswick clubs saw themselves as constitu-

14 For the identification of Nicholas Vincent as sheriff in 1830, see F.H. Tuckey, *The county and city of Cork remembrancer: or annals of the county and city of Cork* (Cork, 1837), p. 313.

15 *Kerry Evening Post*, 17 Sept. 1828. Vincent was elected as a Conservative member of the reformed Cork Corporation in 1841: d'Alton, *Protestant society and politics in Cork*, pp 184, 188.

tional organisations filling the spaces left by the proscription of the Orange Order in the mid-1820s, and defending the civil and religious liberty of an embattled Irish Protestantism against the supposedly seditious onslaught of political Catholicism, personified in the much-vilified figure of O'Connell.[16] Vincent's active membership of the Cork club contextualises his defence of Protestantism at a time when, and in a space (the vestry meeting) where, Anglican privilege was being challenged.

That the question of poor relief, and more specifically who funded it, should arise amidst this exchange of discordant and conflicting views is not surprising. Charity became increasingly sectarian throughout the nineteenth century, reflecting wider polarisation between Catholics and Protestants in Irish society.[17] Catholic–Protestant tensions and suspicions were regularly aroused when public discussions concerned the fate of parochial foundlings and their religious assignment, and the religious education of paupers within the Poor Law Union workhouses. In the post-Famine decades the slums of Dublin became 'battlegrounds', in Jacinta Prunty's term, as Catholic and Protestant missionaries engaged in verbal, and at times physical, struggles centring on the salvation of poor persons' souls and bodies.[18] Among the most common accusations levelled at contentious public assemblies, such as vestry meetings and charities' annual meetings, was that Protestants gave disproportionately more in charity than Catholics, and that distressed Catholics benefited disproportionately more than impoverished Protestants. In the febrile sphere of charity and philanthropy in nineteenth-century Irish urban communities, poor relief became weaponised (in verbal terms), as Catholics and Protestants manoeuvred to ensure the safety of the souls of their own congregants.

Catholics were not the only group carrying, and occasionally expressing, grievances. Dissenters (largely Presbyterians) were also vocal in their criticisms of the vestries and their feelings of injustice arising from this system. It is significant that, according to Ian d'Alton, it was in Holy Trinity parish, where almost one-half of Cork city's Dissenters lived, that organised opposition to the parish cess was fiercest.[19] Dissenter Cork city engineer James Wherland (d. 1845) could not help himself, while voicing

16 Hereward Senior, *Orangeism in Ireland and Britain 1795–1836* (London and Toronto, 1966), pp 225–37; S.T. Kingon, 'Ulster opposition to Catholic emancipation, 1828–9' in *Irish Historical Studies*, xxxiv, no. 134 (Nov. 2004), pp 137–55.

17 Maria Luddy, *Women and philanthropy in nineteenth-century Ireland* (Cambridge, 1995), *passim*.

18 Jacinta Prunty, *Dublin slums, 1800–1925: a study in urban geography* (Dublin, 1998), pp 234–73; eadem, 'Battle plans and battlegrounds: Protestant mission activity in the Dublin slums, 1840s–1880s' in Crawford Gribben & A.R. Holmes (eds), *Protestant millennialism, evangelicalism and Irish society, 1790–2005* (Basingstoke, 2006), pp 119–43.

19 D'Alton, *Protestant society and politics in Cork*, p. 75.

his opposition to an assessment of £25 for the secretary of the church rebuilding committee chairman, from asserting that the Church of Ireland congregation was, during the repair work, accommodated at local Dissenting meeting houses for worship, 'yet they had never contributed a single farthing to the relief of the Presbyterian poor'.[20] Among those aggrieved at the Easter 1830 Holy Trinity vestry was a Mr Osborne, a member of the city's Presbyterian community, whose meeting house was at Prince's Street, located within Holy Trinity parish.[21] The newspaper account of the proceedings reported: 'If he [Osborne] were to apply to the Episcopalians to pay for the organ in Prince's-street, where he went to worship, it would be a monstrous thing, and they would feel very sore at it, and it was quite as unjust that he should be assessed for their Organist.'[22] Similar sentiments were expressed by a Mr Bagley (whose denominational affiliation was not recorded but who may have been a Dissenter). Bagley opposed in the strongest terms the 'disgraceful' assessment of Catholics and Dissenters 'for providing sacred elements' (that is, the bread and wine for divine service). When £15 was proposed for the parish clerk's salary, the motion was opposed by Messrs Fitzgibbon and Osborne, the latter stating that every religion should pay for its own support. To this, a Mr Barber reminded the Presbyterian Osborne 'that the country generally was paying for the support of their own religion' – an implicit reference to the *regium donum* state payment made to Dissenting (especially Presbyterian) ministers since the reign of Charles II, as a means of securing their political loyalty. The question of the clerk's salary was put to a vote and the motion – to assess parishioners for the sum of £15 – was defeated by forty-eight votes to forty-seven.[23] The tight margin by which the motion was decided reflected the divisions present within the parish and how the question of the assessment of parishioners, and the administration of the money thus raised, served as a lightning rod for the underlying sectarian conflict and tensions.

The Holy Trinity select vestry concluded its business sometime before 2pm on Easter Monday, with the election of churchwardens and the levying of a parochial cess on certain items of expenditure – including, but not limited to, the sexton's salary (£120), 'sacramental bread and wine' (£3), 'Lighting the church' (£17) and the organist's salary (£40). At 2pm, the general vestry opened, where Roman Catholics were entitled to vote; at this second meeting, the only two items budgeted for were costs for the fire

20 *CA*, 13 Apr. 1830.

21 The meeting house at 39 Prince's Street is sometimes known as the 'Old Presbyterian Church' and is now (2023) used as a Unitarian place of worship.

22 *CA*, 13 Apr. 1830.

23 Ibid.

engine keeper (£15) and the parochial provision for foundlings (£4 4*s*.).[24] As these final two items of expenditure were seen as benefiting the entire parish, without regard to confessional differences, and as Catholics were entitled to vote to approve or reject this expenditure, this second meeting did not generate discord or conflict amongst those Holy Trinity parishioners present.

Dublin, 1838

The Dublin incident referred to at the beginning of this chapter, and to which we now turn our attention, occurred at the 1838 annual Easter meeting of the select vestry of St Paul's parish on Dublin City's north side. St Paul's, along with St Mary's, was created out of St Michan's parish in 1697 and is located at the northwestern extremity of the city centre. By 1841, St Paul's had a population of 7,550 persons; statistics provided in the 1834 report on public instruction suggests that just less than a quarter of the parishioners belonged to the Church of Ireland, while nearly all the remainder were Catholics.[25] The parish contained the Royal Barracks and the Blue Coat Hospital on Blackhall Place, as well as the notorious slum district of Barrack Street (now Benburb Street). Numerous social surveys in the early- to mid-nineteenth century identify Barrack Street and nearby Church Street (in the adjacent parish of St Michan's) as the hubs of poverty, destitution and 'fever nests' on the north side of the Liffey.[26] James Whitelaw's 1798 survey of the city's population, published in 1805, confirms this fact: of Dublin's parishes located to the north of the River Liffey, St Paul's and its neighbouring parish of St Michan's had a greater proportion of inhabitants described as 'Lower Class' by Whitelaw and his enumerators (76 and 79 per cent respectively), while the respective figures for the three other northside parishes were between 31 and 51 per cent. On the southside, the parishes with the largest proportion of inhabitants in this category were located in the city's southwestern quarter, known as the Liberties, illustrating the geographical concentration of acute

24 'Cork vestries. Returns of the several sums of money assessed in the several parishes in the city of Cork, by the vestries holden during Easter week, in the year 1830 …', p. 2, H.C. 1830 (525), xxxi, 294.

25 'Report of the commissioners appointed to take the census of Ireland, for the year 1841', pp 16–19, H.C. 1843 [C 504], xxiv, 128–31; 'First report, Commissioners of Public Instruction, Ireland', p. 122b.

26 For this general area, see 'A table of the population of Church and Barrack Street', n.d. [c.1817] (National Archives of Ireland (N.A.I.), Chief Secretary's Office Official Papers, OP474/8); Prunty, *Dublin slums*, pp 274–335.

poverty in Dublin's northwestern and southwestern districts.[27] Most of the main thoroughfares in St Paul's – Barrack Street, North King Street and Queen Street – were listed as third-class shop streets in William Wilde's classification of Dublin streets in the 1841 census.[28]

At the annual vestry meeting on Easter Monday, 16 April 1838, a Catholic parishioner, Mr Brenan, was aggrieved. Brenan demanded to be allowed to speak on the matter of the election of churchwardens, among the most imperative issues raised at annual vestry meetings. Brenan began his contribution to the discussion by acknowledging that as a Roman Catholic, he was not entitled to vote at the select vestry; however, he requested that a suggestion of his be heard – namely, that a 'liberal Protestant' named Mr Atkinson be nominated for the position of churchwarden. Brenan asserted to the largely Church of Ireland assembly: 'Though *you* have the exclusive right of electing the churchwardens, I think *we* are at liberty to suggest, if not to vote.' Several Anglican parishioners criticised Brenan for his intervention, asserting that they did not disturb proceedings at the Catholic chapel: '*You* are only allowed to attend here as a matter of courtesy, and *you* cannot interfere in the proceedings.' To this, Brenan replied: '*You* say *you* never interfered with *us* in *our* chapels. I say *we* never interfered with *you* in *your* churches. I think a vestry meeting is a different thing altogether. *It is a temporal matter. We* are in the majority of the rate-payers of the parish, and *we* have a right to interfere.' The *Freeman's Journal*'s account of this exchange reported that upon the conclusion of this initial select vestry meeting, a second (general vestry) meeting commenced, 'which was open to all the inhabitants of the parish'.[29]

In this instance, the conflict between Protestant and Catholic parishioners in St Paul's was limited to heated verbal exchanges. However, episodes of more febrile disagreements and even the outbreak of violence was widely reported in the annual flurry of reports of Dublin's Easter vestry meetings. This incident in St Paul's fell within what John Crawford paints as the most tumultuous

27 Whitelaw divided the city's inhabitants into three categories: 'Upper and Middle Classes', 'Servants of Ditto' and 'Lower Class'. The southside parishes with particularly high rates of 'Lower Class' inhabitants were St James, St Catherine, St Luke, St Nicholas Without, St Michael, St Luke and the deanery of St Patrick's: James Whitelaw, *An essay on the population of Dublin, being the actual survey taken in 1798, with great care and precision, and arranged in a manner entirely new ...* (Dublin, 1805), fold-out table, pp 14–15.

28 William Wilde, 'Special Sanitary Report on Dublin city', 'Report of the commissioners appointed to take the census of Ireland, for the year 1841: Tables of death, section V', pp lxviii–lxviv, H.C. 1843 [C 504], xxiv, 1. A useful analysis of St Paul's parish in the first half of the eighteenth century is presented in Brendan Twomey, *Smithfield and the parish of St Paul, Dublin, 1698–1750* (Dublin, 2005).

29 *FJ*, 17 Apr. 1838. In these quotations, the author has added emphasis through italicisation of text. See also Bob Cullen, *Thomas L. Synnott: the career of a Dublin Catholic 1830–1870* (Dublin, 1997), pp 18–21.

and divisive period in the running of nineteenth-century vestries in Dublin – that is, the mid-1830s to the early 1840s. For instance, Crawford illustrates: 'In 1836, following a series of chaotic Easter vestries, the Tory *Dublin Evening Mail* observed that it could no longer "burden our columns, or offend public taste" by covering such events.'[30] The St Michan's vestry was 'notorious for stormy discussions' in this period, with the police having to attend regularly, while in 1840 an Easter vestry meeting in St Catherine's parish ended in riot, violence, the destruction of property and a four-day hearing before the police magistrates.[31] In 1835 a vestry meeting in the rural County Dublin parish of Lucan was the scene of 'violent proceedings [by] the Roman Catholic inhabitants' owing to their disapproval of the vestry overseeing the allocation of relief measures to the local Catholic poor: it was asserted that the Catholic community could take care of its own poor and that 'Protestant assistance was not needed'.[32] At times, parish vestry meetings could descend into the pantomimic and absurd; grievances and conflict were not limited to more substantive disagreements arising from religious or political rivalries. For example, at the St Bride's Easter vestry in 1838 the beadle was accused of running 'an improper house' and it was suggested that his parochial salary be reduced as a result. In response, the beadle became so enraged that he climbed up on a table and, according to the newspaper report, 'after making repeated efforts to obtain a hearing, he was obliged to content himself with making a series of pantomimic gestures expressive of his wish to exercise his fists in a pugilistic encounter on the faces of the persons who were opposed to his getting 20*l*. a year'. A resolution to reduce his salary to £10 per annum was carried 'if not unanimously, at least without opposition, for a number of the persons present were more occupied in observing the ludicrous conduct of the beadle than attending to the business of the meeting'.[33]

Returning to the St Paul's instance at Easter 1838, we see that this exchange is interesting for several reasons: first, it provides a window into the complex make-up of nineteenth-century parish vestries, especially in urban locations, arising from the coexistence of ecclesiastical and civil parishes from the late-mediaeval/early modern period. The Church of Ireland parish was both an ecclesiastical and civil entity, as were the church building and its vestry room: in the early modern period, for example, contracts and leases were known to be signed in the church porch, a space equally open to parishioners

30 Crawford, *Church of Ireland in Victorian Dublin*, p. 154.

31 Ibid., pp 162, 163–8.

32 Quoted in Patricia Donohoe, 'Protestant philanthropy and social interaction in the 19th century' in Linda Curran *et al.* (eds), *Aspects of Lucan: four historical essays* (Leixlip, 2008), p. 88.

33 Newspaper clipping, dated *FJ*, 8 Apr. 1838, inserted within front cover of St Bride's parish vestry minute book (Representative Church Body Library, Dublin (R.C.B.L.), P 327.3.3).

of all denominations (persons living within the geographical parish, as distinct from Church of Ireland congregants).[34] Brenan's reference to the vestry meeting constituting a 'temporal matter' captures the conflict between the ecclesiastical and civil expenditures overseen by the vestries and the important matter of who was to foot the bill. Grievance over power imbalance at this local level of government was one thing but the imposition of parochial taxes on non-Anglicans for Anglican expenditure pertaining to worship was most commonly the root cause of conflict, disenchantment and public discord. The potential for this financial imposition to generate ill-will was emphasised by Congregationalist minister and journalist James Godkin (1806–79) in his 1867 work *Ireland and her churches*, wherein he argues for religious equality and identifies the pre-Famine vestry system as a source of conflict:

> [T]he parish church was converted into a bear-garden every Easter Monday about the vestry-rate, against which the Roman Catholic ratepayers uproariously contended with the rector and his friends, protesting that they ought not to be compelled to pay for the sweeping of the church, the washing of the surplice, and even for the bread and wine used in the sacrament, which was an outrage upon their consciences.[35]

The evolution throughout the eighteenth century of select and general vestries was in response to growing intercommunity tensions centred on access to local manifestations of political power (including power respecting the levying of local taxes): select vestries were assemblies where only Anglicans could vote, while parishioners of all denominations could vote and (almost) fully participate in the general vestries.[36]

In addition, it is interesting to note that Mr Brenan of St Paul's typified the fact that, while many Catholics held grievances as to their limited rights within the parish vestry system, they nonetheless held positions of authority within the parish: Brenan, possibly the same James Brenan that is listed as a tallow-chandler at 66 Barrack Street,[37] served St Paul's parish as an unpaid officer of health, appointed under the 1819 Contagious Diseases legislation.[38] Catholics and Dissenters often held parochial positions, such as officers of health, as well as overseers of public houses and overseers of deserted children. For instance, at the 1792 Easter vestry in St Catherine's parish, fifteen Catholics and fifteen

34 Ciarán McCabe, *Begging, charity and religion in pre-Famine Ireland* (Liverpool, 2018), pp 128–32.

35 James Godkin, *Ireland and her churches* (London, 1867), p. 274.

36 *Dublin vestries. Returns of the several sums of money assessed in the several parishes in the city of Dublin, 1830.*

37 *Wilson's Dublin directory for the year 1831 …* (Dublin, n.d. [1831]), p. 50.

38 *FJ*, 17 Apr. 1838.

Protestants were elected as overseers of public houses.[39] In her work on the vestry minute books of Finglas in rural north County Dublin, Maighréad Ní Mhurchadha suggests that the appointment of Catholics as sidesmen from the 1720s served to mitigate the difficulties experienced in collecting the parish cess from the largely Catholic parishioners. Catholic cooperation in the administrative functioning of the parish was also courted through their involvement in auditing the parish accounts.[40] There are even rare examples of Catholics serving as churchwardens. One such instance occurred in 1827 in Dunany parish in the diocese of Armagh in 1827; the parish's entry in the relevant parliamentary return includes, under the listing of the two churchwardens' names, the note: '*N.B.* One of the churchwardens is a Roman Catholic.'[41] It is striking that this short note is preceded by the *nota bene* abbreviation, signifying the unusual nature of this arrangement. Presbyterians in Ulster played a greater role in local parish vestries than in other parts of the island, owing to the concentration of Presbyterianism in the northern province. A parliamentary return from the mid-1820s records that, in respect of Bangor, County Down, the 'Body of the Inhabitants of the Parish are Dissenters from the Established Church, and are mostly of the Church of Scotland, who form the great Majority at all Vestries'.[42] These instances of parochial office-holding by non-Anglicans speak to the fact that the workings of the parish vestries did not serve to universally alienate Catholics and Dissenters from the system, and reveal that there was a certain level of 'buy-in' from parishioners who did not belong to the Established Church. This type of conflict, and occasional violence, therefore, contrast sharply with the recurring problem of agrarian protest, which broke out intermittently in rural Ireland from the 1760s onwards, especially as regards the 'respectable' nature of the urban outbreaks of conflict and violence (wherein the aggrieved parties wished for greater access to systems of power) and the 'disrespectable' manner of agrarian disorder (wherein prevailing systems of power and hierarchy were defied).

The St Paul's exchange also attests to the strongly held notions of communal allegiance and identity that were played out at parish vestries. As the most tangible manifestation of localised government power in the community, the annual meetings of parish vestries operated as sites for conflict, and the tensions that underpinned this conflict were most acutely palpable in urban

39 St Catherine's parish, Dublin vestry minute book, 31 May 1792 (R.C.B.L., St Catherine's parish, Dublin vestry minute books, P 117.05.5).

40 Maighréad Ní Mhurchadha, 'Introduction' in eadem (ed.), *The vestry records of the united parishes of Finglas, St Margaret's, Artane and the Ward, 1657–1758* (Dublin, 2007), p. 22.

41 *Parochial rates (Ireland). Returns to an order of the Honourable House of Commons, dated 12th February 1828 …*, p. 11, H.C. 1828 (370), xxii, 285.

42 'Ireland. An account of all sums of money levied in the several parishes of Ireland, by authority of vestry … Part I' (n.p., n.d. [c.1824]), p. 340, consulted at N.L.I. (Ref. Ir274108il).

centres, where members of the Church of Ireland comprised a significant minority of the population. While Oliver MacDonagh painted Irish vestries as being largely unable to operate effectively due to insufficient resources, a more nuanced analysis by David Dickson estimates that a critical minimum of Anglicans comprising between 15 to 20 per cent of the local population was sufficient for the successful management of a parish. This was most relevant in urban centres, where Protestants (albeit in a minority by the nineteenth century) comprised a greater proportion of the local population than rural parishes.[43] Among the most striking aspects of the printed exchange between the Protestant and Catholic parishioners of St Paul's was the way the language used drew explicitly on sentiments of communal allegiances and rivalries. The terms 'you' and 'your' (in the plural sense) were deployed by both Protestant and Catholic contributors, as were 'we', 'us' and 'our'. What was on display at the St Paul's Easter vestry in 1838 was an assertion of conflicting communal identity, framed by disparities in access to local political power, supporting Raymond Gillespie's argument that the 'wider scope of its civil functions ensured that the parish formed one of the key building blocks of local community identity'.[44]

Some reflection on the wider political landscape of Dublin City at the time is useful. These scenes of conflict between Catholics and Protestants were occurring at a time of broader shifts in the positioning of Catholicism and Protestantism in pre-Famine Irish society: the growing assertiveness of the Catholic political nation challenged the declining near-monopoly of public life by members of the Church of Ireland;[45] the rise of evangelical Protestantism and, with the Second Reformation from the early 1820s, growing polarisation between Catholics and Protestants;[46] the early nineteenth century saw the rise to, and ultimately fall from, political significance in Dublin City of a grouping of conservative ultra-Protestants, who were united by their passionate anti-Emancipationist politics and involvement in Orangeism;[47] the

43 Oliver MacDonagh, *Ireland: the Union and its aftermath* (rev. ed., London, 1977), pp 34–5; David Dickson, 'In search of the old Irish poor law' in Rosalind Mitchison & Peter Roebuck (eds), *Economy and society in Scotland and Ireland, 1500–1939* (Edinburgh, 1988), p. 157. See also Gallagher, 'Bishop Thomas Lewis O'Beirne and his church-building programme', pp 215–16.

44 Raymond Gillespie, 'Introduction' in idem (ed.), *The vestry records of the parishes of St Catherine and St James, Dublin, 1657–1692* (Dublin, 2004), p. 9.

45 Thomas Bartlett, *The fall and rise of the Irish nation: the Catholic question 1690–1830* (Dublin, 1992), esp. pp 304–42.

46 Irene Whelan, *The bible war in Ireland: the 'Second Reformation' and the polarization of Protestant-Catholic relations, 1800–1840* (Dublin, 2005).

47 Jacqueline Hill, 'Dublin after the union: the age of the ultra-Protestants, 1801–1822' in Michael Brown, P.M. Geoghegan & James Kelly (eds), *The Irish Act of Union, 1800: bicentennial essays* (Dublin, 2003), pp 144–56.

artisan and lower middle classes of all denominations – but especially Church of Ireland artisans – were hit by the economic downturns of the mid-1820s and the late-1830s/early 1840s, which contributed to fuelling the fires of sectarian conflict (Jacqueline Hill has identified the three years 1839–41 as central to working-class Protestants' loss of status and influence in the city, overlapping with John Crawford's description of these years as the most tumultuous period for the holding of vestry meetings);[48] in Dublin, communal divisions based on confessional allegiance became more clearly defined in response to Daniel O'Connell's Repeal campaign of the 1830s and 1840s, more so than during the Catholic Emancipation campaign of the 1820s; the increasing importance of print culture in fomenting these divisions, with the proliferation of a large number of denominationally based newspapers and journals, not to mention a vibrant trade in pamphlets contributing to discourses of political and religious controversy;[49] and, as Ian d'Alton has observed of Irish Protestantism, 'the awareness of a minority position and an increasing impatience and indifference demonstrated by government and public opinion in Britain created a crisis of morale in the period 1820–40 ... virtually every facet of Protestant ascendancy came under public and parliamentary scrutiny'.[50] Regrettably, the surviving records – predominantly, vestry minute books and newspaper reports – do not give a direct sense of political conflict seeping into the vestry meetings: there is no overt assertion of political rivalries – for instance, between liberal O'Connellites and (Protestant) conservatives – being espoused at these assemblies. As such, it remains to be seen to what extent these divisions were driven by political tensions in pre-Famine urban centres overflowing into the annual Easter vestry meetings.[51]

48 Jacqueline Hill, 'The Protestant response to repeal: the case of the Dublin working class' in F.S.L. Lyons (ed.), *Ireland under the Union: varieties of tension. Essays in honour of T. W. Moody* (Oxford, 1980), p. 48. For the broader context of the decline of Protestant privilege in the 1830s, see D.G. Boyce, *Ireland 1828–1923: from ascendancy to democracy* (Oxford, 1992), pp 15–22.

49 Niall Ó Ciosáin, *Print and popular culture in Ireland, 1750–1850* (Basingstoke, 1997); J.H. Murphy, *Ireland: a social, cultural and literary history, 1791–1891* (Dublin, 2003), pp 21–8, 65–93.

50 Ian d'Alton, 'A contrast in crises: southern Irish Protestantism, 1820–43 and 1885–1910' in A.C. Hepburn (ed.), *Minorities in history: historical studies XII* (London, 1978), p. 76. Many of the themes outlined in this paragraph are explored in Jacqueline Hill's concise and useful, 'Religion, trade and politics in Dublin 1798–1848' in P. Butel & L.M. Cullen (eds), *Cities and merchants: French and Irish perspectives on urban development, 1500–1900* (Dublin, 1986), pp 247–59.

51 For more on this, see Hill, 'Protestant response to repeal'; d'Alton, *Protestant society and politics in Cork*, esp. p. 78.

Conclusion

The first half of the nineteenth century witnessed increasing polarisation between Catholics and Protestants in Ireland. Intercommunity relations were characterised, more and more, by conflict and tension. At the centre of these evolving dynamics was a growing sense of threat and vulnerability felt by Irish Protestants (and, within the Church of Ireland, a gradual loss of privilege), driven, in part, by responses to an increasingly confident and forceful Catholicism: as Jacqueline Hill observes, '[d]eference was now replaced by a new assertiveness'.[52] This chapter concerns itself with the conflict between opposing factions in pre-Famine vestries in Dublin and Cork in the expression of public opinion in increasingly febrile and polarised environments. The removal of certain legal restrictions on Catholics from the mid-1780s offered new opportunities for playing an increased role in urban civic life and in this context, as Hill writes, 'the vestry had acquired a new potential as the expression of public opinion'.[53] Involvement in the parish vestry system was just one of these new opportunities, Yet in urban centres where much of people's everyday lives depended on services provided through the parish, the vestries were arguably the most important realm within the civic sphere for engaged citizens to participate actively within their local community. Owing to the vestry's importance as a source of political power, as well as, crucially, its possessing the power to levy local taxes on parishioners, it was inevitable that vestry meetings generated heightened tensions and outbursts. The injustice of this system was noted by numerous commentators. Among them was Sir John Newport (1756–1843), a banker from a prominent Dissenting Waterford family who publicly supported Catholic Emancipation from as early as the 1790s.[54]

In a speech before the House of Commons in February 1825, Newport castigated the prevailing system of parochial management and cess administration, noting the inequality of levying non-Anglicans against their will for Anglican-specific expenditure, and referring to 'the iniquitous system going on in Ireland, to plunder the Catholics there of their property, by an Ascendancy faction'. Referring to the return of parochial rates levied throughout Ireland in the previous twelve years, Newport slammed: 'These returns were exceedingly voluminous, and disclosed a system of abuse and misapplication of the money raised by the vestries in Ireland, to which, he believed, there was

52 Hill, 'Religion, trade and politics', p. 251.

53 Hill, *From patriots to unionists*, p. 174.

54 Bridget Hourican, 'Newport, Sir (Simon) John' in James McGuire & James Quinn (eds), *Dictionary of Irish biography from the earliest times to the year 2002* (11 vols, Cambridge, 2009–18), vi, pp 902–3.

nothing at all parallel. *The parochial vestries in Ireland set the law completely at defiance.*'[55] Newport provided a litany of examples of unjustified taxation of non-Anglicans for expenditure on, for example, the salary of the Church of Ireland organist (St Peter's, Drogheda, County Louth), decorations for the Anglican place of worship (Thurles, County Tipperary) and prayer books. Such disputes were the most contentious matters discussed at Irish parish vestries prior to 1833: in that year, the Church Temporalities Act prohibited the assessment of non-Anglicans for expenditure specific to the Anglican celebration of divine service.[56] Of our two case studies, the Cork instance occurred three years before the Church Temporalities Act, at a time when parish vestries still possessed the power, as affirmed in the 1826 Church Rates Act,[57] to assess non-Anglican parishioners for Church of Ireland expenditure and withhold (in the case of Catholics) their entitlement to vote against such assessments. By the time of the Dublin instance (1838), this practice had been prohibited and a more concrete system of select and general vestries had taken hold throughout the island.

Interdenominational conflict at vestry meetings was not limited to the pre-Famine period and persisted into the second half of the century. By then, Catholics were no longer being assessed for Anglican-specific expenditure; rather, the most contentious issue was the election of overseers of deserted children within the parish, reflecting each denomination's acute sensitivities over securing the fate of its own flock, especially amongst the vulnerable and supposedly impressionistic poor. For example, at the 1863 Easter vestry meeting in St Peter's parish in Dublin, the discussion on the election of overseers was preceded by the chairman's call for calm and order, in anticipation of a heated discussion. His call, however, was in vain: 'He made a few observations, which, amid the confusion which then prevailed, could not be heard distinctly ... During this proceeding [as people lined up to cast their vote] considerable confusion, noise and uproar was kept up. Not a few were detected on both sides attempting to personate voters, and were pretty roughly handled.' In the end, the announcement that 227 votes were cast for six Protestant candidates and 203 were cast for six Catholic persons, 'was received with hisses and applause'. When the meeting moved on to discuss the assessment of parishioners for the maintenance of deserted children, and the role of Catholics and Protestants in overseeing this maintenance, disorder and affray broke out: 'At this stage of the proceedings a regular fight commenced in the lower end of the school room, and all was soon one scene

55 [Sir John Newport], *A slight peep into the church vestry system in Ireland* (London, n.d. [c.1825]), p. 1. For Newport's full speech, see *Hansard 2*, xii, cols 617–21.
56 3 & 4 Will. IV, c.37, s.73 (14 Aug. 1833).
57 7 Geo. IV, c.72, s.2 (31 May 1826).

of confusion. The inspector of police, who was in the vicinity, entered, and after some time and trouble restored order.'[58] This instance illustrated the fact that as the Irish parish vestry evolved throughout the nineteenth century, as legislation increasingly curtailed its powers in respect of its civil functions, new factors arose that served to resurrect underlying conflict and tensions between Catholics and Protestants.

This chapter focuses on parish vestries in two urban centres – Dublin and Cork cities – which both boasted large Church of Ireland minorities. The question remains as to how interdenominational relations evolved, and how conflict and tensions manifested themselves, in rural parishes, where the Church of Ireland community constituted a smaller proportion of the general population. As demonstrated above, the 1830s and early 1840s was a period of acute conflict within Irish urban parish vestries, owing to broader social, economic and political dynamics. The workings of parish vestries, especially in respect of their annual Easter meetings, serve as a useful vehicle with which to drive an analysis of intercommunity conflict in the pre-Famine decades, and further work will expand the research to other urban centres to facilitate comparative analysis of Protestant–Catholic relations through the prism of the parish vestry.[59]

58 *FJ*, 7 Apr. 1863.

59 This chapter arises from papers delivered at the conference of the Society for the Study of Nineteenth-Century Ireland at University College Dublin in June 2022 and the 'Second Reformation: Bicentennial Perspectives' symposium at Maynooth University in October 2022. I am grateful to Professors Irene Whelan, Jacqueline Hill and Peter Gray for their comments on those papers.

3

J. Duncan Craig and the Sectarian and Agrarian Conflicts of Nineteenth-Century Ireland

Patrick Maume

Introduction

Recent Irish historians of the nineteenth century tend to emphasise change over continuity and segment the era into periods of a few decades. This can obscure how the conflicts of nineteenth-century Ireland were influenced by factions and individuals interpreting contemporary crises as recapitulations of earlier struggles. As Anthony D. Smith argues, 'modernist' theories of nationalism overlook influences from the early modern and even mediaeval periods.[1] Nationalists in the tradition of John Mitchel who saw Lord Clarendon and Earl Spencer as latter-day Cromwells, ultramontane populists identifying with Rinuccini against the temporising Ormondists, Church of Ireland clergymen with experience or traditions of anti-tithe violence and struggling with the failure of the proselytising 'Second Reformation',[2] shared the view that Whig–Liberal promises of a clean start through a shared British identity cleansed of vested interests and incorporating enlightened Catholics was a fraud and that the religious, political and agrarian conflicts of the early modern era were cyclical and could only be escaped by being fought to a conclusion.

This chapter is a case study of how the life and public commitments of John Duncan Craig (1830–1909), Church of Ireland clergyman, Provençal

1 Anthony D. Smith, *Nationalism and modernism* (London, 1998); Patrick Maume, 'The *Catholic Bulletin* 1911–1939 – battle of civilizations or long revolution?' in Mark O'Brien & F.M. Larkin (eds) *Periodicals and journalism in twentieth-century Ireland 2: A variety of voices* (Dublin, 2021).

2 Irene Whelan, *The Bible war in Ireland* (Dublin, 2012); W.J. McCormick, *Sheridan Le Fanu and Victorian Ireland* (Oxford, 1980).

language student, preacher, Orangeman and man of letters in the Fenian and Land War era, were influenced by a vision of Irish history devised in the early modern period, assimilated by ultra-loyalist interpretations of the 1798 Rising and reinforced by pre-Famine agrarian violence and recurring Whig–Liberal attempts to appease Catholic discontent by distancing the state from the embattled Church of Ireland. This vision, vivified for Craig by Protestant siege mentality in mid-Victorian West Cork and Huguenot martyr traditions in Provence, postulated inevitable conflict between civilising Protestant colonists and barbaric Catholic natives dissuadable from priest-incited massacres only by conversion to evangelical Protestantism.

Craig's worldview is explored through three themes: personal identification with the narrative of Protestant beleaguerment and martyrdom; internal Protestant tensions between secularisers, pan-Protestant evangelicals and alleged Romanisers; Craig's response to the Land War and Home Rule conflicts of the 1880s, in pulpit, committee room and newspaper controversies. Craig was opinionated and volatile, fond of exclamation marks, with a preacher's theatricality. He did not always pursue the implications of his statements, but he represented a conspicuous, though declining, subculture whose persistence intensified the bitterness of the 1880s culture wars that accompanied the agrarian struggle and inspired by reaction the 1890s cultural revival and its attempts to articulate a shared Irishness.

Protestant beleaguerment and martyrdom

John Duncan Craig was born in Dublin and grew up at Horsehead House, near Passage West on Cork Harbour. He descended from Scots gentry who claimed Robert the Bruce and covenanting martyrs as ancestors; his father ran a French steamship line before becoming a bank manager. Craig entered Trinity in 1847 to study engineering but transferred to divinity in response to a friend's death.[3] Dublin, just before the abortive 1848 rising, with John Mitchel and others publishing treasonable newspapers and crowds threatening soldiers and loyalists, left a permanent impression and preoccupation with seditious print culture as an engine of conflict. 'Rebel ballads were sung by itinerant melodists, each surrounded by a choice gathering of the well-wishers of the Irish Republic. Rebel literature was sown broadcast throughout the

3 J.D. Craig, *Real pictures of clerical life in Ireland* (London, 1901; first pub. 1875), pp 1–24; *Irish Times* (henceforth cited as *IT*), 12 Apr. 1909. Henceforth all books cited are by J.D. Craig, unless otherwise stated.

land; nor, indeed, has that pernicious poison ever since really ceased from dissemination through Ireland.'[4]

During the Land War Craig exchanged denunciations with nationalist newspapers, and in his Land War novel *Bruce Reynell* (1901), a disreputable journalist rejoices that the government has lost its nerve since 1848:

> I wonder where Parnell would be now if the Freedom's Journal and the rest of them had not taken him up? ... I often wonder that the Government allows our coloured cartoons every week ... A cartoon ... goes everywhere. It is hung up in the garret, and gazed at in the kitchen; it decks the gloomy windows in the liberties of Dublin, and it stirs the Moonlighter's heart; it rouses the Tipperary cabin, and it sends fire into the down-trodden serf of Kerry ... you can suggest so much in a coloured cartoon – so safely, too ... the National movement would be as dull as ditch-water without them ... 'Tis very easy to be a rebel nowadays. Government gives you every facility and immunity ... Write, speak, preach, print, picture, anything you like. They have such a wholesome fear of coercion ... in 1848 one of those same cartoons dared not be published ... the paper would be seized in an hour's time ... I got free quarters in Kilmainham, and it was not champagne and salmon I got there ...[5]

After graduation in 1851 and ordination in 1853, Craig worked in the Dublin Liberties before moving to Munster for health reasons. He held curacies on the Cork–Tipperary boundary, in Kinsale, at St Mary's Youghal and in Crosshaven, before returning to Kinsale as Rector between 1863 and 1872.[6]

A church Craig served in as curate, Templebrady, near Passage West, was partially demolished when a new church was built. Craig was deeply affected by its ruins and produced recurring images of a church, once a centre of paternalist charity and scriptural education, destroyed by Romanism and disendowment – a Protestant counterblast to evocations of ruined monasteries.[7] Craig's duties, described in his fictional and non-fictional sketches *Real Pictures of Clerical Life in Ireland*, included chaplaincy to convicts in Cork Harbour and soldiers in local garrisons (notably Charles Fort in Kinsale, where he tried to quieten rioting Antrim militiamen during the 1859 'Battle of Kinsale').[8] Craig's hierarchical view of society included lifelong military interests, publishing revivalist

4 *Real pictures*, p. 25.
5 *Bruce Reynell, M.A. (locum tenens) or the Oxford man in Ireland* (London, 1901), pp 145–6.
6 *Church of Ireland Gazette*, 8 Apr. 1909.
7 Craig, *Real pictures*, pp 30, 106.
8 *Real pictures*, passim; cf William Butler, *The Irish amateur military tradition in the British Army 1854–1992* (Manchester, 2016), pp 164–5.

hymns for soldiers[9] and fundraising for the Army Scripture-Readers' Society.[10] This underlies his novel *John Maverell* (1898), which features Vicomte Trelcat, French ex-officer turned political convict and Protestant convert[11] (although one reviewer recalled *Les Misérables*,[12] it resembles Alexandre Dumas, with its vengeance-seeking convict – *The Count of Monte Cristo* – and swordsman-turned-intriguing Jesuit – Aramis in *The Man in the Iron Mask*).

His West Cork pastoral activities were interrupted by visiting Provence in 1855, partly for health reasons, as chaplain to crews of British ships transporting Sardinian-Piedmontese soldiers to the Crimean War. In Provence Craig underwent an evangelical conversion-experience,[13] smuggled Gospel translations into Piedmont-Sardinia[14] and developed an interest in the Provençal language. Craig's first novel, *Lady Wilmerding of Maison Rouge* (1869),[15] combines a sensation-novel plot about avenging a man murdered by pirates with digressions (including a chapter-long sermon, two chapters also published separately as religious tracts and the narrative of a Frenchman deceived by the *Tipperary Sunburst*'s descriptions of peaceful peasants into buying an estate with 'good shooting', finding *he* is the 'good shooting').[16]

In 1863 Craig published a *Handbook of the Provençal Language*, officially commended by Napoleon III, leading to correspondence with the Provençal poet Frederic Mistral. Craig translated English-language hymns into Provençal (*La Paroula de la Crouse* (Cannes: H. Vidal, 1866)) and Provençal poetry into English.[17] During an 1876 visit, commemorated in a travel narrative, *Miejour* (1877), Craig was inducted into the Felibrige Provençal literary association.[18] Craig, who inherited mild Bonapartist sympathies and regretted the great Emperor had not re-established the Gallican Church on a Protestant basis,[19] befriended the Irish-Provençal poet William Bonaparte Wyse, grandson of Napoleon's brother Lucien.[20] In 1893 Craig told an Orange meeting 'a distin-

9 *Soldiers of the heavenly camp* (Dublin, n.d. [?1900]).
10 *IT*, 24 Oct. 1894, 19 Oct. 1899, 26 Oct. 1903.
11 *John Maverell: a tale of the riviera* (London, 1898).
12 *IT*, 23 May 1898.
13 *Real pictures*, p. 32.
14 *Real pictures*, pp 76–82; *Miejour: Provençal legend, life, language, literature in the land of the Felibrige* (London, 1877), pp 344–5.
15 *Lady Wilmerding of Maison Rouge: a tale of modern Sardinia* (London, rev. ed. 1901; first pub. 1869).
16 Ibid., pp 140–4.
17 *Real pictures*, p. 13;*Miejour*, pp 253–61; *Bruno! With other ballads of the Irish Reign of Terror* (Dublin, 1888), pp 41–4.
18 *Miejour*, pp 447–8.
19 *Real pictures*, p. 13.
20 *Miejour*, pp 432, 445, 477; Bridget Hourican, 'William Charles Wyse' in *DIB* (https://www.dib.ie/biography/wyse-william-charles-a9149-a) (accessed 18 Jun. 2022).

guished member of the Bonaparte family, a nephew of the great Emperor … told him, "Home Rule means suicide for England and hell for Ireland"'.[21] This may have been Bonaparte Wyse.

Craig studied Hebraeo-Spanish dialect for conversionist purposes (he belonged to the Society for Promoting Christianity among the Jews).[22] *John Maverell* features conversionism in one of its numerous subplots, set in the run-up to the Franco-Prussian War amidst shadowy intrigues (including a projected Irish uprising, described in *Bruce Reynell*) among Jesuits, Jews and revolutionaries. Although individual Jewish characters receive some sympathy,[23] and Craig protested against the persecution of Jews in Russia,[24] he ignores the implications of calling Jewish dispersion punishment for deicide and presenting Jews fomenting European war to reacquire the Promised Land as a nucleus of a Jewish empire.[25]

His view of Ireland was shaped by his West Cork experiences. He married twice into West Cork gentry families, in 1860 and 1866.[26] He recalled visiting a sick Protestant in the fishermen's quarter of Kinsale and almost being beaten to death by friends of the patient's Catholic wife.[27] He described pro-Fenian crowds challenging police and soldiers before the 1867 Fenian rising and isolated Protestant farming and gentry families fleeing to towns.[28] Craig criticised the government's failure to enlist these refugees as mounted auxiliaries, as used by the post-unification Italian government against Southern bandit-insurgents[29] (John Sandys Bird, father of Craig's first wife, fought the Rockites as a mounted volunteer at the Battle of Keimaneigh Pass in 1822, celebrated from the Rockite perspective by the poet Máire Bhuí Ní Laoghaire;[30] in *Bruce Reynell* a battle at the 'Pass of Keim-an-Ree' combines the 1822 battle with the 12 July 1849 Orange and Ribbon clash at Dolly's Brae, County Down).[31]

21 *Freeman's Journal* (henceforth cited as *FJ*), 13 Mar. 1893.
22 *IT*, 23 Apr. 1873, 14 Apr. 1875.
23 *John Maverell*, pp 246–51.
24 *IT*, 15 Feb. 1882.
25 *John Maverell*, pp 67–71, 250.
26 Rolf & Magda Loeber, *A guide to Irish fiction 1650–1900* (Dublin, 2006), pp 306–7; *FJ*, 8 Mar. 1866.
27 *Real pictures*, pp 287–91; *Cork Examiner* (henceforth cited as *CE*), 16 Mar. 1871, 16 Apr. 1971.
28 *Real pictures*, pp 122–7, 217–27, 292–6.
29 Ibid., pp 292–6; *Bruce Reynell*, p. 70.
30 *Real pictures*, pp 318–19; Lesa Ní Mhunghaile, 'Máire "Bhuí" Ní Laoghaire' in *DIB* (https://www.dib.ie/biography/ni-laoghaire-maire-bhui-a6189) (accessed 18 Jun. 2022); James S. Donnelly Jr, *Captain Rock: the Irish Agrarian Rebellion of 1821–1824* (Madison, Wisconsin, 2009), pp 68–71, 374–5.
31 *Bruce Reynell*, pp 102–24.

Reiterating that British rule in Ireland was colonial, and equating Ireland with India[32] and the Royal Irish Constabulary with an army of occupation,[33] Craig ridiculed *The Times*'s campaign for the RIC to become a civilian police force – 'mere thief-takers' could never have played their vital paramilitary role in suppressing Fenianism.[34] Liberal attempts to conciliate the irreconcilable majority merely weakened the Loyalist minority. 'In this land they had neither fortress nor army opposing the forces of the Queen, but there was in three millions of people that had been against them for 600 years, and which all the bayonets of the world could not reach, a hatred for British rule and a desire for National independence.'[35]

His celebrations of imperial conflicts, such as 'The Last Man at Isandula', depict isolated evangelical-military heroes resisting hordes of heathen savages. The 'Isandula' verses inspired a celebrated painting by the artist and unionist propagandist R.H. Moynan,[36] whose grotesque portrayal of Zulus' features was evoked in Craig's description of close-quarter combat between Prussian soldiers and French Arab troops – 'The faces of the combatants ... like the creations of Richard Moynan's ... weirdest moments'.[37] Craig maintained the eighteenth- and early nineteenth-century view that Irish Protestants *were* the Irish nation since Catholics were too ignorant, lawless and priest-ridden to be citizens.[38] He invoked living memories of 1820s Rockite conflicts and the violent campaign against tithes in the 1830s, which embittered a generation of Church of Ireland clerical families.[39] Clerics murdered for collecting tithes were celebrated by sympathisers – including Presbyterian leader Henry Cooke – as martyrs;[40] Craig memorialises two such clerics, Charles Ferguson of Timoleague in West Cork and Irvine Whitty of Golden, County Tipperary.[41] George Bond Lowe, hardline County Cork magistrate and pursuer of Whiteboys – the alleged 'Doneraile Conspiracy' to murder him provoked several trials, one featuring Daniel O'Connell – is eulogised

32 *IT*, 13 Oct. 1883; *Real pictures*, pp 294–5, 312.
33 *Lady Wilmerding*, p. 72.
34 *The Ochlocrat in Ireland! Lord Chancellor Bacon versus Mr Gladstone on the Irish Church. Has she failed in her mission? The Soi-Disant prophecies of S. Columb-Kille the real cause of fenian outbreaks in Ireland* (London, 1869), p. 2. Ochlocracy = mob rule.
35 *Irish Daily Independent* (henceforth cited as *IDI*), 10 Feb. 1893.
36 'The Last Man at Isandula' [with note] in *Bruno!* pp 36–8; cf Ian Knight, *Zulu rising: the epic story of Isandlwana and Rorke's Drift* (London, 2010), pp 490–1; Ian F.W. Beckett, *Rorke's Drift and Isandlwana* (Oxford, 2021).
37 *John Maverell*, p. 304.
38 *Belfast Newsletter* (henceforth cited as *BN*), 7 Nov. 1891.
39 W.J. McCormack, *Sheridan Le Fanu and Victorian Ireland* (Oxford, 1980).
40 William McComb, *The repealer repulsed*, ed. Patrick Maume (Dublin, 2000; first pub. Belfast, 1841), p. 184.
41 Craig, *Real pictures*, pp 45–7, 236–8.

ambivalently.[42] Craig compares Lowe to John Graham of Claverhouse, who repressed Craig's revered Scottish Covenanters, both seen by peasant adversaries as ruthless persecutors protected by the devil.[43] William Carleton's tale of ribbon violence, 'Wild Goose Lodge', is cited[44] and Craig's claim that the Fenian Rising was inspired by prophecies ascribed to St Colmcille recalls 1820s Rockite co-option of Pastorini's interpretation of the Book of Revelation prophesying the downfall of Protestantism.[45]

Craig joined the Orange Order in West Cork, seeing its role as a gathering point for scattered Protestants.[46] He later transferred to Dublin-based Lodge, 1505, and preached or prayed at Dublin Orange meetings, one of several deputy grand chaplains of Ireland and a Royal Black Preceptory deputy grand chaplain.[47] *Bruce Reynell* compares West Cork Orangemen to *camisards* (Huguenot guerrillas resisting persecution) of post-1685 southern France. During the Land War, Craig predicted that Ulster Orangemen would rescue their southern brethren:

> It was proposed to substitute as the Irish flag the hyena, and for a motto 600, 60, and 6. When the Home Rule Parliament came they would meet them at the Boyne 100,000 strong ... Lord Erne [Orange Grand Master, 1885–1914] would take the late train to Dublin and go to the new Parliament and order the key to be turned in the lock, and take the key and the hyena banner and throw them into the Liffey ...[48]

Citing Sir Robert Musgrave's history of 1798 to assert that English appeasement encouraging Catholic rebellion and massacre of Protestants recurred in Irish history, Craig maintained that eighteenth-century Whiteboys and 1,798 rebels were led by foreign officers and priests such as Fr Nicholas Sheehy.[49] He portrays villainous priests called 'Fr Murty' who incite sedition to distract their flocks from clerical dues. The name echoes Fr John Murphy, the Wexford rebel leader of 1798. Archbishop King's *History of the Protestants*

42 Daniel Owen Maddyn, *Ireland and its rulers since 1829* (London, 1844).

43 Craig, *Real pictures*, p. 53; Donnelly, *Captain Rock*, p. 269; Patrick Geoghegan, *King Dan: the rise of Daniel O'Connell* (Dublin, 2010).

44 *Real pictures*, pp 51, 163; Terence Dooley, *The murders at Wildgoose Lodge* (Dublin, 2007) overlooks this reference.

45 *Ochlocrat*, pp 13–16; Donnelly, *Captain Rock*, pp 119–49.

46 *Real pictures*, pp 319–20.

47 *IT*, 15 Jul. 1876, 13 Jul. 1878, 9 May 1879, 27 May 1882, 13 Jul. 1883, 15 Jul. 1890, 14 Jul. 1893, 13 Jul. 1895; *FJ*, 5 Nov. 1883, 13 Jul. 1886, 13 Mar. 1893; *CE*, 13 Jul. 1886; *BN*, 14 Jul. 1894, 20 Sept. 1897; *IDI*, 14 Jul. 1894, 22 Sept. 1896.

48 *FJ*, 13 Mar. 1893.

49 *Real pictures*, pp 228–32, 318.

under King James's Government provided further evidence of persecution.[50] This led back to the 1641 massacres. Craig's antidisestablishmentarian pamphlet *The Ochlocrat* [i.e. Gladstone] *in Ireland* cites Bishop Bedell's laments about ubiquitous Catholic priests to argue that before 1641 Ireland experienced Catholic rather than Protestant ascendancy, similar to the nineteenth-century situation, using inflated estimates of massacre victims to claim that without these massacres Ireland in 1868 might have a Protestant majority.[51] He asked how the Prophet Elijah would have responded if told that since only seven thousand in Israel had not knelt to Baal, Baalism should replace the worship of God.[52] Craig called the growing network of confraternities a clerical army preparing a new 1641.[53]

The evangelicalism that Craig advocated believed itself so obviously true, and Catholicism so false, that the slightest exposure to biblical text would produce conversion.[54] This attitude was reinforced by seeing people taking clay from a priest's grave in Ahinagh, County Cork, to cure ailments and priests using horsewhips on unruly congregations.[55] Craig claimed older gentlemanly priests influenced by French Jansenism acquired Protestant virtues, including political loyalty,[56] but ultramontane Maynooth priests of the Cullen era are portrayed – inverting Catholic images of the self-sacrificing Soggarth Aroon and patriot priests – as peasant ignoramuses ludicrously convinced of their own and the Pope's infallibility while double-dealing to advance their temporal and spiritual interests.[57] Craig contrasts this with Church of Ireland clergy families living on turnips during the Famine[58] and financial self-sacrifice to maintain rural parishes even before disestablishment.[59]

50 Ibid., p. 299.
51 *Ochlocrat*, pp 5–6.
52 Ibid., p. 7.
53 *Real pictures*, pp 127–8.
54 Miriam Moffitt, *The society for Irish Church Missions to the Roman Catholics, 1849–1950* (Manchester, 2010); Charlotte Elizabeth Tonna, *Irish recollections*, ed. Patrick Maume (Dublin, 2004).
55 *Real pictures*, pp 318, 244n.
56 Ibid., p. 243; *Bruce Reynell*, p. 223.
57 *Real pictures*, pp 118–19, 128–33, 150–9, 185–94, 239–49, 309, 314; *Bruce Reynell*, pp 30–1, 41–5, 77, 108–10, 113–20, 141–8, 178–80, 191–3, 196, 199–200, 223–4, 226–31, 260–3, 267.
58 *Real pictures*, pp 30, 38–9, 344–51.
59 Ibid., pp 58–9, 233–5.

Internal Protestant tensions

Why had more Irish Catholics not become Protestants? Craig offered standard explanations, such as intimidation, suggesting that Catholics who lapsed after emigration became crypto-Protestants in Ireland, and belated and limited Irish language evangelisation.[60] He supported the Irish Society (a clergyman in *Bruce Reynell* conducts an Irish language class to teach the peasantry to read scripture), but unlike Provençal he ignored Irish as a literary medium (although it was useful for detecting seditious conversations).[61] Craig's association with proselytism was mentioned in the cross-examination of the forger Richard Piggott at the Parnell Commission; Craig lived beside Piggott in Kingstown, and Piggott tried to make the Catholic Archbishop receptive to begging letters with an anonymous letter claiming that Craig (with whose activities Walsh was assumed to be familiar) tried to bribe Piggott to send his children to Protestant institutions[62] (veiled threats of conversion were a favourite tactic of begging-letter writers addressing clergymen).[63]

Craig attributed the failure of Protestant conversionism primarily to the national school system. He thought the early nineteenth-century Kildare Place Society and bodies using the Bible as a textbook gradually influenced Catholic pupils and staff. Craig fantasised (inconsistently with his awareness of agrarian violence) about an era when Church of Ireland rectories dispensed paternal charity accompanied by scriptural instruction, until the 1830s Whig government appeased Catholic bishops by funding only schools which separated secular from religious education and exempted pupils from religious lessons at parents' request.[64] This was compounded by some churchmen led by Archbishop Whately of Dublin cooperating with national schools rather than demanding assistance for the Church Education Society (CES).[65] The CES was a defining issue of early Victorian Irish conservatism;[66] even after disestablishment and the CES allowing individual schools to join the national system, a hard core, including Craig, advocated strict denominationalism. He explained Land War violence:

60 *Ochlocrat*, pp 12–14.
61 *Real pictures*, p. 349.
62 *IT*, 23 Feb. 1889; Donal P. McCracken, *You will dye at midnight: threatening letters in Victorian Ireland* (Dublin, 2021), pp 25–6.
63 Lindsay Earner-Byrne, *Letters of the Catholic poor: poverty in Independent Ireland, 1920–1940* (Cambridge, 2017), pp 107–17.
64 *Real pictures*, pp 42–3, 293–4, 300, 326–7; *Bruce Reynell*, pp vii–viii, 241.
65 *IT*, 1 Nov. 1883, 3 Nov. 1888, 17 Apr. 1890, 31 Oct. 1895; *FJ*, 27 Oct. 1877.
66 Andrew Shields, *The Irish Conservative Party 1852–1868: land, politics and religion* (Dublin, 2007).

> [W]hen the National system was introduced its object was to put a new stamp on the youth of Ireland ... They saw that stamp in the murder of Lord Mountmorres, in the slaughter of the Huddys ... the massacre of the Joyces on the hillside of Connemara ... National schoolmasters had been the very foremost to write those publications and those murderous threatening letters that had disgraced the country.[67]

When a CES member noted the inconsistency of complaining that Catholic-managed schools influenced Protestant pupils against their parents' beliefs while seeking to proselytise Catholic children at CES schools, Craig retorted, 'no priest, no minister, no parent or guardian should come between a child and its God'.[68] Craig called the precarious position of Irish Protestantism divine punishment for acquiescing in national schools:

> Soon, perhaps, in the South and West of Ireland they would get a Protestant and put him under a glass case, he would be such a rarity ... a sad change had taken place in the Church of Ireland ... contempt and irreverence for the greatest and noblest works which God ever gave His servants ... the work of education ... God was removing the candlestick of the Church of Ireland ... they could see the handwriting on the wall ...[69]

In 1870 Craig was a volunteer chaplain with the Prussian Army during the Franco-Prussian War. He was shot through a lung and spent time in a German hospital, describing his experiences in a short memoir, *La Debonado: Scenes, Sketches and Incidents in France and Germany During the War* (London, 1871); he gave illustrated lectures on the war.[70] In 1872 Craig became chaplain to the Molyneux Asylum, a Dublin home for elderly Protestant ladies recently moved from Peter Street in the Liberties to Leeson Park, south of the Grand Canal. His duties included ministering in the Peter Street church formerly attached to the asylum, the Albert Chapel.[71] In 1884 Craig transferred to Trinity Church in Lower Gardiner Street in the north inner city, operated and endowed by trustees and with a tradition of evangelical preaching.[72]

In these churches Craig kept alive underfunded congregations in poor

67 *IT*, 1 Nov. 1883; see also *FJ*, 3 Nov. 1888. McCracken, *You will dye at midnight*, pp 25–50: McCracken argues that schoolteachers rarely wrote such letters.

68 *IT*, 31 Oct. 1895.

69 Ibid., 17 Apr. 1890.

70 Ibid., 14 Jan. 1873. See also Donall Ó Luanaigh, 'The Rev. J. Duncan Craig: an Irish chaplain in the Franco-Prussian War' in *Dublin Historical Record*, l, no. 1 (1997), pp 76–8.

71 *IT*, 9 Sept. 1939.

72 Ibid., 17 Oct. 1901, 18 Jun. 1902, 9 May 1914.

areas through his own resources (he owned property in Cork[73] and received compensation for his life interest as last rector of Kinsale) and ability to attract non-local congregants. Craig had a high reputation as a preacher, speaking at churches and charitable institutions across Dublin and occasionally in Belfast (he possessed a keen awareness of soundbites). Craig belonged to a network of evangelical groups, charitable societies and discussion groups.[74] He regularly published newspaper appeals for the poor of the areas surrounding his churches and was respected for personal and financial charitable work.[75] In accordance with contemporary middle-class Catholic and Protestant attitudes, he emphasised decayed gentlefolk impoverished by business and health failures, rather than long-term poor.[76] During the Land War he encountered members of dispossessed landed families. The title poem of his collection *Bruno!* describes a landlord's daughter dying of starvation in a tenement.[77] In 1888, he claimed, '[o]ne of the officials of a lunatic asylum told him that part of the asylum was filled chiefly by ladies who had been driven mad in consequence of losing their property'.[78]

It is not clear how far Craig's reputation extended outside Ireland; some of his published works have an element of self-funded vanity publication, but he was able to insert reviews from several British local and religious papers as advertisements among the endpapers, and the *Irish Times* noted his publications respectfully. Within the Dublin archdiocese Craig was prominent among a hardline evangelical milieu for whom clerical and lay politics overlapped. He favoured an evangelical pan-Protestant identity transcending denominational divisions, expressed in multi-denominational prayer meetings and the revivalist services of the globe-travelling American preacher Dwight Moody and his hymn-singing accompanist, Ira D. Sankey.[79] Craig eulogised Methodists and regretted they ceased to take communion in the Church of Ireland after disestablishment;[80] he dismissed complaints when Methodists built schools near Church of Ireland schools in working-class areas – 'there was no danger of loss of faith to be feared as regarded the Presbyterians or Methodists, but there was a danger to the faith of Protestant children from

73 *CE*, 10 Feb. 1888; *Miejour*, p. 282n1.

74 e.g. YMCA (*IT*, 22 Jun. 1874); Stewart Institution (*IT*, 30 Jan. 1875); Protestant Orphanage Refuge Society (*IT*, 9 Apr. 1875), Dublin City Mission (*IT*, 3 Apr. 1877).

75 *IT*, 12 Jan. 1889, 30 Dec. 1890, 24 Dec. 1891, 24 Dec. 1892, 22 Dec. 1893, 24 Dec. 1894, 18 Jan. 1897, 17 Dec. 1898, 23 Dec. 1899, 21 Dec. 1900.

76 *IT*, 26 Mar. 1874, 20 Nov. 1874, 30 May 1877, 7 Oct. 1877, 13 Nov. 1880; Earner-Byrne, *Letters of the Catholic poor*, pp 133–69.

77 'Bruno! An Episode of a Dublin Garret' in *Bruno!*, pp 16–17.

78 *IT*, 30 Oct. 1888.

79 *Real pictures*, pp 300–1; *FJ*, 9 Jan. 1883.

80 *Real pictures*, pp 255–6.

the Roman Catholic teaching'.[81] Craig sometimes preached in Presbyterian churches.[82] His evangelical and Orange activities brought contact with the populist Orange MP William Johnston of Ballykilbeg (whose temperance work Craig admired)[83] and future Ulster Unionist Party leader Edward Saunderson,[84] both Church of Ireland members.

From the 1870s to the 1890s Craig was a maverick member of the senate of Dublin University. In a characteristic incident Craig, with an eye for publicity, interrupted the Senior Proctor, Samuel Haughton, in proposing honorary degrees:

> Rev Dr Craig said ... he thought it a great pity that [African explorer] Henry Stanley was not granted a degree of this University. He asked the representatives of the Press to mention this ... [Arguments over points of order]
>
> Dr Haughton – Very well. Then I'll do what you did. (Addressing the reporters.) The gentlemen of the Press will be pleased to say that Dr Haughton thought this great nonsense ... [Further altercations][85]

He saw Trinity as the centre of Protestant civilisation in Ireland and mourned its secularisation: '[h]e hoped the time would come when they would get Trinity College back again ... they were getting Protestant bishops at last who could be true Orangemen ... he hoped the time would come when these bishops would have the whole direction of the Divinity School in their hands.'[86] For Craig, portraits of famous graduates in the Examination Hall (where the senate met) symbolised Trinity's Protestant traditions. Opposing an honorary degree for John Tyndall because though a unionist, he was an outspoken agnostic, Craig remarked, '[I]t would be a pity that ... the university of such men as Berkeley and Ussher, whose portraits adorned the walls of that hall, should ... lend its sanction to such a school of thought, notwithstanding the great scientific standing of this distinguished Irishman.'[87] When an honorary degree was proposed for Arthur Balfour, Craig 'could almost fancy, looking round at those great old portraits, that they smiled down in approval'.[88]

Craig resisted alleged Romanising trends within Anglicanism. He supported post-disestablishment efforts to amend Church of Ireland

81 *IT*, 21 Oct. 1899.
82 Ibid., 20 Oct. 1873.
83 Ibid., 30 Jan. 1875; *BN*, 4 Dec. 1884, 20 Sept. 1897.
84 *FJ*, 3 Apr. 1878.
85 *IT*, 21 Jun. 1890.
86 *FJ*, 15 Jul. 1879.
87 *IT*, 24 Jun. 1886.
88 *FJ*, 4 Feb. 1891.

regulations to eliminate ambiguities exploited by Ritualists in England.[89] In 1877 Craig organised a protest against a spiritual retreat for Dublin clerics as resembling Romanism. He recited satirical verses hoping those responsible would 'retreat' from Ireland; a hostile clergyman suggested Craig should sing it.[90] Craig complained that restoration of Dublin cathedrals included restoring features removed at the Reformation[91] and denounced the ritualism of St Bartholomew's Church, Ballsbridge.[92]

The Land War and Home Rule conflicts of the 1880s

Though consistently opposing Home Rule, Craig took pride in Grattan's Protestant Parliament. *Real Pictures* argues that Grattan's Parliament did not solve the country's problems or end popular unrest,[93] but Craig complained that 'the man who dared to compare Ireland in 1882 with Ireland in 1782, and to place side by side with the great Henry Grattan the men now in Kilmainham ... in a cartoon he had seen the other day ... made the greatest of all historical blunders'.[94] Craig, like many Irish Tories, complained that the Union progressively deprived local Protestant elites of administrative and paramilitary roles in favour of centralising bureaucrats and British statesmen ignorant of Irish conditions.[95] In *Bruce Reynell*, Trelcat equates Irish Tory localism with Provençal revivalism:

> Here in Ireland you have centralization ... which renders Dublin a deserted village ... that you may make London a Babylon of wealth – the golden one, as the prophets call her. Then you have also in Ireland a decentralization power, which allies itself to crime, to rapine, to murder and assassination itself, vainly thinking thus to compass its object. You have in France and in Paris a centralization force which acts precisely upon the departments as the same force in London acts upon Ireland. And in the revival of the grand old Provençal language, in its crowd of modern troubadours, in its noble poems of a Mistral ... the decentralisation protests, but expressed with the sweet Provençal

89 *IT*, 16 Mar. 1875.
90 *IT*, 29 Sept. 1877; *FJ*, 1 Nov. 1877.
91 *FJ*, 3 Apr. 1878.
92 *IT*, 1 Nov. 1890, 31 Jan. 1894.
93 *Real pictures*, pp 312–20.
94 *IT*, 23 Dec. 1881.
95 Charles Lever, *The Knight of Gwynne* (London, 1847); Anthony Malcolmson, *Virtues of a wicked earl: the life and legacy of William Sydney Clements, 3rd Earl of Leitrim* (Dublin, 2008).

> music sounds, not with the moonlighter's rifle, the Invincible's dagger, the Home Ruler's self-seeking rhetoric, or the Roman priest's altar denunciation.[96]

The novel's suggested remedies include agricultural protection for Irish produce and a new plantation of English unemployed.[97] Craig endorses the suggestion (originated by Henry Maunsel in the 1840s) that the British Parliament should rotate triennially between Westminster, Edinburgh and Dublin.[98] In 1875 he complained that Gladstone's 1870 Land Act left it uncertain whether landlord or tenant owned the land.[99] While Craig endorsed 'constructive unionist' measures, even in 1899 he thought peasant property ownership dispossessed the landlords, mainstay of the British garrison, in favour of irreconcilable Catholic farmers.[100] Although Craig admits some landlords committed injustices[101] he generally exculpates them; he depicts most victims of agrarian violence as Protestants. The protagonist of 'The Old Squire's Death' laments:

> I have made myself a pauper, borrowed money at high rate,
> To fence and drain, their houses build, all over the estate;
> I don't mind telling *you*, Fitz, poor Jack to College can't go;
> And the girls – well their old dresses are shabby enough you know.[102]

Craig's depiction of the Land War (and earlier conflicts) is more akin to older Tory-evangelical depictions of Rockism as a centrally directed Catholic conspiracy[103] rather than other contemporary treatments that emphasise a more ground-up source for the conflict (though writers who emphasise a breakdown in former paternal relations between landlord and tenant were seeking an alternative source for the fellow feeling that Craig saw as achievable through evangelical conversion).[104] For Craig, agrarian conflict in 1880–83 was assimilated to the pre-existing Protestant narrative of massacre,

96 *Bruce Reynell*, pp 66–7.
97 *Bruce Reynell*, p. 70.
98 Ibid., p. 233.
99 *Real pictures*, p. 312.
100 *Bruce Reynell*, pp 142–3.
101 *Real pictures*, pp 95–6.
102 'The Old Squire's Death' in *Bruno!*, pp 11–15.
103 e.g. Charlotte Elizabeth [Tonna], *The Rockite: an Irish story* (London, 1829); Patrick O'Sullivan, 'A literary difficulty in explaining Ireland: Tom Moore and Captain Rock, 1824' in Sheridan Gilley & Roger Swift (eds) *The Irish in Britain: 1815–1939* (Dublin, 1989), pp 239–74.
104 Several literary treatments are analysed in Heidi Hansson & James H. Murphy (eds), *Fictions of the Irish Land War* (Oxford, 2014).

beleaguerment, seduction of unwary Protestants and betrayal. 'Did they forget that the celebrated Charles Stewart Parnell was a member of that Synod ... they ought to come out the more unhesitatingly?', he protested at the 1880 Dublin diocesan synod.[105] Craig complained that Dublin Protestants ignored the siege conditions brethren endured in the south and west. He endorsed the complaint of Standish James O'Grady ('an Irish gentleman ... a scholar ... an historian') that Irish landlords were shamefully passive, and landlord organisations were dominated by big landlords indifferent to smaller proprietors.[106] When the Dublin University Senate condemned the Phoenix Park murders, Craig complained that it ignored numerous agrarian murders in the past two years, without even the excuse available to Land League leaders of having been in prison.[107]

The role of newspapers was emphasised:

> The origin of this disease, which had so long cursed Ireland, was ... the unbridled licence of the Press – the treasonable Press of the United States of America, and ... Dublin itself ... He knew what it was to be placarded all over Dublin, by aid of the leading papers, in a manner calculated to mark him out for the hand of the assassin ... The men who circulated those papers, and ... cartoons they saw week after week were in some measure responsible for the awful tragedy that had disgraced Ireland ... infamous cartoons ... spread over the length and breadth of Ireland, calling in the most vile and awful manner the attention of exasperated people to able men, statesmen, and politicians who were doing their duty.[108]

Craig had a symbiotic relationship with the *Freeman's Journal* of the type analysed by Lucy McDiarmid.[109] The *Freeman* denounced his accusations:[110]

> Dr Craig ... incontinently inundated the Synod Chamber with the turbid torrent of his fanatical loquacity. 'The Romish doctrine of assassination', 'hayricks burning,' and rifles hanging round the ministers' residences in the South of Ireland are some disjecta membra hurried down the stream of his impetuous diatribe of yesterday ... even those ... prepared to vote for his resolution ... took care to dissociate themselves from his language ... we pass over ... Dr Craig's references

105 *CE*, 29 Oct. 1880.
106 *IT*, 23 Dec. 1881.
107 Ibid., 12 May 1882.
108 Ibid., 12 May 1882: *FJ*, 12 May 1882.
109 Lucy McDiarmid, *The Irish art of controversy* (Dublin, 2005).
110 *CE*, 29 Oct. 1880.

> to ourselves ... Nothing could induce us to incite anybody to harm a hair of Dr Craig's head ... we cannot but admire the ingenuity which endeavours to cast upon another the odium of language which Dr Craig himself used when he spoke ... of a Protestant army marching and sweeping disaffection from the land ... the mistake the landlords had made in not planting their lands with Protestants, and of 'the Romish doctrine of assassination,' ... which he had ... to withdraw even in the Protestant Synod.[111]

This ridicule (coupled with veiled threats towards Trinity under Home Rule)[112] further stimulated Craig:

> The *Freeman's Journal* had taken him personally to task, stating that although a bishop could make a clergyman he could not make a gentleman ... though a bishop could not make a man a gentleman by an ordination, still according to the testimony of one who was dead – James Carey – the editor of the *Freeman's Journal* could make out of a living man – out of a living gentleman – a dead man.[113]

Bruce Reynell ridicules '*Freedom's Journal*' and the *Sunburst of Erin* (the Parnellite weekly *United Ireland*). The *Sunburst*'s claims that moonlighters attacking a farmer's dwelling were seeking a light for a pipe when shot at by panic-stricken loyalists parodies nationalist claims that unionist scaremongers exaggerated Irish violence.[114] Craig notes thinly veiled intimidation in League resolutions published by the *Sunburst*, describing 'the runner of the League' who circulates resolutions too incendiary for print (the messenger's costume resembles Carleton's Phelim O'Toole).[115] Some features – a drunken journalist, an American general leading an abortive uprising, a discussion on an American ship off the coast – parody *When We Were Boys*, an 1890 novel about the Fenian Rising by *United Ireland*'s founding editor, William O'Brien.[116] The polemics of the Irish political press in the 1880s exhibit why 1890s cultural nationalists believed they had experienced civil war and sought to articulate a deeper shared Irishness.[117]

111 *FJ*, 29 Oct. 1880.
112 Ibid., 4 Feb. 1891; *Nation*, 7 Feb. 1891.
113 *IT*, 2 Nov. 1883.
114 *Bruce Reynell*, pp 56–7.
115 Ibid., 55–6, 126–8.
116 Patrick Maume, 'In the Fenians' wake: Ireland's nineteenth-century crises and their representation in the sentimental rhetoric of William O'Brien MP and Canon Sheehan' in *Bullan: an Irish Studies Journal*, iv, no. 1 (1998), pp 59–80.
117 Patrick Maume, 'The *Dublin Evening Mail* and pro-landlord conservatism in the age of

In 1883 Craig warned that Home Rule was an imminent danger, telling 'loyal Catholics ... repeal not the Union with England, but the Union with Rome, and let heart and soul go together under the sceptre of Queen Victoria'.[118] He met Gladstone's first Home Rule bill in 1886 with predictions of divine deliverance as in 1690,[119] warnings that Catholics were raffling the farms of Protestant neighbours,[120] and an undercurrent of near-despair.[121] His morale was revived by unionist victory at the 1886 general election, the firm administration of Arthur Balfour and the Parnell split, with his praise for Parnellites[122] quoted by anti-Parnellites as proof that John Redmond's followers allied with Orangemen.[123]

In 1888 Craig published political verses including *Father Ulick's Letter,* a satirical description of Ireland under Home Rule that the *Belfast Newsletter* praised as suitable for recitation in Orange lodges.[124] Father Ulick arrives in Dublin where Parnell, 'President of te Republic', is opening Parliament escorted by 'Moonlighter Dragoons' – parodying the Lord Lieutenant. Father Ulick's hotel has neither tea nor coal fires because of a boycott of British goods:

> I met our great Archbishop [Walsh] driving out from Trinity,
> Six as coal-black horses drawing him as ever you did see;
> He'd been selling off the Library, and Quaritch [book dealer]
> has the lot,
> And cruel chape I hear all the volumes he has got ...
>
> Now where is Edmund Burke gone? Why 'tis Sexton I declare!
> And instead of Goldsmith's statue, there stands our great
> Lord Mayor![125]
> In place of old King William, on his charger who was seen,
> Our own illustrious Michael [Davitt] stands a guarding
> College Green!

Gladstone and Parnell' in *Irish Historical Studies*, xxxvii, no. 148 (2011), pp 550–66; Myles Dungan, *Mr Parnell's rottweiler: censorship and the United Ireland newspaper 1881–1891* (Dublin, 2014); J.H. Murphy, *Ireland's Czar: Gladstonian governance and the lord lieutenancies of the Red Earl Spencer* (Dublin, 2014).

118 *IT,* 30 Oct. 1883.

119 Ibid., 22 Oct., 26 Oct. 1886.

120 *FJ,* 1 Mar. 1886.

121 Ibid., 9 Apr. 1886.

122 *BN,* 7 Nov. 1891; *IT,* 18 Feb. 1892.

123 *FJ,* 18 Mar. 1892; *Nationalist & Leinster Times,* 5 Mar., 12 Mar., 9 Apr. 1892.

124 *BN,* 3 Jan. 1888.

125 Thomas Sexton (1874–1932) – a prominent Irish Party orator. Lord Mayor T.D. Sullivan (1827–1914) – a prolific author of patriotic verse.

I entered then the gateway – no 'Fellows' could I see,
For the Provost and Professors had fled from TCD.
Well, the students seemed raal *omedhauns*, their manners
so uncouth,
And all the teaching staff, I heard, had come up from Maynooth!

An inquisition operates in St Stephen's Green (presumably in the Catholic University premises); bibles (and their owners) are burned in the park. The Home Rule government declares war on Ulster, with Davitt leading an army including continental revolutionaries (implying that ultramontane Catholicism would, as in France, produce revolution and atheism):

There are Nihilists from Russia, the Petroleuse from France;
The Lyons' Marianne, and moonlighters advance;
The Knights of Labour join them, with many a Dynamard;[126]
All the Orange Scarfs in Ulster our progress won't retard!

The invaders are routed by an army of Irish Protestants and imperial volunteers led by the ghosts of William III and Schomberg:

Three thousand then came marching with axes by their side,

And rifles on their shoulders, advancing like the tide
That sweeps across the bay its water onward fast;
And I heard the people mutter, 'They're the Shipwrights of
Belfast!'

…

There were men from Tipperary, sons of the Palatine,
The yeomanry of Wicklow advancing line by line;
From far Kinsale and Bandon and Pass of Keim an Eigh,
The Protestants came marching, a gallant band that day!

I saw each regiment tramping on, their Chaplain marching too;
The Presbyterians filing on 'neath Covenant flag of blue,
And Church of Ireland sweeping past, with Orange banners high,
And Wesleyans hasting onward, with triumph in their eye!

126 *Petroleuses* – allegedly frenzied female arsonists during the 1871 Paris Commune (cf. *John Maverell*, pp 348, 350). *Marianne* – symbol of the French Republic. *Knights of Labour* – semi-secret American-based trade union with significant Irish membership.

Home Rule and the Inquisition are abolished, scriptural education made compulsory; Father Ulick emigrates – 'In Ireland, Rome's power forever is done!'[127]

While Craig was confident that Gladstone's Second Home Rule Bill would be defeated, his long-term outlook remained gloomy.[128] He supported hardline independent unionist candidates in Trinity College (1895, as did Standish James O'Grady)[129] and South Dublin (1900).[130] In 1897 he inherited £60,000 from his sister (widow of a Derby banker),[131] which enabled him to give generously to charities, publish his collected works and acquire a mansion in San Remo on the Ligurian coast where he spent winters after retiring from Trinity Church (he returned to Dublin in summer to preach). He died of a heart attack at San Remo in 1909 and was buried in Deansgrange Cemetery.[132]

Conclusion

The career of John Duncan Craig is a reminder that attitudes associated with Irish society in the first half of the nineteenth century survived in certain quarters for decades afterwards, allowing later nineteenth-century conflicts to incorporate older loyalist narratives, but it also displays the fantasy and half-concealed despair of political and cultural intransigence. *Bruce Reynell* runs backwards in time, beginning with the Land War (and nationalist manipulation of legal procedure and public opinion) to pre-political popular violence of the pre-Famine era and the 1867 and 1798 rebellions, suppressible by straightforward military force. At the end of the novel the Irish-speaking peasantry show signs of conversion to Protestantism, while priests and 'patriots' die, convert or emigrate; this retrospective wishful thinking looks back to earlier decades when conversionist projects and military reconquest seemed plausible, and hopes that these opportunities are not permanently lost. Craig fantasises about deporting Catholic clergy and nationalist politicians on a gigantic steamship:

> For mine's the opinion, that Rome's the foundation
> Of two-thirds our trouble, our discord, our woe;
> And that Ireland would be the cream of creation
> If the Priest and the 'Patriot' from Ireland would go ...

127 'Father Ulick's Letter' in *Bruno!*, pp 22–32.
128 *BN*, 9 Feb. 1893, 20 Sept. 1897.
129 Ibid., 9 Nov. 1905.
130 *IT*, 2 Oct. 1900.
131 *Evening Echo*, 26 Apr. 1897.
132 *Church of Ireland Gazette*, 8 Apr. 1909, p. 351; *BN*, 3 Apr., 7 Apr. 1909; *IT*, 2 Apr. 1909.

Then I watched the Great Eastern far away gliding,
Till sunlight at once, 'stead of midnight, did gleam.
My country at last, I have some sort of pride in.
Alas! I awoke, and 'twas only a dream.[133]

Craig's political and religious projects may ultimately appear as fantasies, but he was in some respects a sophisticated man with a particular though idiosyncratic European outlook, centred on international Protestantism and a philanthropic social commitment inspired by his paternalist beliefs. An approach to Irish history that investigates personalities rather than periods has acknowledged disadvantages, but it can be used to explore how personal and communal memories and interpretations of conflict formed in early life allowed these attitudes and perceptions to exert residual influence decades later, how conflicts normally presented from the perspective of those seen as representing the future were also shaped by the persistence of forces associated with an earlier age. This case study of Craig allows us to see, for example, how semi-military local associationalism, encouraged by the everyday presence of Crown forces, remained part of Irish Protestant culture outside Ulster late into the nineteenth century; how the open sectarianism of the 1820s and 1830s continued to shape some perceptions of the theoretically unsectarian land conflicts of the 1880s; how the verbal and visual violence of nationalist and unionist print culture proved mutually reinforcing; and how late Victorian unionist and Protestant culture experienced continuing conflict between liberal and hardline forces when renewed challenges from below might have emphasised the need for compromise and unity.

133 'A Dream of the Great Eastern' in *Bruno!*, pp 19–20.

Conflict in Society

4
Douglas Hyde and his Inner Conflicts

Máire Nic an Bhaird and Liam Mac Mathúna

Introduction

Douglas Hyde was a Roscommon man. He was also a folklorist, a poet, a philologist, a playwright, a literary historian, a university professor, a leader of the Gaelic Revival, an antiquarian, a pioneer of the Irish literary revival, an Irish Free State senator and Ireland's first President.[1] Hyde was born at Longford House, Castlerea, County Roscommon, while his mother, Elizabeth (1834–86), was on a short visit there. He then lived in Kilmactrannagh County Sligo for the first seven years of his life. In 1867, Douglas Hyde's family relocated to Tibohine, Frenchpark, County Roscommon, owing to his father's career as a rector. This move would ultimately exert a profound influence on Douglas Hyde's life and career trajectory.

His father, Arthur Hyde, whose family were originally from Castlehyde, Fermoy, County Cork, was Church of Ireland rector of St Thomas's Church of Ireland, Kilmactrannagh, from 1852 to 1867. The family lived in the adjacent Glebe House, which was constructed in 1816.[2] There is a plaque for Douglas Hyde and his father in the church: 'Douglas Hyde First President of Ireland, born 1860 – died 1949, who spent the first 7 years of his life in Kilmactrannagh Parish where his father the Rev Arthur Hyde was rector from 1852–1867.' There is also a newly erected plaque near to the church, which reads: 'Carrickard, Carraig Ard. Douglas Hyde, Dúbhghlas de hÍde.'[3]

1 Máire Nic an Bhaird & Liam Mac Mathúna, 'Early diary insights into Roscommon's impact on Douglas Hyde, Ireland's first President' in *Roscommon history and society: interdisciplinary essays on the history of an Irish county* (Dublin, 2018), pp 515–37.

2 Mrs Bríd Martin currently lives in the Glebe House in Kilmactrannagh and kindly showed Professor Liam Mac Mathúna and me around the house, St Thomas's Church and the local area in March 2020.

3 For information on Hyde's early years, see Nic an Bhaird & Mac Mathúna, 'Early diary insights'.

Hyde's early years in Tibohine were shaped by his father and aunt who home-schooled him owing to a childhood illness. This unexpected turn of events proved to be a fortuitous one, as it ignited Hyde's fascination with the Irish language, particularly the way in which it was spoken by the older generation in his locality. As a result of his fervent passion for language, Hyde pursued higher education at Trinity College Dublin (TCD), where he distinguished himself as a scholar of great merit. Through his tireless dedication to academic excellence, Hyde earned a BA, MA and LLD, cementing his reputation as a formidable intellectual force. Throughout his childhood and college years, Hyde became fluent in a range of languages including Irish, French, Latin, German, Greek and Hebrew.[4]

Douglas Hyde was a cultural influencer during a tumultuous time in Irish history. He kept thirteen diaries spanning 1874–1912, all of which are housed in the National Library of Ireland.[5] These diaries give the reader an intimate understanding of his life as a young boy in Frenchpark, highlighting how he acquired the Irish language. Without this upbringing in Roscommon and his connection with the local inhabitants of Frenchpark, many of whom were native Irish speakers, Ireland's cultural revival may have taken a very different path. These ego-documents also reveal how conflict permeated Hyde's life during the late nineteenth century. This chapter will analyse these many inner conflicts relating to issues such as self-identity, interpersonal relationships, politics, culture and the Gaelic Revival, and assess their significance in moulding the man who would come to play a pivotal role in creating modern Ireland.

The inner conflict of character formation

Douglas Hyde had a Protestant upbringing, with many of his ancestors being clergymen who studied in TCD since the 1600s. Hyde was home-schooled, which fortuitously enabled him to spend many hours of every day in the company of the local Irish speakers of Tibohine, thus exposing himself to the world of Irish language and folklore. As a youth, he was eager to learn about Irish folklore and to perfect his acquisition of Irish, and though his family didn't champion the language, his father, Rev. Arthur Hyde, did pay for Douglas to travel to Dublin on 17 August 1878 so that he could attend an auction of Irish books held on 19 August.[6] It is ironic, perhaps, that one of his Christmas presents in 1876 was in fact a Bible in the Irish language, an item

4 Nic an Bhaird & Mac Mathúna, 'Early diary insights'.

5 To view the digitised diaries see National Library Ireland (NLI), Douglas Hyde Papers (not given in subsequent references), MS G 1036–48.

6 'Diary of Douglas Hyde, 1878–80' (NLI, MS G 1038).

that connected two aspects of his life: his linguistic identity and his religious identity. He wrote of this in his diary on Christmas Day that year: 'Fuair mé bronntannusa, Biobla Gaoideilge agus Stair na hEagluise na hEirionn agus dhá giota don phioban.'[7] These aspects were conflicting, however, owing to his desire to be immersed in the Irish language and culture and to follow a different path to his familial predecessors who worked in the church. The Irish language Bible in question therefore holds profound symbolic significance, as it represents the intricate interplay of cultural conflicts already experienced by Hyde at such a young age.

Hyde's daily life in Tibohine in the 1870s would have been spent hunting and shooting, pastimes enjoyed mostly by the Anglo-Irish gentry. The young Douglas was also at ease on the tennis court or playing croquet on neighbouring Lord De Freyne's land.[8] Yet because of Hyde's pursuit of Irish language fluency, two personae begin to take shape in his diary entries during the period 1874–1876: his Anglo-Irish persona and his Irish-speaking persona. The expression of his Anglo-Irish persona is evident in his first diary. On 9 April 1874, for example, he wrote: 'Shot a rook for Lavin with a home-made cartridge which answered admirably.'[9] He also had easy access to porter, whisky and tobacco, and he was a keen marksman, all traits of a privileged Anglo-Irish upbringing.[10] However, on 28 March 1874, Douglas also introduced the reader to his Irish-speaking persona when he wrote his first sentence in the Irish language, using a phonetic approach.[11]

Hyde therefore belonged to two worlds growing up: the world of his family, which was the Anglo-Irish world; and the world of the native Irish speakers of Tibohine, with whom he felt a strong connection. There were different conflicts at play here – religious, cultural and linguistic – and Hyde was trying to seamlessly dance in and out of these two distinctly different worlds. This journey would help him successfully navigate different social circles throughout his career. He could socialise with ease with the Anglo-Irish aristocrats, but was just as comfortable mingling with the local workers and

7 'I received presents, an Irish Bible and the History of the Church of Ireland and two pieces for the pipe' ('Diary of Douglas Hyde, 1874–6' (NLI, MS G 1036)).

8 For daily accounts of Hyde's hunting successes see his 1874–1876 diary (NLI, MS G 1036).

9 'Diary of Douglas Hyde, 1874–6' (NLI, MS G 1036).

10 See, for example, his diary entry for 15 May 1874: 'went to Hanly's for tobbaco [sic]'. In 'Diary of Douglas Hyde, 1874–6' (NLI, MS G 1036).

11 For more on Hyde's Irish language acquisition, see Máire Nic an Bhaird & Liam Mac Mathúna, 'Douglas Hyde (1860–1949) – the adolescent behind the diarist' in R.A. Barr, Sarah-Anne Buckley & Muireann Ó Cinnéide (eds), *Literacy, language and reading in nineteenth-century Ireland* (Liverpool, 2018), pp 28–50.

Irish speakers of Tibohine. Prominent Gaelic Leaguer and novelist Mary Butler recalls the following about him:

> The eyes were the only attractive feature in his face and they made one forget all the rest! Their colour seemed to change like his expression, according to his mood. They would blaze with anger when he spoke of Ireland's wrongs, or be tender when he pleaded for the saving of her soul; a moment later they would be twinkling mischievously as he poked fun at some 'West British' affectation of country people ... He really seemed to possess some gift of drawing people and captivating them, whatever it was.[12]

It was this uncanny ability to adapt to social situations and the facility of putting at ease whomever was in his company that propelled Hyde's profile onwards and upwards. There is also a certain acceptance by Hyde himself of the duality of his personality and a distinction between the English and Irish self are seen in his early diary entries.

During the 1870s, Douglas Hyde adeptly navigated the complex dual nature of his existence, which entailed engaging with rural inhabitants of Tibohine, such as Seamus Hart, Johnny Lavin and Mrs Connolly, and participating in a wider societal context. The emotional connections forged with these individuals in Tibohine were instrumental in nurturing Hyde's aspirations for cultural independence. This formative period of his youth, characterised by personal relationships and experiences, set the stage for his subsequent educational pursuits at Trinity College, where a similar undercurrent of cultural autonomy continued to shape his perspective. This enduring commitment to the preservation of Irish cultural heritage found manifestation in the public sphere, notably exemplified by Hyde's renowned lecture titled 'The Necessity for De-Anglicising Ireland', which he delivered on 25 November 1892 on behalf of the Irish National Literary Society in Dublin.[13] This lecture serves as a prominent demonstration of Hyde's resolute advocacy for the revitalisation of Ireland's native cultural traditions and language and is often credited as being a catalyst for the foundation of the Gaelic League in 1893. Hyde was co-founder and first president of the Gaelic League, one of the most influential cultural organisations in Ireland at a time of increased cultural conflict. His force of personality enabled him to bring his concern for the future of the Irish language and its culture to centre stage in the public sphere at the end of the

12 In G.W. Dunleavy & J.E. Dunleavy, *Douglas Hyde: A maker of modern Ireland* (Oakland, CA., 1991), p. 202.

13 Available in Breandán Ó Conaire (ed.), *Language, lore and lyrics: essays and lectures* (Dublin, 1986).

nineteenth century. However, it was the tension that manifested because of his contrasting cultural and linguistic standpoints, arising from his Irish language persona and his Anglo-Irish persona, that strengthened his understanding of his own identity during his formative years.

Douglas Hyde harboured private Fenian sympathies, which were nurtured by those around him in Frenchpark. Janet and Gareth Dunleavy noted in their 1991 publication *Douglas Hyde: A Maker of Modern Ireland* that as he came of age Hyde 'chose for his friends and informal tutors Irish-speaking, card-playing, snuff-taking, poteen-sampling, Fenian-loving Frenchpark countrymen and women of stone cottages and bog cabin.'[14] Most notable in this regard was Seamus Hart, Lord De Freyne's game-keeper, who was the first person to teach Hyde Irish.[15] The Dunleavys noted how Hart, 'with his fluent Irish, his talent for reciting poems, his rich store of Irish historical and cultural tradition, his knowledge of the natural world of Frenchpark and environs, his Fenian sympathies, his calm strength and his capacity for warmth and affection', was a central figure in shaping Hyde's identity.[16] Hart became a father figure to Douglas and his death at the end of 1875 affected the then fifteen-year-old more than any other.[17] Hart had opened up the Irish language world to Hyde; a world of folklore, stories and history, and his impact both in a cultural and linguistic capacity was immense. He is mentioned on the very first page of Hyde's first diary in 1874 and references continue throughout until Hart's death, illustrating a close bond formed through simple outdoor pursuits and through language.[18] On 29 December 1875, Hyde refers to the death of Seamus in his diary and the detail of the time of his death, at 8pm, is very emotive, giving the reader considerable understanding of Hyde's

14 Dunleavy & Dunleavy, *Douglas Hyde*, p. 9.

15 For more information on Seamus Hart see Liam Mac Mathúna, 'Douglas Hyde the scholar' in Pádraig Ó Macháin (ed.), *The Book of the O'Connor Don* (Dublin, 2010), p. 197.

16 Dunleavy & Dunleavy, *Douglas Hyde*, p. 45.

17 On a sunny afternoon in 2018, Professor Liam Mac Mathúna and I were brought out by Mícheál Mahon, of the Mahons of the cottages just outside the gates of Ratra, where Hyde lived from 1893. Mícheál Mahon's family had taken care of Ratra house and gardens. Mícheál Mahon brought us down bog roads to find the ruins of Seamus Hart's house, where Douglas Hyde learned his first words of Irish and where he was imbued with a deep love of the land. In 2018, Professor Liam Mac Mathúna and I collaborated with the National Folklore Collection, University College Dublin, and interviewed Mícheál Mahon about his family's involvement with Douglas Hyde.

18 See for example diary entries for 18 March 1874: 'Hart gave me a black-thorn'; and 20 April 1874: 'Lent Hart the spade, learn'd some Irish from him.' In 'Diary of Douglas Hyde, 1874–6' (NLI, MS G 1036). See also Dunleavy & Dunleavy, *Douglas Hyde*, pp 49–81.

emotional state of mind during a very significant moment in his young life: 'Hempul ochd clug foor Sémuis bás. Foor sé Sémuis bás.'[19]

Alongside Hart featured other local workers such as William Connolly and Johnny Lavin, who also contributed to mould Hyde's future ideas and thoughts. According to the Dunleaveys, Hyde found in Lavin a 'new and needed friend', with his fluent Irish and Fenianism again being very significant.[20] In his diary on 21 February 1877, for example, the seventeen-year-old Hyde describes an evening in Johnny Lavin's house spent sitting fireside with a man who recounted his memories of 1798 and the three French frigates carrying over a thousand men that landed at Kilcummin Head, on the west shore of Killala Bay, County Mayo.[21] On 27 February 1877, Douglas was again at Lavin's and listened to a report of a Fenian meeting held in Frenchpark that everyone had deemed to be a great success.[22] Hyde was astute and careful enough to understand that he could not share these stories with his father, however, and he kept any Fenian sympathies to himself. Here we can see the beginning of Hyde's management of his inner and outer self, an ability that would stand to him in his later career as a statesman. He had started to learn that the best policy was sometimes discretion and to study your audience and work with them to avoid unnecessary personal and professional conflict.

Hyde's first (1874–76) and second (1877) diaries[23] therefore clearly show how, from an early age, he was mixing with local inhabitants who constituted the last generation of native Irish speakers in Roscommon and were connected or sympathetic to the Fenian movement. Through this exposure to Fenianism as a teenager, Hyde developed his own strong nationalist ideals during the late nineteenth century, which he then expressed vehemently in Irish-language poems between 1877 and 1882. Around 1878/9, he adopted the pseudonym 'an Craoibhín Aoibhinn' ('the Pleasant Little Branch'), and published poems in Irish in newspapers at home and in the United States, for example in *The Shamrock* and *The Irishman*, both edited by Richard Pigott.[24] This pseudonym, 'An Craoibhín Aoibhinn', afforded Hyde the freedom he needed to express strong anti-English sentiment in his poetry. For example, he dedicated an 1880 poem in Irish to Fenian Jeremiah O'Donovan Rossa, and a similarly

19 'Around eight o'clock Seamus died. He, Seamus died' ('Diary of Douglas Hyde, 1874–6' (NLI, MS G 1036)).

20 Dunleavy & Dunleavy, *Douglas Hyde*, p. 54.

21 'Diary of Douglas Hyde, 1877' (NLI, MS G 1037). E.A. D'Alton, 'The French in Mayo, 1798' in *Journal of the Galway Archaeological and Historical Society*, iv, no. 4 (1906), pp 219–22.

22 'Diary of Douglas Hyde, 1877' (NLI, MS G 1037).

23 NLI, MS G1036 and MS G1037, respectively.

24 For biographical information about Richard Piggott see *DIB* (https://www.dib.ie/biography/pigott-richard-a7335) (accessed 25 Oct. 2022).

revolutionary message can be found in an 1880 marching song titled 'Come Boys to Camp, We'll Sprightly Tramp'.[25] His views gradually shifted towards a more public, non-partisan approach, however, and the Fenian sympathies that he developed were later hidden behind other pseudonyms, as will be discussed anon. This was particularly true during his tenure as president of the Gaelic League from 1893 to 1915. Hyde championed the revival of the national language and culture, but wished to detach this from the politics of the time and promoted an apolitical stance, without which the Gaelic League may not have flourished to such a degree.

The conflict of the father–son relationship

Hyde's relationship with his father, Rev. Arthur Hyde, was a complex one. During his childhood, Douglas hunted and went swimming and rowing with his father in Lough Gara, near their home in Tibohine, as documented in his first diary (1874–76). On the opening page, in an entry for 10 March 1874, for example, he wrote: 'I shot a jackdaw. Pa shot two snipe. Pa shot a jackdaw';[26] on 20 August 1874, he noted being '[o]ut shooting with Pa'.[27] As well as documenting his hunting achievements through the years, these diaries also highlight the conflict that existed between Douglas and his unpredictable father. Douglas was home-schooled and he successfully managed to negotiate a study plan and his relationship with his father by working hard and concealing any ideas or feelings that would not meet his father's approval. As already mentioned, he kept any Fenian or Parnellite leanings secret for fear of the fierce friction this would cause in the Glebe house. He couldn't, for example, attend a local victory celebration for Parnell in 1879. He did, however, get second-hand accounts of these events from a Tibohine workman named Dockry who also had strong Fenian sympathies.[28]

Douglas's diaries reveal how the strong views his father held in relation to Douglas's own career pathway were also a major source of tension between the two. The Rev. Hyde was awarded a BA from TCD in 1839, he referenced Latin and Greek and used them with his children, and he also had a library in the Glebe house in Tibohine.[29] He had followed his own family's tradition of religious service and became the fourth Rev. Arthur Hyde of the Church of Ireland. He therefore wished to have his eldest son, also called Arthur, follow

25 Dunleavy & Dunleavy, *Douglas Hyde*, p. 107.
26 'Diary of Douglas Hyde, 1874–6' (NLI, MS G 1036).
27 Ibid.
28 Dunleavy & Dunleavy, *Douglas Hyde*, p. 55.
29 See Doiminic Ó Dálaigh, 'The young Douglas Hyde' in *Studia Hibernica*, no. 10 (1970), pp 108–35.

in his footsteps. Young Arthur refused, however, as did another brother, Oldfield. The Rev. Hyde thus focused his efforts on his youngest son. Indeed, Douglas's diary entry of 7 July 1876 states that he went with his father to the bishop to discuss his future as a clergyman, but Douglas himself wished to avoid conflict and thought he could deal with this at a later date.[30] Hyde's father also wanted Douglas to complete a degree in theology in TCD as a stepping stone to a career in the church and so, in 1880, Douglas entered TCD. This was not too distressing, however, as his preferred subject of Irish was also offered in the same faculty of divinity. Hyde's diaries reveal how his Theology lectures did little to inspire him. Of his first lecture on 2 November 1882, he wrote: 'Och! Mar thit mo chroidhe ….'[31] After the next lecture, on 6 November, he complained again about the Theology lecture and his fellow students: 'Bhí sé na athfhuathmhaireacht dam. Is grána liom na daoine tá liom ann.'[32] As his studies progressed and his own linguistic identity was nurtured, Hyde became more vocal about not pursuing the career his father desired for him. Writing on 9 August 1883, he recalled having a 'titim amach diabhalta'[33] with his father. On 2 October 1883, Rev. Hyde threatened to cut Douglas off if he did not follow him into the Church. However, we see in his diary entry that Douglas defended himself, threatening to go to London and become a Bohemian, a prospect that certainly would have horrified his father.[34]

Douglas Hyde's many personal and inner conflicts can be clearly seen in such entries, but his diaries also helped him strengthen his own philosophical and ethical positions. In October 1883, the Rev. Hyde took a step back and gave Douglas Hyde some space to think about another career, provided it was one that met his father's approval. The Rev. Hyde viewed language and literature as a hobby and he would have preferred his son to enter the army. However, Douglas regarded that as an immoral profession. Ironically, this contradicts some of his early poetry, which glorified militant nationalism and contained a call to violence. This ongoing conflict with his father was intense and really affected him, so much so that he wrote in his diary that his state of mind was so awful that he would not wish it on a dog.[35]

Rev. Arthur Hyde was not an easy person to live with; he was easily angered, especially after drinking. Hyde's brother, Oldfield, also had similar problems with alcohol, as documented in Douglas's diaries. An entry for

30 'Diary of Douglas Hyde, 1874–6' (NLI, MS G 1036).
31 'Oh, how my heart sank …' ('Diary of Douglas Hyde [1882]–1885' (NLI, MS G 1040)).
32 'I hated it, and hated the people who were with me' (ibid.).
33 'a terrible falling out' ('Diary of Douglas Hyde [1882]–1885' (NLI, MS G 1040)).
34 For a detailed account of the difficulties between Rev. Hyde and Douglas Hyde read his 1883 diary from July to October, in 'Diary of Douglas Hyde [1882]–1885' (NLI, MS G 1040). See also Dunleavy & Dunleavy, *Douglas Hyde*, chap. 6.
35 'Diary of Douglas Hyde [1882]–1885' (NLI, MS G 1040).

8 August 1878 described how Oldfield and Rev. Hyde had been drinking heavily and how dinner was barely over when Oldfield swayed upstairs and fell asleep, only to wake up vomiting.[36] On 15 August 1878, he wrote: 'Ma was not well and the Master was bad enough as usual for the same reason – too much of the full jug.'[37] Throughout October, November and December of 1879, Douglas described his father's drunken episodes more frequently and with less tolerance for his violent angry tendencies towards his family. He wrote on 30 October 1879 that the 'sinner' amongst us is very ugly, referencing his father.[38]

These diaries evidently allowed Hyde to reveal his most private thoughts and feelings and to process and reflect upon them too. However, the careful discretion over personal and political views that would come to define his later public career was not in evidence here. On occasion, Hyde wrote accounts of events that, one feels, he knew would one day be published, such as his 1916 diary housed at TCD.[39] But these earlier, personal diaries were not for public consumption and they highlight to readers the raw conflict that existed between father and son as Douglas negotiated his way through numerous battles, eventually winning the war when he followed his heart and mind as an Irish language academic and cultural revivalist. Upon the death of Rev. Arthur Hyde in August 1905, a newspaper sent condolences to Douglas on the passing of his father but ended the paragraph with a subtle reference to the underlying conflict that permeated their relationship throughout the latter half of the nineteenth century: 'Doctor Hyde's father and grandfather were Protestant rectors, and he himself took the degree of Bachelor in Divinity in Trinity College and won a theological exhibition, but Irish Ireland claim him.'[40]

Conflicting personae: the political company of Douglas Hyde during his journey to Northern America in 1890–91

By 1890, the thirty-year-old Douglas Hyde had gained an international reputation as a key player in the growing field of Irish folklore owing to his academic publications, published poems and translations. With his appointment as Interim Professor of Modern Languages at the University of New Brunswick for 1890, his conflicting personae moved towards North

36 'Diary of Douglas Hyde [1878–80]' (NLI, MS G 1038).

37 Ibid.

38 Ibid.

39 See 'Diary by Douglas Hyde covering events of Easter week, 1916' (NLI, MS 17,770) and 'Diary of Easter week dictated by Douglas Hyde and typed by Nelly O'Brien' (TCD, MS 10343/7). See also Máire Nic an Bhaird, 'Reading between the lines. Hyde's writings, 1916' in *Éire-Ireland*, liii, no. 1&2 (2018), pp 48–63.

40 *Evening Telegraph*, 1 Sept. 1905.

America and his time in Canada is documented in his diary for 1890–93.[41] His appointment in the Fredericton College saw him replace William F. P. Stockley,[42] who had attended TCD during Hyde's own college years and who is mentioned as a contemporary in Hyde's diaries from 1882 on.[43] Stockley publicly identified as a nationalist and supporter of Home Rule; he also enjoyed the company of Fenians and revolutionaries such as John Boyle O'Reilly in Boston, who in 1867 had been sent to Western Australia owing to his membership of the Irish Republican Brotherhood.[44] Hyde also documents in his 1890–93 diary how Colonel Maunsell, a Limerick man who had strong nationalist views and was a relative of William Stockley's, had helped Hyde purchase alcoholic beverages as he had placed him on the officers' mess list during his time at the University of New Brunswick.[45] The Scott Act prohibited the sale of alcohol in Canada at the time.[46] These relationships reveal the nature of the political company Hyde was keeping.

According to his diary, Hyde left Fredericton on 3 June 1891, and headed by train to Boston.[47] He then left for New York on 9 June 1891, again documenting the trip in his diary: 'Got at 8 in the evening on board an enormous floating palace of a steamer which brought me to N York at 7 next morning.'[48] There, on 11 June 1891, he 'breakfasted' with fellow Irish revivalist Thomas O'Neill Russell, who had left Ireland for America in 1867 under suspicion of involvement in the Fenian Rising.[49] More than thirty years Hyde's senior, O'Neill Russell was a pioneer of the Irish language revival, who regarded himself as Hyde's mentor ever since the then seventeen-year-old Hyde joined the Society for the Preservation of the Irish Language (SPIL) in Dublin in 1877.[50] This demonstrated that there was no reluctance on Hyde's part to keep the company of those with forthright political positions. In New York in 1891, Hyde wished to meet his boyhood hero, Jeremiah O'Donovan Rossa.[51] Unfortunately, when he called to his office on 11 June, O'Donovan Rossa was out and so Hyde left a note for him: 'I spent most of the day

41 'Diary of Douglas Hyde, 1890–3' (NLI, MS G 1043).
42 For biographical information on W.F.P. Stockley see *DIB* (https://www.dib.ie/biography/stockley-william-frederick-paul-a8321) (5 Oct. 2022).
43 'Diary of Douglas Hyde, 1890–3' (NLI, MS G 1043).
44 Ian Kenneally, *From the earth, a cry: the story of John Boyle O'Reilly* (Dublin, 2011).
45 'Diary of Douglas Hyde, 1890–3' (NLI, MS G 1043).
46 C.D. Boyce, 'Prohibition in Canada' in *The Annals of the American Academy of Political and Social Science* (Philadelphia, 1923), p. 225.
47 'Diary of Douglas Hyde, 1890–1893' (NLI, MS G 1043).
48 Ibid.
49 Ibid.; for biographical information on Thomas O'Neill Russell, see *Bunachar Náisiúnta Beathaisnéisí Gaeilge* (https://www.ainm.ie/Bio.aspx?ID=292) (accessed 5 Oct. 2022).
50 'Diary of Douglas Hyde, 1890–1893' (NLI, MS G 1043).
51 Ibid.

with him in Cumann na Gaedheilge and hunted in vain for O Donabháin Rossa …'[52] O'Donovan Rossa seems to have been equally keen to meet the younger man. The esteem in which Hyde was already held in advanced nationalist circles in New York is clear from a letter Joseph Cromien sent to Pádraig Ua Birn on 10 June 1891; this letter also highlights that O'Donovan Rossa was a controversial figure:

> I think it was very thoughtful and kind of Craoibhín Aoibhín to call to see Rossa and much as I esteemed the gentleman before now it was but small thoughts to the place he holds in my heart now. It makes me feel like hugging C.A. if I should meet him to think that he has a heart above and beyond the mob who want to let the world know that they are Irishmen while they would with the same breath shout on Rossa Crucify him; Crucify him.
>
> Dear P. I am so delighted with this act of C.A. that I could dilate a long time on it but I don't want to bother you
> I am sincerely
> Yours J Cromien
> 2715 8th Ave.[53]

Hyde's admiration for O'Donovan Rossa was reciprocated by the old Fenian, who sent Hyde a verse invitation to attend dinner at his home in Brooklyn. The verse was composed in Irish on *United Irishman* notepaper on 15 June 1891:

> THE UNITED IRISHMAN
> NO. 12 SPRUCE STREET
> P. O. Box 2197
> New York, Mithimh 15 1891
>
> Craoíbhín Aoíbhin – Croidhe na feile
> Badh mhaith liom cheile,
> A's liom leanbhuídhe léithe
> Tu feiscint féinig
> Sul imtheóghair go h-Érin.
> Innis dam, tráth,
> Aon uair, aon lá
> Go mbeidh aig tusa

52 Ibid.
53 'Verse letter in Irish from Jeremiah O'Donovan Rossa to Douglas Hyde requesting a meeting in New York, and associated letters' (NLI, MS 17,295).

Cead do chosa
Dul go dtíghe – Rossa
1009 Hancock St. Brooklyn
Bridge Elevator to Brooklyn.
Elevator Road to Halsey St. Station.
1009 Hancock St. is one block – one street back.
Do léigheas do leabhar goleir a ndé,
Diarmuid.[54]

Hyde and Rossa then joined forces and spent the best part of a day trying to persuade Patrick Ford, editor of the *Irish World*, to support the Irish language. Hyde felt that they succeeded as Ford later helped him a great deal, with Hyde writing in his diary on 13 June 1891: 'Chuaigh go h-O Donabhán Rossa air maidin agus bhí caint fhad agam agus deochanna agus do rug seisean mise go Padraig Forde [*sic*] ann a oifig (Irish World) agus bhí caint fhada agam leisean.'[55]

The aforementioned Stockley, who had been the catalyst for Hyde's move to Canada in 1890/91, also reappears in Hyde's life in February 1905, when Hyde attended a lecture delivered by Stockley in Queen's College, Cork. The chair of English Literature had just become vacant, and William Stockley suggested Hyde for the post.[56] Again this would support the argument that Hyde was comfortable being in the company of, and being associated with, Irish Republican Brotherhood (IRB) sympathisers up to this time. However, the conflict between Hyde's two personae decreased during the early years of the twentieth century as his public pronouncements on behalf of the Gaelic League, from at least 1900, invariably championed the apolitical line. Hyde had started to censor himself as his understanding of how best to achieve a cultural revival grew. This is evidenced, for example, in his reaction to a famous lecture titled 'The Turning of the Tide', which was given by the San Francisco-based priest, Father Peter Yorke, to the Gaelic League's newly organised Central Branch on 6 September 1899.[57] An editorial in *An Claidheamh Soluis* the

54 'Craoibhín Aoibhinn – Ever generous/ My wife/ And my children too/ Would like to see you yourself/ Before you go to Ireland./ Tell me, the time,/ Any hour, any day/ That you will be free/ to go to – Rossa/ 1009 Hancock St. Brooklyn/ Bridge Elevator to Brooklyn./ Elevator Road to Halsey St. Station./ 1009 Hancock St. is one block – one street back./ I read all your book yesterday,/ Diarmuid.' (Ibid.).

55 'I went to O Donovan Rossa's this morning and I had a long talk with him and drinks and he brought me to Patrick Forde's office and I had a long talk with him too.' ('Diary of Douglas Hyde, 1890–3' (NLI, MS G 1043)).

56 Dunleavy & Dunleavy, *Douglas Hyde*, p. 257.

57 See *An Claidheamh Soluis* (henceforth cited as *ACS*), 16 Sept. 1899. See also Liam Mac Mathúna et al. *Douglas Hyde: my American journey* (Dublin, 2019), p. 83.

same month highlights the impact this lecture, which was held in the Antient Concert Rooms in Dublin, had on the twelve hundred attendees:

> [E]very person in the audience must have felt like one who had lived in darkness for years and stepped forth suddenly into the light and glory of a brilliant summer day, or like one just released from the noisome and foetid atmosphere of a dungeon who stands on the seashore and inhales the fresh breezes blowing around him and listens enraptured to the music of the waves. We have never heard yet anything like it.[58]

For Hyde, however, the speech was a cause of inner conflict as the speaker, Yorke, had shared advanced nationalist views. Hyde therefore publicly avoided Yorke to ensure that he was not connected with controversial viewpoints, only revealing years later in his book, *Mise agus an Connradh*, that he had never heard anywhere an orator to equal Yorke:

> He spoke sharply, angrily, fiercely. He attacked priests, nuns, politicians, newspapers, schoolmasters and school managers, fathers and mothers, and spared none of them. He said the things we badly needed to have said, the things I myself would have liked to say but that I was afraid to do it! I did not know beforehand what he was proposing to broadcast; but anyhow, since I was not personally acquainted with him, I thought it would be safest for me to stay away and I kept entirely apart from him.[59]

The Irish language controversy of 1899

The Irish language formed the basis of an important national controversy at the turn of the twentieth century and Hyde was at the centre of it. The dispute began in 1899 with the Vice-Regal Inquiry into Intermediate Education to examine and reform secondary education in Ireland. The Gaelic League saw this as timely and wished to place emphasis on the Irish language and to boost its status in the curricula at primary, post-primary and third level. However, this inquiry was also seen as timely by senior academics in TCD, who viewed it as an opportunity to exclude the Irish language from the education system. As stated by P.J. Matthews, '[t]his controversy was one of the most significant

58 *ACS*, 16 Sept. 1899.
59 Douglas Hyde, *Mise agus an Connradh* (Dublin, 1937), p. 72.

battles in Irish academic history and embroiled many of the country's leading intellects in heated dispute.'[60]

One of the TCD academics who led the attack on Irish language and literature was Sir John Pentland Mahaffy, and this inquiry highlighted the turbulent relationship that already existed between Hyde and Mahaffy and took it into the public forum. Sir John Pentland Mahaffy was Professor of Ancient History in TCD from 1871, later Provost from 1914.[61] At TCD in 1882, Hyde was already associated with revival of Irish through his affiliation to the SPIL. Mahaffy criticised SPIL's successful 1878 campaign to introduce modern Irish, albeit as an extra subject, into the national school curricula.[62] A point of interest is that Mahaffy, in 1882, would not have made the connection between Douglas Hyde and the poetry, in Irish or English, of 'An Craoibhín Aoibhinn' that advocated physical force nationalism. Mahaffy and his colleague, Professor Robert Atkinson,[63] who held the chair of Sanskrit and Comparative Philology, spoke against Irish, stating that it was useless as a language and that there was no merit in its literature. They recommended that Irish be taken off the intermediate school programme altogether. Hyde fought vehemently for the Gaelic League and received support from Irish scholars around Europe. By 1899, the connection between Dr Douglas Hyde, the public man, and 'an Craoibhin Aoibhinn', the public persona of Hyde's private Irish self, was as well known to the Ascendancy as to Irish Ireland, although the extent of his Fenian connections and sympathies seems not to have been recognised outside nationalist circles, even by some who were closest to him.

Mahaffy testified at the Vice-Regal inquiry that teaching Irish was a waste of time and supported only by foolish sentimentalists. Mahaffy concluded with this statement: 'I am told by a much better authority than any of them in Irish that it is almost impossible to get hold of a text in Irish which is not religious or which is not silly or indecent.'[64] Hyde sent off Mahaffy's testimony to renowned Celtic scholars, who in return sent their arguments against Mahaffy's statement while expressing disbelief and outrage. Professor Atkinson also came before the committee, asserting that Irish must be considered deficient as it lacked standardisation of spelling and grammar, that the literature was indecent and that the collection of folklore lacked academic

60 P.J. Mathews, 'Hyde's first stand: the Irish language controversy of 1899' in *Éire-Ireland*, xxxv, no. 1&2 (2000), p. 173.

61 For biographical information on Sir John Pentland Mahaffy see W.B Stanford & R.B. McDowell, *John Pentland Mahaffy: biography of an Anglo-Irishman* (Dublin, 1971).

62 See Séamus Ó Buachalla, 'Educational Policy and the Role of the Irish Language from 1831 to 1981' in *European Journal of Education*, xix, no. 1 (1984), pp 75–92.

63 For biographical information on Professor Robert Atkinson see *DIB* (https://www.dib.ie/biography/atkinson-robert-a0265) (accessed 17 Nov. 2022).

64 In Dunleavy & Dunleavy, *Douglas Hyde*, p. 210.

credibility. Contemporary newspapers such as the *Freeman's Journal, Daily Express* and *An Claidheamh Soluis* followed the conflict with great interest.

It is safe to say that Hyde did not respect the opinions, academic work or academic leadership of Mahaffy, nor did Mahaffy hold respect for Hyde or his scholarly work. In an article titled 'The Recent Fuss about the Irish Language', published in August 1899 in the British monthly literary magazine *The Nineteenth Century*, Mahaffy attacked Hyde as one of those people he judged to be 'self-developed enthusiasts', who teach Irish because they hope to earn their living and achieve fame by leading the new movement.[65] In a creative response in 1903, Hyde wrote a sharply satirical bilingual play *Pleusgadh na Bulgóide, or The Bursting of the Bubble*, about the continuing battle over education in Irish; its targets were easily identified as Mahaffy and Atkinson, enemies of the Irish language. 'Bulgóid' [*gen. Bulgóide*], as the 'notes' to Hyde's Irish text point out, is suspiciously similar to 'Tríonóid' [*gen. Tríonóide*], the Irish for Trinity. In the Irish version of the play, Hyde uses the name 'Mac Eathfaidh' for one of the protagonists, christening him 'Magaffy' in the English translation. This 'Magaffy' and his colleague 'Hatkin' i.e. Atkinson, are given lines that only slightly exaggerate the charges made by their real-life counterparts in their 1899 testimony before the Vice-Regal inquiry into secondary education. Hyde's utilisation of satire serves as a testament to his adeptness in navigating and mediating conflict, while concurrently harnessing conflict as a source of inspiration. Moreover, this instance of satire exemplifies an early Irish drama that derived its thematic material from contemporaneous events associated with the Revival movement, as opposed to relying on historical subject matter. As such, the satire assumes a distinctive and consequential position within the realm of Irish dramatic literature.[66]

Despite Mahaffy's efforts, Hyde and the Gaelic League were victorious and the place of Irish within the curriculum was secured with the Intermediate Education Amendment Act of 1900. Hyde also campaigned vigorously to have Irish recognised as an essential element in the new National University, where in 1910 Irish was made a compulsory subject for matriculation.[67] Led

65 John Pentland Mahaffy, 'The recent fuss about the Irish language' in *The nineteenth century* (London, August 1899).

66 For a standardised version of *Pleusgadh na Bulgóide*, together with some explanatory notes and instances of contemporary reaction, see Éadaoin Ní Mhuircheartaigh & Nollaig Mac Congáil (eds), *Drámaí thús na hathbheochana* (Galway, 2008), pp 191–209. For discussion of this satirical play's significance at the time of its composition, see the editors' introduction in the same source, p. 19.

67 Douglas Hyde, 'The new National University in Ireland and the Irish language' in *Celtic Review*, no. 5 (1909), pp 319–26. See also Brendan Walsh, 'Frankly and robustly national': Padraig Pearse, the Gaelic League and the campaign for Irish at the National University' in *Studies: An Irish Quarterly Review*, ciii, no. 411 (Autumn 2014), pp 318–30.

by Hyde, this was undoubtedly a major achievement for the Gaelic League, with its importance acknowledged by Irish nationalists at home and abroad. The *Gaelic American*, for instance, proclaimed on its front page that it was the 'most significant achievement in the history of the Gaelic League ... that had the moral support of the whole country.'[68]

Pseudonyms: 'Hyding' behind the pen

Throughout his public career, Hyde cleverly used the pseudonyms 'an Craoibhín Aoibhinn' and 'an Géagán Glas' to enable him to portray what he considered controversial political opinions or ideals. These writings highlight how intercommunal conflict and his inner conflicts in relation to his public apolitical stance as president of the Gaelic League were expounded, albeit surreptitiously, through his writings. The elements of the name 'an Géagán Glas' mirror those of 'an Craoibhín Aoibhinn', *géagán* having the same meaning as *craoibhín*, i.e. 'little branch', while the adjective *glas*, meaning 'green', is set against *aoibhinn*, meaning 'pleasant'. As Professor Liam Mac Mathúna has unearthed, 'an Géagán Glas' makes his first appearance in a booklet with three pieces from the 1901 Oireachtas.[69] The first two items – a prose allegory in both Irish and English, and the second, the Oireachtas Ode (an Anglophobic poem in Irish) – are both attributed to 'an Craoibhín Aoibhinn', while the third marks the first appearance of 'an Géagán Glas'. Entitled 'Mallughadh an Bhóeir ar Shacsanaibh' ['The curse of the Boer on the English'], it is a bitter anti-English poem in which he attacks Queen Victoria for the crimes committed in her name against Irish, Boer and Indian alike.[70] 'An Géagán Glas' also penned a long letter to *An Claidheamh Soluis* in 1902 on the position of Irish in the education system, in which he argued vehemently against Professors Mahaffy and Atkinson of Trinity College.[71] Hyde evidently chose to attribute his more controversial and anti-British pieces to 'an Géagán Glas', a fact confirmed by a note entered by Hyde into a scrapbook copy of a piece of

68 *Gaelic American*, 18 Jun. 1910.

69 Liam Mac Mathúna, 'Na róil a bhí ag an gCraoibhín Aoibhinn, an Géagán Glas agus "G. G." i gcumadh agus in aistriú *Pleusgadh na Bulgóide; Or the Bursting of the Bubble* (1903)' in Éadaoin Ní Mhuircheartaigh, Róisín Ní Ghairbhí & Pádraig Ó Liatháin (eds), *Ó chleamairí go ceamaraí: drámaíocht agus taibhealaíona na Gaeilge faoi chaibidil* (Dublin, 2021), pp 19–33.

70 See Cathal Billings, 'Cogadh na mBórach agus an pholaitíocht forbartha náisiúnach i gConradh na Gaeilge' in *Éigse: a Journal of Irish Studies*, xli (2021), pp 212–35.

71 This letter is reprinted as an appendix in Gaelic League Pamphlets, No. 29, *Irish in university education: evidence given before the Royal Commission on University Education, 1902* (Dublin, 1902), pp 50–6.

comic verse titled 'The Song of the Galway Shoneen'; the note read: 'Mise do sgríobh!'[72] This verse was published in *The Leader* on 31 January 1903, again under the pen-name 'an Géagán Glas'. Hyde's aforementioned satirical play, *Pleusgadh na Bulgóide*, was published in 1903 by Gill & Son in Dublin along with its English translation. Up to now, commentators had assumed that this play, like others by Hyde, was translated by Lady Gregory, but it was in fact translated by 'G.G.', an intialisation of 'an Géagán Glas'.[73] As Mac Mathúna notes: 'Away from the spotlight, buttressed by a vitriolic opposition to Trinity College's ethos, there continued to be indications of the Fenian leanings of the younger Hyde that were hidden behind his second – and less widely addressed – nom de plume, "An Géagán Glas".'[74]

Hyde also used 'an Géagán Glas' when writing in the bilingual Church of Ireland periodical, *The Gaelic Churchman*.[75] *The Gaelic Churchman* allowed its readers to hear about the aims of Cumann Gaedhealach na hEaglaise (the Church of Ireland Gaelic Society) and the campaign to make Irish language services available for Church of Ireland congregants. The campaign was successful, and in November 1919 service in Irish for the Church of Ireland was approved. Though he would write for the same publication under his acknowledged pen name 'an Craoibhín', the need for anonymity arose when Hyde engaged in debate over a subject that might be regarded as contentious. Thus it was 'an Geaghan Glas' who in April 1921 launched a severe critique in *The Gaelic Churchman* of 'the Northern Celt', who had previously written an article titled 'Founding of the National Church'. Drawing on his frustrations as a former student of Theology at TCD, Hyde remarked: 'A chara, I fear Northern Celt never paused to verify some of his quotations. I have noticed that this is a common failing amongst theologians.'[76] Concluding his response with the initials 'G.G.', Hyde further affirmed the employment of a pseudonym to shield himself from direct public confrontation.

Subsequently, 'the Northern Celt' replied to Hyde, and their correspondence was published in June 1920 under the title 'Correspondence – The Early Celtic Church':

> A chara, I regret to ask you of space for a reply to the letter of 'An Géaghan Glas' in the April number of the Magazine.

72 'I wrote this!' ('Scrapbook compiled by Douglas Hyde', NLI MS 42,685). See also Liam Mac Mathúna, 'Great War strains and Easter Rising breaking point: Douglas Hyde's ideological ambivalences' in *Éire-Ireland*, liii, no. 1&2 (2018), pp 24–5.

73 Douglas Hyde, *Pleusgadh na Bulgóide* (Dublin, 1903), p. 1.

74 Mac Mathúna, 'Great War strains', pp 7–8.

75 *The Gaelic Churchman* was first published in March 1919. See Dr Caird Collection, housed in the Church of Ireland RCB Library, MS 2000.

76 *Gaelic Churchman*, Apr. 1920.

> When a critic asserts with such confidence that the facts of history have not been correctly and honestly presented the first writer is compelled to give further time and labour for the purpose of removing any misapprehensions in the minds of the readers engendered by the defective antiquarian and historical knowledge of the critic. I did not intend to go into this subject specially again and hope that your readers will recognise that I have been drawn into it further by my critic's want of knowledge. An GG claims that I have not paused to verify some of my quotations. An Géagán Ghlas endeavours to entrap me by the ridiculous enquiry if I am quoting from Theiner's 'Einführung der erzwungenen Ehelosigkeit bei den Geistlichen' of 1828 or the 'Vetera Monumenta Hibernorum et Scotorum' of 1864 as regards a bishop of Connor who as late as 1233, was 'the son of a priest and begotten in priesthood.' He will see the full papal letter in the last-named vol.[77]

This episode serves as another manifestation of Hyde's compulsion to adopt a pseudonym to avoid overt public disputes. Such an approach allowed him to maintain a statesmanlike demeanour in his political and social endeavours, while concurrently enabling him to articulate his perspectives publicly, albeit under the veil of anonymity.

Hyde's ideological development can thus be seen in a few parts: from 1874 to 1890, he acquired Irish from Fenian supporters in Tibohine and he idolised O'Donovan Rossa; from 1893 to 1915, he relentlessly promoted the apolitical stance of the Gaelic League but resigned in 1915 as president of the Gaelic League as the apolitical policy was overturned by the IRB members within the Gaelic League executive.[78] He did, however, maintain a lifelong emotional attachment to Fenian views, albeit privately, and these feelings only occasionally reached the public through his pen and through the little-known pseudonym of 'an Géagán Glas'.

Conclusion

Hyde lived through a tumultuous period in Irish history. He had tremendous foresight to take an apolitical public stance on the Gaelic Revival and his nationalist ideals, which thus catapulted him to the position of Ireland's first president in his later years. He managed to navigate his way successfully through various conflicts in his early life: his successful management of his

77 Ibid., Jun. 1920.

78 See Aindrias Ó Cathasaigh, *Athrú ag teacht: Conradh na Gaeilge, Ard-Fheis 1915 agus Éirí Amach na Cásca* (Baile Átha Cliath, 2016).

father regarding his career pathway; his victorious campaign for an improved visibility and status for the Irish language in the education system; and his clever use of pseudonyms to ensure anonymity when putting forward a controversial political stance. Having to traverse two different worlds through his childhood, and to find his place in both, strengthened Hyde's resolve and allowed him to connect seamlessly with people during his collecting of folklore, his travels, in the lecture theatre, on stage and, finally, in Áras an Uachtaráin. Douglas Hyde's life and legacy serve as a testament to the power of identity, community and language. His upbringing in rural Roscommon, his academic pursuits and his political activism all contributed to his unique perspective on Irish culture and society. Hyde's commitment to promoting the Irish language and culture was not merely an academic pursuit, but a deeply personal one, shaped by his own experience of social, linguistic and cultural conflict. His ability to navigate these tensions and to channel his social and emotional intelligence in his political and cultural work allowed him to become a true statesman and Ireland's first president.

5

'To Instigate Them to Talk English': The *Bata Scóir*, a Weapon of Linguistic, Psychological and Cultural Conflict in Nineteenth-Century Ireland

Kerron Ó Luain

Introduction

Albert Memmi, the French-Tunisian colonial theorist, noted how a 'mythical and degrading portrait ends up being accepted and lived with to a certain extent by the colonised. It thus acquires a certain amount of reality and contributes to the true portrait of the colonized.'[1] In the Irish context, *an Drochshaol*, or the Great Famine of 1845–52, seared into the minds of many Irish people a self-portrait of a naturally impoverished people – a notion advanced, for example, in Malthusian thinking and promulgated by British propagandists and politicians.[2] The link between the Irish language and regions with high mortality and emigration during the Famine accelerated the process by which the peasantry began to turn their backs on the language, and its attendant culture, in large numbers in the post-Famine years – a process Breandán Mac Suibhne describes in *The end of outrage: post-Famine adjustment in rural Ireland* as 'walking away from their dead … figuratively through cultural change'.[3] This, in tandem with the belief that English was required to 'get on in life', saw the language rapidly decline in the second half

1 Albert Memmi, *The colonizer and the colonized* (London, 2021), pp 131–2.

2 Hazel Waters, 'The Great Famine and the rise of anti-Irish racism' in *Race & Class*, xxxi, no. 1 (1995), pp 106–7.

3 Breandán Mac Suibhne, *The end of outrage: post-Famine adjustment in rural Ireland* (Oxford, 2017), p. 279.

of the nineteenth century. When writing to the Folklore Commission in the 1930s about his own upbringing in Doolin, County Clare, in the 1880s, Seán Mac Mathghamhna stated that it was well known 'that the parents at home fifty years ago discouraged the speaking of Irish in this district ... Even the most illiterate of parents imagined their children were all right and fully fit to face the great, strong world if they knew a little broken English ... But as for Irish they reckoned it was only a slaves' gibberish.'[4] The process of language shift had begun in earnest, of course, in pre-Famine times, and education had played a key role. The macro-economic, political and cultural forces that drove language shift have been evaluated by several scholars.[5] Such larger trends of language shift over time – which occurred in the social, political and economic realms, as well as in educational and ecclesiastic institutions – were driven by smaller instances of everyday linguistic, psychological and cultural conflict.

The focus of this chapter is the tally stick, or *bata scóir* (*pl. bataí scóir*). A seemingly innocuous material object, the *bata scóir* was used both at home and within the national education system to coerce children to shift from Irish to English and it became emblematic of the eradication of the Irish language in nineteenth century Ireland. The *bata scóir*, described as being up to twelve inches long and one inch in circumference, was notched with the number of times a child had erred by speaking Irish and then a corresponding number of lashes were administered for the transgression – a punishment that exacted a cruel psychological toll on the child, cultivating stigma and attaching shame to the speaking of Irish. Although first-hand accounts of its use are difficult to find, by the turn of the twentieth century the *bata scóir* had become a symbolic focus for revivalists and nationalists in their campaign to halt and reverse the language shift. The process of language shift was thus interpreted as having been driven almost entirely by the education system. As one historian of Irish education, John Coolahan, has argued, this was not without good reason. The National Board of Education fiercely resisted attempts in the last quarter of the nineteenth century to allow Irish to be taught within the school system.[6] The resistance, however, was not

4 Questionnaire response on the *bata scóir* of Seán Mac Mathghamhna, Doolin, Co. Clare, 24 Mar. 1936 (UCD Folklore Archive (henceforth cited as UCDFA), MS 495), pp 151–4.

5 Tom O'Donoghue & Theresa O'Doherty, *Irish speakers and schooling in the Gaeltacht, 1900 to the present* (Switzerland, 2019); Mac Suibhne, *The end of outrage*; Gearóid Ó Tuathaigh, *I mbéal an bháis: the Great Famine and the language shift in nineteenth-century Ireland* (Hamden CT., 2015); Angela Bourke, 'The baby and the bathwater: cultural loss in nineteenth-century Ireland' in Tadhg Foley & Seán Ryder (eds), *Ideology and Ireland in the nineteenth century* (Dublin, 1998); Seán de Fréine, *The great silence* (Westport, 1965).

6 John Coolahan, 'Education as cultural imperialism: the denial of the Irish language to Irishspeakers, 1831–1922' in *Education and Ethnicity, Paedagogica Historica*, xxxvii, no. 1 (2006), pp 32–3.

constant and symbolic gestures were made, but only following campaigns by Irish language activists. Ó Buachalla, for example, has highlighted that although the commissioners agreed in 1878 to include Irish as an 'extra' subject on the programme for schools following a campaign by the Society for the Perseveration of the Irish Language (SPIL) 'no provision was made to train the necessary teachers until 1897 when the language was permitted as an "optional subject" in the Training Colleges'.[7] The overall hostility of the Board would have policy consequences when the Free State was founded in 1922 and education, rather than society and the economy at large, was identified as the key locus by which to reverse language shift.[8]

In this chapter I will first examine accounts, both first- and second-hand, of the use of the *bata scóir* in the nineteenth century. Much of the evidence provided in this first section is derived from the National Folklore Commission and the work of Séamus Ó Duilearga who adopted a Swedish questionnaire system to use in Ireland. The School's Scheme of 1937–38 thus provided a network of enthusiastic teachers throughout the state to act as correspondents.[9] I will then examine language revivalists' perceptions of the *bata scóir* before finally turning to the psychological, even cognitive, impact of its use.

Use of the *bata scóir*

Seán Ó Suilleabháin of the Irish Folklore Commission traced the use of the *bata scóir* in Ireland from the Jesuit colleges of the European continent in the seventeenth century. He contended that teachers in the national schools founded in 1831, and perhaps hedge school masters before them, already aware of corporal punishment and the use of a stick in attempting to instil Latin in the place of vernacular languages, imported the practice to Ireland to be applied against the Irish language.[10] However, primary sources detailing its use are rare. One of the few accounts of the use of a tally stick found in the provincial press relates not to its use in an educational setting, but within the realm of work. At Lorrha petty sessions in North Tipperary in the summer of 1864 the *Nenagh Guardian* reported that:

7 Séamas Ó Buachalla, 'Educational policy and the role of the Irish language from 1831 to 1981' in *European Journal of Education*, xix, no. 1 (1984), pp 75–92.

8 Coolahan, 'Education as cultural imperialism', pp 32–3.

9 Mícheál Briody, *The Irish Folklore Commission 1935–1970* (Helsinki, 2016), p. 281.

10 Seán Ó Suilleabháin, 'Bataí scóir' in Eóin Ua Riain (ed.), *Féil-sgríbhinn Eóin Mhic Néill: tráchtais léigheanta i n-onóir do'n ollamhain Eóin Mac Néill do sgríobh cáirde d'á cháirdibh i n-am a dheichmhadh bliadhna agus trí fichid, an cúigmhadh lá déag de mhí na Bealtaine, 1938* (Dublin, 1940), pp 551–2.

> Darby Donohoe obtained a decree against Thomas Mannion, of Ballyhoctor, for 5s. and costs for labour performed. Darby, who is one of the old school of labourer, now nearly extinct, exhibited his account on a tally stick, having a notch for each day except Saturday, the mark for this day crossed the other five, and completed the full week. It took some trouble from the Bench to become properly initiated into Darby's mode of single entry.[11]

Seán de Fréine's assessment on the changeover from Irish to English encouraged, or, rather, enforced, by parents may offer a clue as to the scant availability of sources on the *bata scóir* as a means of punishment. 'When we contemplate the physical and psychological implications of what they did', he writes, 'it becomes perfectly understandable why the experience was buried in the recesses of the subconscious of the individual and social memory.'[12]

One of the only extant first-hand accounts of the use of the *bata scóir* for punishment and language change comes from Sir William Wilde, surgeon, author and father of Oscar Wilde. Writing in one of his travel books entitled *Ireland: her wit, peculiarities, and popular superstitions* published *c.* 1850, Wilde offered the following snippet that occurred on the shores of Lough Inagh in Connemara:

> Our guide conducted us to a neighbouring village, where we were received for the night with that hospitality which has ever been the characteristic of those wild mountaineers. While supper was preparing and the potatoes laughing and steaming in the skieh, the children gathered round to have a look at the stranger, and one of them, a little boy about eight years of age, addressed a short sentence in Irish to his sister, but meeting the father's eye he immediately cowered, having to all the appearance committed some heinous fault. The man called the child to him, said nothing, but drawing forth from its dress a little stick, commonly called a scoreen or tally, which was suspended by a string round the neck, put an additional notch in it with his penknife.
>
> Upon our inquiring into the cause of this proceeding, we were told that it was done to prevent the child speaking Irish, for every time he attempted to do so a new nick was put in his tally, and when these amounted to a certain number summary punishment was inflicted upon him by the schoolmaster.[13]

11 *Nenagh Guardian*, 8 Jun. 1864. It survived in this use, though not widely, until the 1920s; see R.J. Welch, 'Survival of the tally-stick in Ireland' in *The Irish Naturalists' Journal*, ii, no. 5 (September, 1928), p. 101.

12 De Fréine, *The great silence*, p. 149.

13 Sir William Wilde, *Ireland: her wit, peculiarities, and popular superstitions: with anecdotes, legendary and characteristic by distinguished Irish writers* (Dublin, c.1850), chap. 1; also

Another account from a teacher, who was said to have used the *bata scóir* on his pupils, is perhaps more interesting because of his denial. David O'Callaghan, the resident teacher at Fearann an Choirce (Oatquarter) National School on the Aran Islands, took umbrage at his portrayal by Gaelic League organiser, Thomas Concannon, as someone who used the tally stick on children. In 1899 he wrote to Eoin Mac Néill, then editor of the Gaelic League weekly *An Claidheamh Soluis*, to fight his case. A previous issue of the paper had stated that Concannon had received 'many a cut' from O'Callaghan's cane for 'venturing, now and then, to speak a word in the only language he knew; and, even at that early age, his heart would swell with indignation at the injustice against which he dare not protest'. Yet according to O'Callaghan it was some parents whom he knew who had engaged in the practice, and it certainly had not gone on in the school:

> My heart swells with indignation at reading the above untrue statement, and I dare protest against it. I taught the Inishmaan school from September, 1880, to October, 1884. During the four years I pledge my word that I never punished Master Thomas Concannon nor any other pupil of mine for speaking Irish.[14]

His retort is illustrative either of an element of constructed memory and propagandising by revivalists such as Concannon surrounding the tally stick or, perhaps, of the rise of Gaelic revivalism and attempts by teachers who might have used the *bata scóir* in the past to distance themselves from its use later.

The National Folklore Collection in University College Dublin, which sent questionnaires to folklore collectors in the 1930s, provides far more bountiful examples on the *bata scóir* than the press or literary sources of the nineteenth century. The responses show some of the local idiosyncrasies in its use (see Figure 1). For example, at Oldcourt near Skibbereen, County Cork, the respondent, Mícheál Ó Cuileanáin reported that although none of the old people in the area had ever seen a *bata scóir*, they all commented that they knew of its existence. It was known as a 'signum' in that part of the country and was not used on girls.[15] In Cathair Dónall (Caherdaniel), County Kerry, the signum 'was shaped like a log for a vicious dog, with a rope running through' the wooden device, similar to a collar.[16] Just to the north, in the

cited and discussed as *Collection of information* in *An Claidheamh Soluis* (henceforth cited as *ACS*), 31 Aug. 1912.

14 *ACS*, 7 Oct. 1899.

15 Questionnaire response on the *bata scóir* of Mícheál Ó Cuileanáin, Oldcourt, Skibbereen, Co. Cork, 1 Feb. 1936 (UCDFA, MS 495), p. 159.

16 Questionnaire response on the *bata scóir* of Pádraig Ó Cuinneagáin, Caherdaniel, Co. Kerry, n/d (UCDFA, MS 647), p. 72.

townland of Killagurteen, it was called a 'signal' or 'an capall bán', i.e. the white horse, and was still in use *c.* 1870.[17] Meanwhile, Daithí Ó Ceanntabhail, from Croom, County Limerick, received details of the *bata scóir* from a Mrs Moore, who resided near Shronell, County Tipperary, and that information was passed through her mother, who saw them in use in the 1860s. In that locality, the stick was made of larch or birch. According to Moore 'there was a number of nails driven into the wall of the school and on each nail was hung by the free loop, a *bata scóir*. The name of the child was written on the wall under its own bata. Accordingly the school wall held rows of them.'[18] By contrast, in Woodgraigue, County Wexford, according to Seán de Buitléir, 'there was a cord from one end of the stick, and this had a loop on the end, and this was tied around the boy's neck. Of course he always carried the stick and cord with him.'[19] Other responses note that in some cases both the schoolmaster and the parents would administer punishment. P. de Búrca, who collected information from three women – Brighid Ní Mháille, Máire Ní Shomacháin and Nóra Ní Maoildhia – from Corr na Móna (Cornamona), County Galway, and Tuar Mhic Éadaigh (Toormakeady), County Mayo, noted 'go raibh na h-aithreachtaí agus na máthaireachaí chomh mór in aghaidh na Gaedhilge an uair sin le muintir Shasanaí'.[20] Indeed, this corresponds with a similar account given by the abovementioned O'Callaghan to *An Claidheamh Soluis* in 1899:

> A parent one day came to complain to me that his son *Páidín,* though two years at school, had no English, and I was the cause of that, because I did not put a *score* round his neck, as was done in his time. This was the first time I ever heard of the *score.* He also complained that I permitted the children to talk Irish in the school. I had no Irish then, and had to get the above at second-hand from a person brought by the parent for that purpose, who explained to me the meaning of the *score.* I was not then two months on the island, and the parent's main reason for making complaint was that I allowed the children to speak Irish at will. I told him that he did not seem to have benefited by the *score* being used in his day as he had no English, that if he prevented his child from talking Irish at home he would do him far more harm than good. I said I should not like to be punished every time I spoke English, and that I was anxious to be able to speak Irish as he was that his son should talk

17 Ó Suilleabháin, 'Bataí Scóir', p. 558.

18 Questionnaire response on the *bata scóir* of Daithí Ó Ceanntabhail, Croom, Co. Limerick, Mar. 1936 (UCDFA, MS 495), pp 162–6.

19 Ó Suilleabháin, 'Bataí scóir', p. 556.

20 'that the fathers and mothers were so much against the Irish language that time as were the English' (questionnaire response on *bata scóir* of P. de Búrca, Co. Mayo, 28 Mar. 1936 (UCDFA, MS 495), pp 181–3).

English. I also told him that if I were the child I should make short work of the *score*. All this through our interpreter. I saw by the man's appearance that I had provoked him very much; he spoke angrily and quickly. I asked what he was saying, and was told that it was not at all complimentary, and 'that I was a quare schoolmaster surely'.[21]

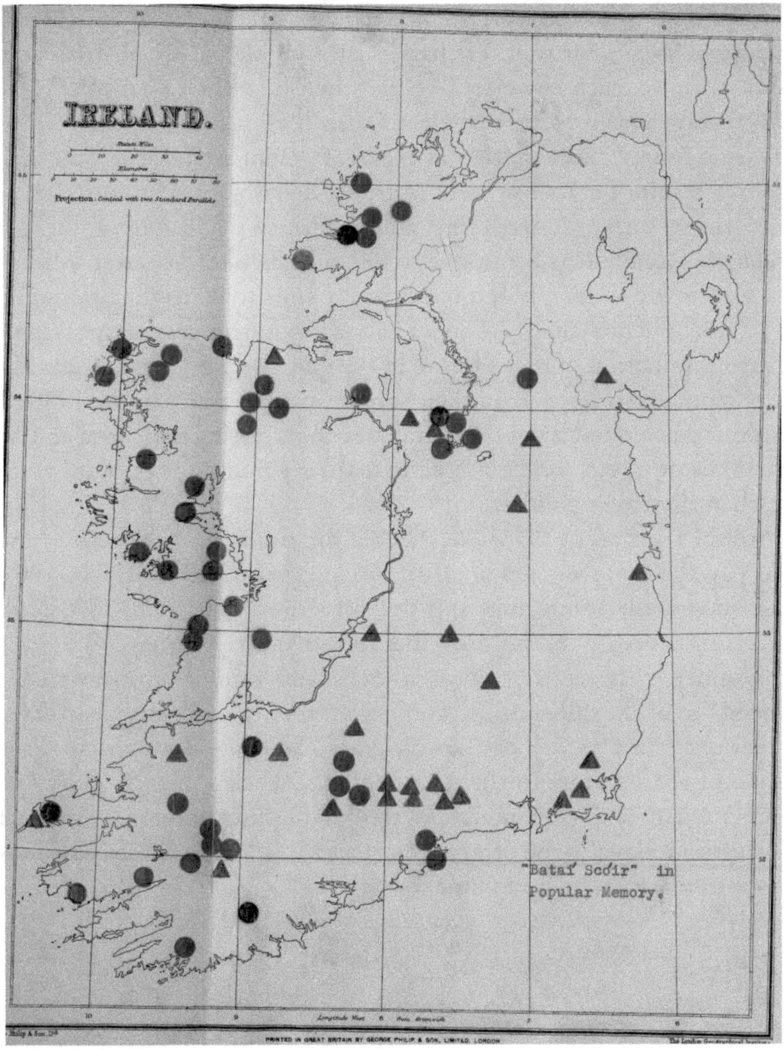

Figure 1 Dispersion of positive results (circles) and negative results (triangles) from use of the *bata scóir* and other methods of discouraging the use of Irish by children in Ireland. Courtesy of the National Folklore Collection, UCD.

21 *ACS*, 7 Oct. 1899.

Elsewhere in the responses we can deduce the geographical spread of the use of the *bata scóir* and the timespan in which it was used. For example in Tipperary, Máirtín de Búrca, BA, a teacher at Clonmel and a former student of Séamus Ó Duilearga, Professor of Folklore at University College Dublin, recounts how 'Pat's Power' of Newcastle Parish in the county who attended national school from 1864 'never remembers any attempt to put down the Irish language in the local national school – except in so far as it was neither taught nor used in the school', He never knew 'bataí sgóir to have been used, nor any practice similar to it. He had learned all his prayers in Irish at home, but was made re-learn them in English when he went to school.'[22] It seems logical to state that in places where English had gained supremacy, the *bata scóir* was no longer used. Indeed, as Figure 1 demonstrates, the concentration of positive results for its use were in the still Irish-speaking districts in the west of the country. Indeed, the aforementioned allusion in the *Nenagh Guardian* to Donohoe as being 'one of the old school of labourer' who, by the 1860s, was nearly extinct, is of interest, as it points towards the *bata scóir* being a pre-Famine phenomenon. As to its use as a punishment for speaking Irish, from my examination of the material in the questionnaires it seems that many of the respondents who were in their seventies and eighties in the 1930s either barely remembered its use in the national schools during their own childhoods in the 1850s or 1860s, or recounted that their parents spoke of it being used often when they were children.

It would then seem that, like the use for counting work-related matters such as pay, the *bata scóir* as a linguistic weapon was also more of a pre-Famine phenomenon with some lingering use into the 1860s and 1870s. This is unsurprising since in both cases the spread of paper that occurred from the mid-nineteenth century onwards in Ireland would have superseded the continued use of the tally stick.[23] Another reason for its demise may have been a generational shift as well as the accelerated language shift that occurred in the wake of the Famine. In the townland of Carheeny Beg, County Galway, Seán Ó Flannagáin documented how 'the *bataí scóir* ceased to be used in 1866' in New Quay following the death of one teacher, a Mr Connolly, who used the *bata scóir* in order 'to make a name for himself'.[24]

22 Questionnaire response on the *bata scóir* of Máirtín de Búrca, Clonmel, Co. Tipperary, Mar. 1939 (UCDFA, MS 495), pp 175–7.

23 *Irish Times*, 15 Jan. 1996. Paper production doubled between 1838 and 1852.

24 Ó Suilleabháin, 'Bataí scóir', p. 561.

The *bata scóir* and Irish nationalism

That the *bata scóir* still exists in the national consciousness for many people is underlined by the appearance, in recent years, of a song and a poem detailing its use. In 2017, Joe Canning, a poet from Strabane, County Tyrone, wrote the poem 'A message to Mr Poots', most likely in response to Democratic Unionist Party member Edwin Poots and his many anti-Irish language pronouncements. The poem's opening stanzas refer to the *bata scóir*, the first of which is as follows:

> The tutor warned them every day,
> that Gaelic sounds they must not say
> or canes would strip the flesh from tiny hands.
> A wounding lash for every notch,
> for utterance of a Gaelic word
> forbidden by the power that ruled the day.[25]

Similarly, a song entitled 'An Bata Scóir / The Tally Stick' and penned in 2021 by songwriter and poet Frank Callery, a native of Dublin, details at length the practice of using the *bata scóir* as a means of punishment for use of the Irish language and the wider colonial context in which it operated:

> Silence was no salve, and no safe option,
> The stick accounting each sharp notch of pain.
> In the language of a brutal, forced adoption
> There was little comfort, little gain.
>
> Their hands were raw, their minds were cleared –
> Like the lands they'd owned – of wise Gaelic lore;
> And the bitter words, that stick they feared,
> Notched the very tongue they loved the more.[26]

In the same vein, an internet meme with several facts about the *bata scóir* and its use in the national school system is shared widely on social media from time to time. Included is a picture of a tally stick, possibly from the continent.[27] These examples demonstrate the enduring powerful symbolism of the *bata*

25 Joe Canning Facebook page (https://www.facebook.com/joe.canning.39/posts/4154724847919848) (accessed 3 Sept. 2022).

26 Frank Calleary Soundcloud (https://soundcloud.com/frankcallerysongs/an-bata-scoir-the-tally-stick) (accessed 5 Nov. 2022).

27 Cassidy Slang Scam web page (https://cassidyslangscam.wordpress.com/tag/bata-scoir/) (accessed 16 Oct. 2022).

scóir and the perception of the national education system as the primary factor in the decline of the Irish language. Unsurprisingly, this perception emerged in the nineteenth century among cultural nationalists.

Recent scholarship has tempered the notion of the National Schools being the main driver of language shift, however. For Nicholas Wolf, in the first two decades of the National School system's existence 'the language question was far less pressing on the school administrators than it might have been had the system's growth not been so slow in precisely the same regions where Irish speaking was strongest'. In other words, he says, 'the commissioners could get away with ignoring Irish because of the uneven spread of the system'.[28] Yet the focus on the National Schools as a threat to the Irish language and Irish nationality went as far back at least to the era of the Young Irelanders. In December 1849 *The Nation* opined that 'if the National Schools were once remodelled in a truly national spirit, there would be sure hope and speedy redemption for Ireland'. Drawing on Thomas Davis's earlier pronouncement regarding a language being a 'surer barrier, and more important frontier, than fortress or barrier', the paper proclaimed that 'the National Schools may be made more serviceable to Ireland than the military schools of France were to Napoleon'.[29] Later, SPIL would continue in the same vein. When it issued its sixth annual report in 1883 the Society's emphasis on education was clear. The report noted its disappointment that 'very little progress has been made in a quarter deemed, on all sides, *the* [my emphasis] most important to the preservation of the national language – namely, the National schools'. The SPIL could not be blamed, perhaps, for its emphasis on the schools. But the report, which contained testimony from national teachers, noted there were several debilitating obstacles to teaching Irish. One of these included 'the restrictions on teaching the language to the junior classes'. Also noted was that Irish was not included in the 'payment by results' system. Positive recommendations were made by the SPIL, and, in subsequent years, the barriers to Irish gaining ground in the national school system remained clearly at the forefront of the Society's minds.[30] Twenty years later, in 1903, the *Meath Chronicle* noted how Archbishop McHale 'foretold that the National Schools would be "the graves of the Irish language"'. The paper continued, 'we have now had seventy years experience of those schools and it is safe to say that they have done more than all other agencies combined to kill our native tongue'.[31] One outcome of this emphasis on National Schools as the chief destructive force regarding

28 N.M. Wolf, *An Irish-speaking island: state, religion, community, and the linguistic landscape in Ireland, 1770–1870* (Madison, WI, 2014), pp 141–2.

29 *The Nation*, 22 Dec. 1849.

30 Ibid., 29 Mar. 1884.

31 *Meath Chronicle*, 24 Jan. 1903.

the language was a belief that if they could be repurposed for the teaching of Irish then the revival could see major gains. Such a belief was in the ascendant when Gaelic League organiser Thomas Concannon (mentioned above) visited Tyrone and the parish of Donaghmore in 1901 where previously 'there was absolutely no talk of the Irish language'. However, a young Catholic cleric named Father Rogers and a teacher called Mr McNelis had made inroads. 'They pinned their faith to the teachers', Concannon wrote, and 'if they could only get them to learn sufficient[ly] to introduce it in their schools the day would be won'.[32]

The memory of the use of the *bata scóir* was also transported to America. *The Winslow Mail* of Arizona noted in 1910 how the Home Rule politician T. P. O'Connor related 'the curious story of how the "tally stick" crushed out the remains of the ancient Irish language among Irish children'. O'Connor proclaimed 'when the English were determined to make all Ireland over into a sort of England ... they used some unusual means. Among these was the "tally stick".' The Home Ruler concluded with an anti-imperial comparison: 'every time [the child's] parents heard him say a word of Irish they were supposed to cut a notch in the stick, just as the American trappers of the old days are said to have notched the stocks of their guns every time they killed an Indian.'[33] Away from the political platforms of Irish nationalists, Irish-American academics also promulgated the story of the *bata scóir*. Dr Joseph Dunn of the Department of Celtic Languages and Literature of the Catholic University, Washington, writing in an article entitled 'The Revival of Gaelic' in the October 1905 issue of the *University Bulletin*, noted that the *bata scóir* was one of 'the vile methods that were invented to repress Irish feeling and to crush the souls of Irish children who were the principal victims'.[34]

This emphasis on the National Schools and the *bata scóir* was sometimes tempered by writers and journalists with a more judicious view of the language's decline that had material factors at its core. For example, in his 1893 book *Irish Ideas*, William O'Brien, agrarian agitator and Home Rule MP, homed in on the socio-economic causes for the decline of the Irish language. O'Brien viewed the fortunes of the language through the lens granted to him by his background in social struggle. 'Bitter things have been said of those who in the last fifty years were used to chide Irish school-children caught lapsing into their own mother tongue; and no doubt it was a sorry spectacle', he wrote, 'but it was emigration, not the ferule[35] of the old pedants, that drove the Irish

32 *ACS*, 7 Dec. 1901.
33 *The Winslow Mail*, 29 Oct. 1910.
34 *Irish Standard*, 18 Nov. 1905.
35 A flat ruler with a widened end, formerly used for beating children.

language out of fashion.'[36] In November 1901, P. T. MacGinley gave a lecture before a crowded town hall in Strabane on the topic 'How we are Englished'. His message, by focusing on the spiritually destructive nature of colonialism, was one common to revivalist themes at the time. 'To be Englished ... means a lessening of intellectualism, of self-respect, of individuality and of initiative', he stated. MacGinley also remarked upon the decline of the language and the use of the *bata scóir*, noting that it prefigured the establishment of the National School system in 1831:

> Even before the national schools came up, the hedge-school masters were often encouraged to use gross cruelty to children for speaking their own language; and parents sometimes tied wooden tallies round their children's necks as a mark of degradation for speaking Irish, just as you might tie a clog to a dog's tail for some canine misdemeanour. Then they rushed their children to the national schools regardless of the character of the instruction imparted, and in a score of ways have manifested their willingness to be Englished and still more to have their children Englished. It is the madness of a degenerate people demoralized by ignorance and slavery.[37]

Likewise, writing in *An Claidheamh Soluis agus Fáinne an Lae* in 1901, the editor, Eoghan Ó Neachtain, highlighted the social, educational, legal and commercial spheres as being central to the marginalisation of Irish and the dominance of English. In the process he also took aim at those he believed should know better – fellow nationalists:

> now in Ireland we do not require penal laws to spurn the Irish language. *Nationalists* do it for us at public meetings, managers and teachers do it in public schools, Galway solicitors and magistrates do it in the law courts, and railway companies do it for us in business; so in one guise or another we humbly eat the bread of slavery.[38]

Thus, in an age before sociolinguistic research had really developed, many homed in on education and the *bata scóir* as the root cause of the language shift, but some were also beginning to put the various pieces of the puzzle together in a more rounded way. These views were documented in detail during the Gaeltacht Commission of 1926 when numerous testimonies from teachers

36 William O'Brien, *Irish ideas* (London, 1893), p. 65.
37 *Ulster Herald*, 23 Nov. 1901; see also *ACS*, 7 Dec. 1901.
38 *ACS*, 7 Dec. 1901.

and clerics noted that Irish-speaking parents linked economic advancement to the acquisition of English.[39]

The psychological impact of cultural conflict

To assess the psychological, even cognitive, damage that the violent use of the *bata scóir* method produced in Ireland, it is useful to allude to similar examples in colonised countries globally. Declan Kiberd in *Inventing Ireland* misinterprets several factors when he foists the blame for the decline of Irish onto the populace itself and not the sociolinguistic conditions arising from the colonial context. Kiberd stated that 'Irish declined only when the Irish people allowed it to decline. Brit-bashing mythology which cites the tally stick, National Schools and Famine as the real causes was designed by politicians to occlude this painful truth.'[40] Similar arguments have been made by those of a more revisionist hue – that Irish parents, in a dawning of clarity and altruism towards their children, made the personal choice, *in vacuo*, to abandon the language.[41] By contrast, Bill Rolston and Robbie McVeigh have recently focused on the matter of the colonial project. They assess the language shift in more structural, and internationalist, terms by casting their eye not just on Ireland but on Scotland and Wales too. The authors refer to 'the clearance of the Celtic Fringe'. For them, 'in this reading "North Britain" and "West Britain" are not simply internal colonial ideological spaces but also determinedly *material* projects of Union'. They contend that 'over its 220 years of existence, the Union certainly attempted to clear this fringe of native language and thought and politics and agency'.[42] Similarly, James McCloskey notes how 'it is surely no accident that the loss of local languages has been most thorough-going in those parts of the world where English has been the colonial language. English, wherever it has gone in the world, has travelled on an ideological wave of great intolerance for bilingual ability and practice.'[43] Tomás Mac Síomóin, philosopher and Irish-language activist, bolsters this structuralist view. He rebukes not just British colonialism but also institutions such as the Catholic

39 For one example see John Walsh, *Díchoimisiúnú teanga: Coimisiún na Gaeltachta 1926* (Dublin, 2002), p. 117.

40 Declan Kiberd, *Inventing Ireland: the literature of the modern nation* (London, 1996), p. 616.

41 See discussion on John Edwards's and R.V. Comerford's depiction of language shift as 'voluntary' in Feargal Mac Ionnrachtaigh, *Language, resistance and revival: republican prisoners and the Irish language in the North of Ireland* (London, 2013), pp 62–4.

42 Robbie McVeigh & Bill Rolston, *'Anois ar theacht an tsamhraidh': Ireland, colonialism and the unfinished revolution* (Belfast, 2021), p. 133.

43 James McCloskey, *Voices silenced: has Irish a future?* (Dublin, 2001), p. 20.

Church, as well as the capitalist economy, for the erosion of the Irish language. When it comes the impact of these processes he suggests that:

> for many individuals and families in 'postcolonial Irish society', these mechanisms have left a deep psychological legacy of trauma along with consequences of: dependency; fear; ambivalence toward the colonizer; suppression of anger and rage; a sense of inferiority; self-hatred; loss of identity, horizontal violence, and vulnerability to psychological distress, all endemic to PTSD symptomology.[44]

Indeed, several documented incidents as they relate to the bata *scóir* illustrate several of the traits mentioned by Mac Síomóin. When the Sir William Wilde spoke to the father of the boy in Connemara a dependency trait and an understanding that identity was being lost was evident:

> We asked the father if he did not love the Irish language – indeed the man scarcely spoke any other. 'I do', said he, his eye kindling with enthusiasm, 'sure it is the talk of the ould country and the ould times; the language of my father and all that's gone before me – the speech of these mountains and lakes and all these glens where I was bred and born, but you know', he continued, 'the children must have larnin' and as they tache no Irish in the National School, we must have recourse to this [use of the *bata scóir*] to instigate them to talk English.'[45]

Elsewhere, there is evidence of cognitive impairment arising from the use of the *bata scóir*. The schoolmaster on the Aran Islands, David O'Callaghan, when denying that he used the *bata scóir* noted that it was the parents who did so with 'the result that, there were a few children, 8 to 10 years old, who seemed to have no language. They feared their parents to speak Irish, and they had no English.'[46] The hostile attitude of some parents to the language being taught in the schools persisted into the twentieth century. The testimony of a Father Hugh MacDwyer, parish priest of Gort an Choirce (Gortahork), County Donegal, to the Gaeltacht Commission in 1925 related how one parent 'launched an attack' against the Irish in his presence and that of an Inspector's.[47] A Folklore Commission response from Seán Ó Dúbhda in Corca Dhuibhne in West Kerry, which highlights a type of colonial horizontal

44 Tomás Mac Síomóin, *The broken harp: identity and language in modern Ireland* (Nuascéalta, 2014), p. 145.
45 *ACS*, 31 Aug. 1912.
46 Ibid., 7 Oct. 1899.
47 Walsh, *Díchoimisiúnú teanga*, p. 72.

violence, mentioned that although they had not come across the *bata scóir*, they were prevented from speaking Irish in the national school: 'Cuirtaí cuid aca a' faireadh ar a' gcuid eile féachaint a' mbeidís a' labhairt na Gaedhilge. Bhíodh [spiairithe] amuigh ag an máistir chun [sgéitheachaimh] ar lucht labhartha na Gaedhilge'.[48] This chimes with the observations of African decolonial writer, Ngugi Wa Thiong'o on his native Kenya:

> A button was initially given to one pupil who was supposed to hand it over to whoever was caught speaking his mother tongue. Whoever had the button at the end of the day would sing who had given it to him and the ensuing process would bring out all the culprits of the day. Thus children were turned into witch-hunters and in the process were being taught the lucrative value of being a traitor to one's immediate community.[49]

For Wa Thiong'o, this active coercion of English into the child's mind, 'resulted in the dissociation of the sensibility of that child from his natural and social environment, what we might call colonial alienation'.[50] The method of passing the button was also used in Brittany, where French was being imposed upon speakers of the Breton language, the object being called a *sabot*. The aforementioned Dr Dunn of the Catholic University, Washington, recorded this comparison with Brittany 'where the same blind infatuation for the dominant speech and the same disdain for the native tongue were, and are still, found as in Ireland.' In Britanny:

> a 'sabot' was given at the opening of the class to one of the boys who was to pass it over to the first of his comrades caught speaking Breton and he, in turn, was to keep it until he had caught another flagrante delicto. And thus the 'sabot' passed from hand to hand, from group to group, like a spy trapping the unwary into speaking a word of the proscribed tongue. At the stroke of the bell the boys fell into line and the schoolmaster asked in a severe tone, 'who has the Wooden Shoe?' The poor culprit was brought in, his schoolmates hooted at him and, as the 'sabot' was made and called the 'symbole' of the old tongue of his fathers so the punishment for its use was equally symbolic, namely, to clean the closets.[51]

48 'Some of the students were made to watch the other students to see would they be speaking Irish. There were spies deployed by the schoolmaster to inform on Irish speakers' (questionnaire response on the *bata scóir* of Seán Ó Dúbhda, Corca Dhuibhne, Co. Kerry, Mar. 1936 (UCDFA, MS 495), p. 149).

49 Ngugi Wa Thiong'o, *Decolonising the mind: the politics of language in African literature* (Suffolk, 1986), p. 11.

50 Ibid., p. 17.

51 *Irish Standard*, 18 Nov. 1905.

Figure 2 Examples of Welsh Nots. Image courtesy of Amgueddfa Cymru / National Museum of Wales.

In Wales the Welsh Not served the same purpose, although it seems to have been used as a sort of 'pass the parcel' punishment, rather than being used as a tally method, with the child holding it at the end of the day being punished.[52] The 1850s saw the expansion of the number of elementary schools in Wales and in 1861 a 'revised code' standardised teaching, introduced inspections and capitation grants and placed emphasis on the reading of English and arithmetic. The code did not prohibit the use of Welsh, according to Janet Davies, 'but as the livelihoods of teachers depended to a large extent upon whether or not their pupils had at least a mechanical knowledge of English, they had pecuniary interest in boycotting the Welsh language'.[53] Some teachers, says Davies, 'actively persecuted children who spoke Welsh in school, but the "Welsh Not" ... was probably not as widely used as twentieth-century mythology would suggest'.[54] Unlike the *bata scóir*, there exist several samples of artefacts of the Welsh Not as seen in Figure 2.

52 People's Collection Wales (https://www.peoplescollection.wales/items/24360) (accessed 6 Aug. 2022).

53 Janet Davies, *The Welsh language: a history* (Cardiff, 2014), p. 75.

54 Ibid., p. 76.

Physical and psychological punishment were also used in Kenya. As Wa Thiong'o states; 'one of the most humiliating experiences was to be caught speaking Gikuyu in the vicinity of the school. The culprit was given corporal punishment – three to five strokes of the cane – or was made to carry a metal plate around the neck with inscriptions such as I am stupid or I am a Donkey.'[55] This type of shaming practice persists in parts of Africa, having occurred as recently as 2014 in Uganda. In that year, a story emerged that two children were forced to wear sacks, which appeared to be made from coarse flax, for speaking an Indigenous language called Luganda in school. As Bwesigye bwa Mwesigire explains:

> In various schools in Uganda, and some other parts of Africa, children as young as five are punished for speaking African languages, indigenous languages and mother tongues at school. The modes of punishment differ. The most common one in Uganda is wearing a dirty sack until you meet someone else speaking their mother tongue and then you pass the sack on to them. In some schools, there are specific pupils and students tasked with compiling lists of fellow pupils and students speaking mother tongues. This list is then handed over to a teacher responsible for punishing these language rule-breakers. According to Gilbert Kaburu, some schools have aprons that read: 'Shame on me, I was speaking vernacular' handed over to an offender of the No Vernacular rule, who then is tasked with finding the next culprit to give the apron. Most of the punishments in their symbolism emphasise the uselessness of the African languages.[56]

The element of shame, and self-hatred, was also in evidence in Ireland in the responses sent to the Folklore Commission. In the townland of Waterville, County Kerry, Tadhg Ó Murchadha documented how a friend of his informant's father was caught 'speaking in Irish and he got the rope from the master. The poor boy was ashamed and downcast.'[57] In addition to the psychological impact of shame, at least one account in the collection documents the wielding of property rights against the language. Cáit Bean Uí Bhrádaigh of Granard, County Longford learned from Patrick Dolan that 'if the parents continued to speak the language, or if they failed to mark the tallies, they were often given a notice to quit, and then evicted. The landlords did as much to

55 Thiong'o, *Decolonising the mind*, p. 11.

56 'This is Africa' website, 'Why are schools punishing children for speaking African languages?' (https://thisisafrica.me/african-identities/schools-punishing-children-speaking-african-languages/) (accessed 26 Aug. 2022).

57 Ó Suilleabháin, 'Bataí scóir', p. 557. Author's translation.

kill the language as the Government.'[58] These examples demonstrate that the experience across hundreds of years of colonialism and various colonised, and formerly colonised, countries around the globe is too remarkably similar to be able to dismiss the language shift as a mere individualised phenomenon driven by 'forward-thinking' parents. Clearly, the colonial and capitalist context was, and continues to be, the main driver of the whole process.

How, then, were these forces tackled? To return to the nineteenth century and Irish revivalists, *An Claidheamh Soluis agus Fáinne an Lae* recognised the international imperial dynamics that drove language shift. In 1901, the paper drew a comparison on the point of cultural conflict that counterposed dominant and subjugated languages with reference to the *bata scóir*. It stated that

> [t]he Poles have their penal days at present under the Germans for refusing to become Germanised. Polish school children are being flogged for refusing to say their Catechism in German, a language they do not understand ... Many Irishmen will compare this flogging with that which they received when the tally stick hung round their necks in their school days.[59]

To combat this subjugation in Ireland revivalists sought to tackle the element of shame attached to the language by methods such as the *bata scóir*. One article, carried in *An Claidheamh Soluis agus Fáinne an Lae* in 1907, and written under the pen-name 'Tír-Fhiachrach', noted the difficulty of encouraging children to speak Irish when they had been reared from the 'cradle' in English. As a countermeasure the writer put forward an idea: 'suggested by the "score" or "tally" used to kill the language, but in this case reward is substituted for punishment. In any school where the children have been learning Irish for, say, two or three years, let those who have acquired some power of Irish conversation be entered for a prize to be awarded at the end of the year.'[60] Similarly, P. Lonergan, Catholic parish priest of Ballinamult, County Waterford, a supporter of the Gaelic League, wrote to the *Freeman's Journal* in 1900, perhaps foreshadowing later arguments about the cognitive abilities of bilingualism and multilingualism.[61] These ideas, of course, were scientifically proven towards the close of the twentieth century and are now a staple selling point of most minority language education sectors.[62]

58 Ibid.
59 *ACS*, 7 Dec. 1901.
60 *ACS*, 17 Oct. 1907.
61 Such ideas were further developed by Pádraig Pearse after he founded Scoil Éanna in 1909. See, for example, Norman Atkinson, 'The educational ideas of Patrick Pearse, 1879–1916' in *Comparative Education Review*, xi, no. 1 (1967), pp 70–1.
62 Viorica Marian & Anthony Shook, 'The cognitive benefits of being bilingual' in *Cerebrum*, no. 13 (2012), *passim*.

Lonergan contended that 'the acquisition of a knowledge of Irish brings out the mental Powers'.[63] It is noteworthy that the now well-established benefits of bi- and multilingualism were identified by a turn-of-the-century revivalist. Ultimately, what is interesting about these final accounts is the emphasis of revivalists on reversing language shift and on correcting the psychological impact inflicted by the *bata scóir* method through positive reinforcement and bilingual education, which foreshadowed the work of the *Gaelscoileanna* (Irish-medium schools) that emerged over half a century later.

Conclusion

The last scholarly investigations of the *bata scóir* were published over half a century ago or more, and only amounted to several pages. For an object that loomed so large in the revivalist conception of language shift, and still resonates with people in contemporary society when they think of the Irish language in the colonial context, it is perhaps an anomaly that more modern scholarly analyses had not been attempted until now. Nevertheless, there exists an opportunity for further research into the numerous respondents' questionnaires – if analysed both qualitatively and quantitatively these might tell us something more about the language shift. Such an analysis is beyond the scope of this chapter but I hope that this offering sets out the direction for more in-depth research on the topic soon.

The use of the *bata scóir* seems to have petered out in the post-Famine era. This may have occurred due to the larger and more all-pervasive forces of emigration, rural depopulation, the diminished status of the Irish language in the public sphere and economic imperative accelerating the language shift. These forces seem to have superseded the *bata scóir* and meant that the cruel practice of physically banishing Irish from the mouths of children was no longer thought 'necessary'. Changes to the economy in the post-Famine era that saw the spread of paper may have also diminished the prevalence of the *bata scóir* in wider society for the means of work, thus curtailing its use in the classroom. Corporal punishment, of course, continued well into the twentieth century and was not abolished in the Republic of Ireland until 1982. Further investigation is therefore warranted on language dynamics in Irish classrooms from the demise of the *bata scóir* in the late nineteenth century to the foundation of the Irish Free State in 1922. Indeed, Irish educational history, usually more concerned with legislation and curriculum changes, still awaits a bottom-up approach that analyses in depth the experiences of children and teachers during the nineteenth century. Better still, a history of this nature

63 *Freeman's Journal*, 17 Feb. 1900.

could use global comparators – of which there are many – to tease out the effects of colonialism on children, on educational systems and on language. In Africa, where these practices still exist today, research into the psychological impact on children is still a possibility and could assist in understanding the past. Such an analysis in Irish terms is not possible given that the practice died out long ago, but an historic analysis is also made more difficult by the continued refusal of the Department of Education to open its files to the public. These might shed much light on individual and collective experiences of language shift in the classroom and the linguistic, cultural and psychological implications that ensued from that shift. The impact of that shift on the national psyche, and its reverberations from the nineteenth through to the twenty-first centuries, have yet to be fully understood.

6

Conflicts of Interest: The Importance of the Coroner during the Great Famine, 1845–52

Michelle McGoff-McCann

> We have lost those unimpeachable evidences of the hideousness of our condition, presented by the records of coroners' inquests, and the verdicts of coroners juries. Why? Because Grand Jurors, moved by selfishness for their class more than by economy [in] regards [to] the people's money, have recommended that Coroners should no longer hold inquests upon subjects believed to have died of starvation. No wonder they should not wish to have any such testimony of their misdoings.

Introduction

The inquest during the Great Famine was a site of conflict as public opinion varied as to the value offered by the investigation of death. Inquests exposed the failure of inadequate legislation, the slow response of local landholding elites and officials to address the needs of the poor, and restrictive local relief policies that placed coroners at the centre of controversy. Coroners worked within the political framework of gentrified 'officialdom', which was still monopolised by the local elite, a group of which they themselves were members. As the death toll increased, the usefulness and purpose of the coroner was questioned. While some government officials and clergy demanded the investigation of starvation and Famine-related deaths, grand juries comprised of local elites found inquests into the 'obvious' deaths of the destitute unnecessary. Inquests that resulted in verdicts of death from 'starvation', 'want of food' and 'want of the common necessaries of life' reflected a society in decay and one that was politically polarised.[1] This chapter aims to reveal conflicting attitudes to the inquests of the poor, and the social and political conditions that impacted coroners in executing their role in death investigation during the humanitarian crisis.

The utility of coroners during the Great Famine has not attracted much scholarly attention. Inquests were used as evidence of the conditions under which a person died in sudden, suspicious or unusual circumstances, and particularly during those difficult years, they only comprised a portion of deaths that occurred. Coroners kept records of their investigations and were required by law to send annual returns to the Lord Lieutenant's Office. The destruction of the Public Records Office in 1922 leaves a gap in these historical records of coroners for nearly all of the nineteenth century. The most readily available documentation of inquests taken include newspaper reports, official government reports and correspondence between local and administrative officials. Much rarer sources include the original casebooks of individual coroners. All these materials reveal regional variations that help define the effects of the Famine and provide the opportunity to examine the use of the inquest in those communities. The work of the coroner was intended, in part, to support the investigation of homicide by identifying suspects in cases of murder, and legislation was passed to reform and support the office.[2] When thousands began to die from starvation, inquests exposed the failures of administrative policy and the moral and ethical ambiguity of the local elite as reflected in their attitudes to the lives and deaths of the poor.

Attitudes to the poor: legislation and providence

Legislation imposed by the administration was resented by grand juries, comprised of the landed elite, who felt that the costs imposed upon them to care for the poor were too difficult to bear. The Irish Poor Law Act of 1838 addressed Irish poverty and rural inequality, as well as providing moral regulation, reformation and social stability.[3] Poor Law districts were established in each geographical region in the country and workhouses constructed to provide institutional reform to support vulnerable and marginal

1 *Freeman's Journal* (henceforth cited as *FJ*), 20 Feb. 1847; *FJ*, 20 Mar. 1847.

2 9&10 Vict. c.37 (27 Jul. 1846), Coroners (Ireland) Act; 9&10, Vict. c.62 (18 Aug. 1846), Act to Abolish Deodands and Fatal Accidents Act, 9&10 Vict. c.93 (26 Aug. 1846).

3 1&2 Vict. c.56 (31 Jul. 1838), Poor Relief (Ireland) Act; Peter Gray, *Famine, land and politics: British governmental Irish relief, 1845–50* (Dublin, 1999), p. viii.

groups in society. The implementation of the law also contributed to the social conditioning of the local elite imposing costs on them to support their poor.[4] The adoption or rejection by grand juries of legislation and costs reveals attitudes towards the poor themselves and the administration.

Although the function of the coroner was not outlined in the Poor Law Act, its implementation and execution during the Famine had a close relationship with the office of coroner. The Coroners Act of 1846 provided the coroner with reinforced powers including authorising payment for witnesses, care of the body, exhumation, interment, coffins, fees for medical examinations, etc.[5] Coroner's districts were established for each geographical region and county in Ireland.[6] It was a powerful piece of legislation, which also reinforced that all costs for inquests would be paid by local grand juries as would fines for jurors who refused to participate when summoned.[7] Like the Poor Law Act, the Coroners Act served as a form of social conditioning for the local elite who challenged payment for the services of coroners, as inquests were often conducted on the poorest and most disadvantaged groups.

Beliefs amongst Irish landlords were grounded in the need for free trade, laissez-faire policies, self-reliance and, ultimately, non-interference in their management of labour, goods and land.[8] The belief in providentialism combined with the resentment of the Poor Law, when applied to the deaths of thousands of paupers, indicates that attitudes towards costs incurred in the investigation of their death by coroners would not be a priority for local elites. The Irish poor were considered at least partly responsible for the mortality suffered during the Famine.[9]

Sir Robert Peel's administration (1841–46) had laboured under the weight of the Great Famine since the first reports of the failure of the potato crop in Ireland in the autumn of 1845. Peel's decisions to secretly purchase Indian corn to feed the poor and abolish the Corn Laws to remove the tax on imported food saved lives but not his role as the head of government. In July 1846, when the Whig–Liberal administration led by Lord John Russell (1846–52) took

4 Peter Gray, 'Conceiving and constructing the Irish workhouse, 1836–45' in *Irish Historical Studies*, xxxviii, 149 (2012), pp 23–4.
5 9&10 Vict. c.37 (27 Jul. 1846), Coroners (Ireland) Act.
6 Ibid.
7 Ibid.
8 W.J. Smyth, 'The longue dureé – imperial Britain and colonial Ireland' in John Crowley, W.J. Smyth & Mike Murphy (eds), *Atlas of the great Irish Famine* (New York, 2012), p. 55, pp 46–63.
9 Jonny Geber & Barra O'Donnabhain, '"Against shameless and systematic calumny": strategies of domination and resistance and their impact on the bodies of the poor in nineteenth-century Ireland' in *Historical Archaeology*, liv (2020), p. 160, pp 160–83; Peter Nally, *Human encumbrances, political violence and the Great Irish Famine* (Notre Dame, 2011), p. 127.

over, Russell dramatically changed the policies put in place by his predecessor. He accused the former Conservative administration of over-generosity to Irish landlords and peasants and took the advice of his Assistant Secretary to the Treasury, Charles Trevelyan (1840–59), discontinuing the Famine Relief Commission. Trevelyan's confidence in non-interference in the food trade, combined with his belief in divine providence and the government's heavy reliance on his guidance, impacted the programmes of Irish relief.[10]

In August 1846, Russell's government rushed through the Labour Rate Act.[11] The policy was intended to expand public works employment with strict adherence to offering the lowest wages in the locale for non-permanent improvement work, in order not to compete with private business. Only those who could prove destitution would receive the benefit of employment and local relief officers were restrictive. Irish landowners were not availing of government loans offered to supply the poor with employment, so that same month a new Public Works Act was passed. Russell now had the power to compel grand juries to hold presentment sessions and enforce their vote for public works where and when he believed them necessary. The new law demanded 'Irish property will pay for Irish poverty'.[12] As the winter of 1846–47 began, the death toll increased as a direct result of the new government policies and the reluctance of local landowners to enact them. The work of the coroner at the coalface captured the impact of their delayed behaviour and the ensuing crisis.

Winter 1846–47: The coroner and the inquest

As the challenging months of the winter of 1846–47 began, verdicts of death from inquests published in newspapers locally and nationally served as a regular reminder of the failure of Russell's relief policy. On 18 December 1846, nationalist leader and MP for Cork, Daniel O'Connell (1775–1847), spoke at Conciliation Hall, Burgh Quay, Dublin, stating that '47 deaths from starvation in Connaught were authenticated and certified by coroners' inquests, and yet people were not sufficiently aroused'.[13] His statement exposes the attitudes of local elite and their attitudes to the poor, as well as their refusal to acknowledge the official reports of starvation deaths as investigated

10 Peter Gray, 'British relief measures' in Crowley et al., *Atlas of the Great Irish Famine*, p. 85; J.S. Donnelly, Jr, *The Great Irish Potato Famine* (Gloucestershire, 2010), p. 70.

11 9&10 Vict. c.107 (15 Aug. 1846), Poor Employment Act (Ireland).

12 J.S. Donnelly, Jr, '"Irish property must pay for Irish poverty": British public opinion and the Great Irish Famine' in C. Morash & R. Hayes (eds) *Fearful realities: new perspectives on the Famine* (Dublin, 1996), pp 60–76.

13 Gearóid Ó Tuathaigh, 'Daniel O'Connell' in *DIB* (https://www.dib.ie/biography/oconnell-daniel-a6555) (accessed 29 Apr. 2024); *Anglo-Celt*, 18 Dec. 1846.

by Irish coroners. O'Connell further stated that he was 'ashamed of some of the landed gentry of Ireland and the mercantile classes who had done nothing as yet to support the poor in their fight for survival'.[14] Speeches, like that of O'Connell, reflected the widely understood 'officialdom' of the work of the coroner as evidence of death due to the lack of resources and action by local elites around the country.

Coverage and detail of Famine-related deaths captured by coroners in newspapers varied based on the politics of each constituency, and regional variances existed as to the severity of the crisis. On 5 December 1846, liberal newspaper *The Nation* published a letter sent by an anonymous contributor. The author identified only as W.G. reported that deaths by starvation were prevalent in County Mayo, but disease (although Famine related) was also determined by coroners' juries as the cause of death.

> Of course, it is only in rare cases that inquests are held. Inquests are for deaths that are accounted sudden. Starvation comes gradually, is long resisted, is often beaten away for a week, or for a month … and if you ask did such and such a person die of starvation, you answered 'Why, not exactly of starvation; I think I heard 'twas fever, or dysentery, or some such thing he died of', but he died in terrible want and had not a morsel of food in the house when he died …[15]

Although some inquests returned a verdict of death by disease, the root cause of the death was starvation. These reports support the findings of Ó Gráda, who highlighted that while deaths during the Famine were a result of starvation, many victims succumbed to infectious diseases owing to weakened immune systems and social disruption.[16] The deaths captured by inquests were not representative of the actual number of people dying. W.G. highlighted that while a great many deaths were taking place in the country, many would not be reported and would 'never find their way to newspapers at all'.[17] This indicates that starvation as a cause of death and the circumstances or cause for death was considered by some to be unworthy of coroners' inquests. He further stated,

> These [deaths by starvation] are not the only such inquests and verdicts, by a great many, that did not come to the knowledge of the editor, and

14 Ibid.
15 *Nation*, 5 Dec. 1846.
16 Cormac Ó Gráda, 'Varieties of Irish famine death' in James Kelly & Mary Ann Lyons (eds), *Death and dying in Ireland, Britain and Europe: historical perspectives* (Kildare, 2013), p. 203.
17 *Nation*, 5 Dec. 1846.

> that many take place in the country which never find their way to the newspapers at all. If such a number of deaths by starvation are authenticated by *coroner's inquests*, what must be the multitude that are actually occurring![18]

Recognised as *authentic* and *official* evidence, the results of the work of coroners required attention, acknowledgement and action by the government and local authorities. Responsibility for saving the poor from death by starvation was blamed on Russell's administration. The question was posed: 'the decrepit, vacillating Whig government imagines that men will look on this, and tolerate them, or it, or the system out of which both have grown?'[19]

In a series of reports in December 1846, County Mayo district of Ballina coroner, John Atkinson, exposed the number of inquests he was conducting and provided the detail of the circumstances under which people were dying in the liberal *Mayo Constitution*. On 16 December 1846, an inquest took place on the body of Catherine Walsh, who was employed on the public works until the inclement weather set in. Because of her old age she was unable to withstand the cold, was unfit to work and could not earn the money to buy food. The verdict of death was from 'the absolute want of the necessaries of life'.[20] With no outdoor relief provided, Walsh was representative of many who died. Several other inquests reported similar circumstances of persons unable to find employment, indoor relief in the workhouse or outdoor relief to support themselves.[21] Atkinson also wrote to the Lord Lieutenant Bessborough that same month outlining the names of victims of the 'monster hunger', noting that he had enclosed the depositions from the inquests with his letter. The coroner's correspondence appeared in the *Mayo Constitution,* highlighting that food prices were on the increase, and it is 'beyond the means of the poor to purchase'.[22] The reply from Bessborough's office noted that they would 'again … [take] the state of the provision of trade in the Ballina district under special consideration'.[23] Atkinson was representative of other coroners and local government officials in the country using newspapers to publish his inquests and correspondence to the administration's most senior official to alert him of the problems with policy resulting in the unnecessary deaths of society's poorest.

Reports of deaths by starvation continued to flood into senior administrative officials from local officials and clergy around the country. They

18 Ibid.
19 Ibid.
20 *Mayo Constitution* (henceforth cited as *MC*), 15 Dec. 1846.
21 Ibid.
22 *MC*, 15 Dec. 1846.
23 Ibid.

often referenced the work of coroners that reflected the conditions of the regions from which they were reporting. On 4 December 1846, Constabulary Inspector General Duncan McGregor received a letter from Sligo constabulary sub-inspector and ex-officio poor law guardian John Grant, who was concerned by an inquest held on a local man. The coroner's jury had delivered a disturbing verdict:

> County of Sligo
> Riverstown, 11 December 1846
> I have to report that I attended an inquest on the afternoon of the 3rd inst. at Glen, parish of Ballinakill [*sic*], Barony of Tirerrill in the above county on the body of Bryan Waters about 56 years of age and that the coroner's jury returned a verdict, 'the deceased Bryan Waters came to his death by absolute want of food to support life'.
> J. Grant, 1st sub inspector[24]

McGregor acted, instructing a letter to be sent to the Collooney Relief Committee, who were responsible for qualifying the destitute for relief and raising funding to support them. He requested additional information on Waters, indicating that questions were raised as to whether he was known to them, supported or refused. The communications between local and senior government officials indicate that Inspector General McGregor was concerned as to the lack of relief being offered locally. The barony of Tirerrill was representative of many other baronies in Ireland whose local landholding elite had not yet accepted their responsibility to hold baronial presentments and agree to fund employment for the poor.[25] Such delays on the part of local officials resulted in the deaths of people, like Waters, whose desperate circumstances were captured by coroners across the country. The *Sligo Journal* reported that Waters' inquest had been taken by Sligo coroner A. Burrows stating 'Further comment on these everyday tragedies, were we so disposed, is unnecessary. Each such death is a volume against the Premier's mercantile league.'[26]

While some counties reported on the inquests taken in their local districts revealing the direct correlation between policy and lack of intervention by local elites in Famine-related deaths, there was a lack of transparency in County Monaghan. County coroner for Monaghan William Charles Waddell conducted inquests capturing Famine-related deaths that resulted from disease, want, destitution, starvation and exposure with details of local conditions. As a sample, of the ninety-one inquests conducted by Waddell

24 Grant to McGregor, 4 Dec. 1846 (N.A.I., FRC, RLFC3/2/26/42).
25 *Warder and Dublin Weekly Mail*, 19 Dec. 1846.
26 *Sligo Journal* (henceforth cied as *SJ*), 4 Dec. 1846.

from May 1846 through July 1847, at least forty-eight inquests or 53 per cent identify exceptional changes in circumstances leading to starvation and Famine-related death.[27]

Another inquest conducted that month by Waddell was held on a vagrant: those who were viewed as choosing their lifestyle rather than begging as a necessity. This often provoked a negative response from the public.[28] Charity towards beggars or vagrants was conditional during times of Famine or epidemic disease, and they might be unwelcome everywhere.[29] Waddell's inquest held on 'the body of a strange man' provided the sad detail that the deceased had been found near death, lying in a local graveyard. He was taken in by Rev. and Mrs Hurst who offered him some 'light warm food' and 'put a little tea through his teeth with a spoon' but he died shortly thereafter.[30] The *Northern Standard* published some details of the inquest but placed emphasis on the charity of the Rev. J. and Mrs Hurst of Errigal Trough.[31] The political positioning supporting the Protestant minister and his wife opposed to the dire and fatal circumstances of the dead man reflects a society, and specifically the constituency of the *Northern Standard* readership, that was politically polarised and biased towards the poor.

The inquest as 'the voice of the people'

Some national and regional Irish newspapers published verdicts of inquests that reflected negative public opinion of government policy and show how the inquest was used as a platform for 'the voice of the people'.[32] In January 1847, the nationalist newspaper, the *Limerick and Clare Examiner*, reported a coroner's inquest taken at the Galway workhouse,

> We find that the deceased Mary Commons, died from the effects of starvation and destitution, caused by a want of the common necessities of life; and as Lord John Russell, the head of her Majesty's government, has combined with Sir Randolph Routh, to starve the Irish people, by

27 Clones Library, Co. Monaghan. The casebook of William Charles Waddell (1846–55) [CB1]; Michelle McGoff-McCann, *The Irish Coroner: death, murder and politics in County Monaghan (1846–78)* (Dublin, 2023).

28 L.M. Geary, '"The whole country was in motion": mendicancy and vagrancy in pre-Famine Ireland' in Jacqueline Hill & Colm Lennon (eds), *Luxury and austerity* (Dublin, 1999), p. 126.

29 Ibid.

30 CB1, inquest no.16.35, the body of a strange man, 27 Feb. 1847.

31 *Northern Standard* (henceforth cited as *NS*), 13 Mar. 1847.

32 W.E. Vaughan, *Murder trials in Ireland, 1836–1914* (Dublin, 2009), p. 52.

> not, as was their duty, taking measures to prevent the present truly awful condition of the country, WE FIND THAT THE SAID LORD JOHN RUSSELL AND THE SAID SIR RANDOLPH ROUTH, ARE GUILTY OF THE WILFUL MURDER OF SAID MARY COMMONS.[33]

The Galway city inquest jury, comprised of urban middle-class Catholic men, was not fearful of delivering a nationalist anti-government position that policy was killing the people. However, the coroner refused to receive the finding and the jury was forced to return the verdict in a modified form that blamed policy – not Lord Russell or Routh by name,

> We find that the deceased, Mary Commons, died of the effects of destitution and starvation. And we further find that the policy adopted by the present Government, in reference to the supply of food, has been such as to raise to an extraordinary high rate the price of provisions, thus placing food beyond the reach of persons in the rank of life of the deceased, and causing innumerable deaths throughout the country.[34]

In February 1847, the nationalist *Nenagh Guardian* reported forty deaths from starvation of which inquests were held in Bantry, County Cork. The foreman of the inquests' jury announced that he along with his fellow jurors thought 'that they ought to bring a general verdict, inculpating Lord J. Russell as the head of government'.[35] He stated that the minister had the power of keeping people alive but would not, and his policy had fatal consequences. Therefore, the jury 'could bring in no other verdict, but one of wilful murder by Lord John Russell'.[36] Similarly, on 16 February 1847, Dublin City Coroner, Dr Kirwin, led a jury through an inquest on the bodies of husband and wife John and Ellen Mulgerin, who died of starvation in their home. Kirwin stated that he hoped the case would 'arouse the authorities to a sense of their duty and hoped the government would dispense with their cold, political economy and come forward to save the people'.[37] The Dublin inquest jury verdict begged the government, on behalf of their fellow citizens, that they adopt immediate measures and modify their policies to stop the effects of the Famine.[38] Additionally, on 17 February 1847, the *Freeman's Journal* published an inquest held by Waterford coroner Thomas Dennehy on a man referred

33 *Limerick and Clare Examiner*, 20 Jan. 1847.
34 Ibid.
35 *Nenagh Guardian*, 13 Feb. 1847.
36 Ibid.
37 *FJ*, 16 Feb. 1847.
38 Ibid.

to only as Sullivan. The sick and starving man was brought to the gate of the Lismore poorhouse 'in a dying state' and died shortly after arrival from the effects of starvation and cold.[39] The jury found that although Sullivan was admitted immediately and cared for appropriately, saving him was futile. A damning conclusion as to the cause of the poor man's death concluded: 'we further find that his death was caused through the neglect of the government in not sending food into the country in due time.'[40] While the results of the coroners' work exposed life-threatening government policy and local practice in the delivery of relief, how the inquests were valued and measured depended upon the political and social environment in which they were carried out.

Inquests served as a social good contributing to the well-being of society and justice, but contrary opinions existed as to their value if they did not exist solely to identify suspects in cases of murder – a view shared by many local county grand juries.[41] Costs incurred when conducting inquests were often contested by grand juries who complained that accidental deaths and verdicts by 'visitation of God' were unnecessary.[42] Conflicting views emerged over time as to the usefulness of inquests taken on the poor as a result of starvation, as local elite resented the costs of carrying them out. On 19 March 1847, *The Sligo Champion* reported that Sir R.G. Booth stated before the grand jury that he knew of five persons who died of hunger in his neighbourhood, but no inquests had been held.[43] The police had adopted a new rule of not sending for coroners for victims of Famine when there was no doubt that the cause was starvation, and that 'coroners inquests cannot now be looked upon as affording a correct account of the deaths from starvation'.[44]

By mid-April 1847, Cork city coroners had declared their determination not to hold inquests on the bodies of persons dying in the streets from want and fever, to 'avoid the great expense which the innumerable inquests from the causes would bring upon the city'.[45] *The Evening Chronicle* also published

39 *FJ*, 17 Feb. 1847.

40 Ibid.

41 Vaughan, *Murder trials in Ireland*, p. 52; Richard McMahon, *Homicide in pre-Famine and Famine Ireland* (Liverpool, 2013), p. 186.

42 *Irish Examiner*, 30 May 1842.

43 *Sligo Champion*, 19 Mar. 1847.

44 Ibid.

45 The news story appeared in newspapers throughout the United Kingdom and Ireland including: *Southern Reporter and Cork Commercial Courier*, 15 Apr. 1847; *Athlone Sentinel*, 16 Apr. 1847; *Liverpool Reporter*, 20 Apr. 1847; *Shipping and Mercantile Gazette*, 21 Apr. 1847; *Gloucestershire Chronicle*, 24 Apr. 1847; *The Examiner*, 24. Apr. 1847; *Tipperary Free Press*, 24. Apr. 1847; *West Kent Guardian*, 24 Apr. 1847; *Liverpool Standard and General Commercial Advertiser*, 27 Apr. 1847; *Dumfries and Galloway Standard*, 28 Apr. 1847; *Witness (Edinburgh)*, 28 Apr. 1847; *Bath Chronicle and Weekly Gazette*, 29 Apr. 1847; *Wiltshire Independent*, 29 Apr. 1847.

an article that same month reporting that the Sligo grand jury officially instructed the coroners not to hold inquests on those who died of starvation.[46] The liberal *Fermanagh Reporter* also declared 'that death by starvation, more than any other cause, excites scarcely any emotion at the present time ...'

In contrast to reports of attitudes regarding paying for the costs of inquests, the nationalist newspaper, the *Cork Examiner*, published an article with a reminder of the coroners' inquests that brought in a verdict of 'wilful murder' against Lord John Russell. It also reported that Father Maginn and the Catholic clergy of Londonderry would record their own findings. The registries of their diocese recording death would bear the inscription:

> The records of the murders of the Irish Peasantry, perpetrated in A.D. 1846–7, in the 9th and 10th Victoria, under the name of economy, during the administration of a professedly Liberal Whig Government of which Lord John Russell was the Premier.[47]

Circumstantial evidence suggests that the Catholic clergy around the country believed in the institution of the coroner and felt the work they did in recording the deaths of the poor was important. The use of the coroner by the clergy indicates a sense of justice for the dead. On Boffin Island, Fr Thomas McManus, stated that when the Famine made its biggest impact on the population in his community, 'there [was] no coroner or inquest [on] these islands to record these starvation deaths'.[48] He further highlighted, 'Let their legislators, however [they] recollect that there is an infallible Judge before whom and an awful tribunal at which these crying crimes should be tried.'[49] This demonstrates that the clergy valued the coroner and the inquest as 'official evidence' or proof of the inadequate legislation and local mismanagement of the poor that contributed to their deaths.

By June 1847, it was reported in the *Northern Standard* that the corpse of an old itinerant beggar man, a stranger, not known in the Clones neighbourhood, was found lying dead nearby in the townland of Clonfad, County Fermanagh, in a pigsty after eight days unnoticed. The local paper reported that the cause of death was so obviously starvation, 'the authorities did not deem it necessary to have an inquest on the body'.[50] This may indicate that the County Fermanagh coroner refused to take an inquest, not seeing the value or importance of such an investigation. It reflects a shift in the attitudes of

46 *The Evening Chronicle*, 7 Apr. 1847.
47 *Cork Examiner*, 26 Apr. 1847.
48 *Tuam Herald*, 12 Feb. 1848.
49 Ibid.
50 *NS*, 12 Jun. 1847.

the middle-class public in that district of County Monaghan, and potentially also of the County Fermanagh coroner, whereby they purportedly became desensitised to excess deaths or Famine-linked deaths of society's poorest. This attitude was reflected in the lack of local press coverage of the formal investigation into Famine-related deaths in County Monaghan being recorded by Waddell. Inquest findings and local newspaper coverage were intertwined and reflect the politics in specific geographic regions.

The call for the abolition of the coroners' office

While the financial pressures on the local elite and landowning classes to pay for the Famine continued to increase through 1847–48, and at a time when the death rates remained high, a suggestion was made to abolish the coroners' office. On 10 August 1848, County Cork Liberal MP, Thomas Chisholm Anstey, submitted two petitions to the House of Commons on behalf of the high sheriff and grand jury of Cork and Sligo, respectively.[51] The first petition prayed for an amendment to the Irish poor law stating that 'they viewed with great alarm the increase of able bodied paupers'.[52] The appeal for poor law reform indicated their claimed inability to fund the relief of the poor. The second petition prayed for the abolition of the office of coroner in Ireland.[53] They claimed that by eliminating the office of coroner, it would save the cess-payers of Ireland £25,000 per annum.[54] This suggests that the overwhelmingly conservative landholders on the grand juries of Cork and Sligo were looking to reduce costs and the increase in inquests held on paupers were viewed as unnecessary.

Several conservative newspapers throughout the country carried the story, including the *Dublin Evening Mail*, which declared that at this 'present stage of society, [the coroner] is a supernumerary and useless functionary'.[55] The article proposed that the coroner's duties could be left to the discretion of the country gentlemen, local justices, resident magistrates or constabulary officers and encouraged every county in Ireland to adopt the petition.[56] Opposing these views, the liberal editor of the paper Michael Carey convincingly refuted them. He identified that eighty-one coroners received average payments of £100 per year, and that their expenses (costs for running an inquest) would

51 Sidney Lee, revised by K.D. Reynolds, *Anstey, Thomas Chisholm (1816–1873)*, ODNB.

52 *Hansard 3*, ci, 10 Aug. 1848, cc.54–5; *FJ*, 12 Aug. 1848.

53 Ibid.

54 Ibid.

55 *Dublin Evening Mail*, 21 Aug. 1848; *Kerry Evening Post*, 23 Aug. 1848; *MC*, 29 Aug. 1848; *SJ*, 1 Sept. 1848.

56 Ibid.

still have to be met by the local magistrate or person assigned such duties. The resulting national figure of £8,100 for dedicated local resources was negligible. What emerged was Carey's emphasis on the duties and importance of keeping the function of the coroner in Ireland. He stated that it was an injustice to the freeholders of the country to recommend the abolition of 'the only paid officer to which they still have right of presentation'.[57] In a separate article, the newspaper published a short piece on the matter, stating that they agreed fully with the views put forward in the *Leinster Express*, and were convinced that 'the more the question is scrutinised, the stronger the reasons will appear for maintaining this ancient and useful office'.[58]

By contrast, on 16 September 1848, the *Northern Standard* published the meeting of the Monaghan grand jury finance committee, which announced its agreement with the other grand juries that called for the abolition of the office of coroner.[59] They evaluated the mileage fees submitted by the coroners and, with no explanation, imposed a reduction in the reimbursement of mileage due to coroner Waddell as well as his colleague, the coroner of the south district of County Monaghan Hugh Swanzy.[60] As both men were from the local elite and fitted the ideal qualifications for gentlemen coroners, refusing payment of their full bill again demonstrates how the values of the Monaghan conservatives undermined their authority as coroners. This suggests that County Monaghan's conservative leadership, the local elite and local government agents, of which Waddell was himself a member, did not appreciate the social value of the coroners' work. It is reflective of the conflicting ideologies of local conservatives relating to the poor at that time.

Lack of transparency: Inquest numbers queried

On 18 January 1850, barrister and MP Isaac Butt spoke to a large group gathered in Dublin to support Irish industry and reform the poor law in Ireland. He stated

> From 23 April 1848 to the 15 July 1849 [...] over 15 months inquests had been held on persons who died and verdicts of death from starvation had been returned in 589 cases. [These] 589 individuals have died under circumstances so horrible, that coroners' juries declared on their oaths they were starved to death. How many deaths took place

57 *Leinster Express*, 2 Sept. 1848.
58 Ibid.
59 *NS*, 16 Sept. 1848.
60 Ibid.

> from the same cause of which we have no record? How many have perished by the slow and wasting agony of famine?[61]

Butt's speech asserts that death was far more prevalent than was officially recorded, thereby raising the questions as to the importance of the inquest during the years of the Great Famine.

On 28 May 1851, a debate took place in the House of Commons on the proposed Coroner's Bill, which sought to replace payment of coroners with a salary rather than by fees. Dublin Irish Repeal Association MP John Reynolds addressed the House as to the lack of transparency around deaths that happened during the Famine. Reynolds stated:

> In Ireland, I fear it was no exaggeration to say that the number of deaths from want of food within the walls of the workhouses exceeded 1,000 per week. No inquests were held, because those who had the government of the workhouse did not wish, as they sometimes stated, to put the union to the expense, and they did not wish to expose the malpractices that occurred, lest they should be censured by the public. At all events, it ought to be imperative on the governors of all gaols, workhouses, and establishments where human life was destroyed for want of the common necessaries of life, to give notice to the coroner to attend, and not to magistrates with the power of dealing with the salary of the coroner at all, as it would be opening an avenue to favouritism, corruption, and malpractices, which would produce more evils than were produced by the present law, even with all its defects.[62]

This refusal or reluctance to reveal the true conditions in workhouses existed alongside negative attitudes to the poor as evidenced by restricted spending on their care and on the investigation of their death. The bill was defeated.

In 1855, an official government return was published that reported on the coroners in each of their respective districts in Ireland and their associated costs during the years 1842–45 and 1848–52.[63] Notably, the data for 1846

61 *FJ*, 18 Jan. 1850.

62 HC, 28 May 1851, vol. 117, cc.100–13.

63 'Coroners' Inquests (Ireland). Abstract of return to an order of the Honorable The House of Commons, dated 17 April 1855 for, A Return "of the number of inquests held by the several Coroners in Ireland, for each of the years 1843, 1844 and 1845, separately; and of the sums presented each year as payment to those Coroners, and also to medical witnesses; similar turn for each of the years 1848, 1849, 1850, 1851, 1852, and 1853, but distinguishing the sums presented for holding inquests, for mileage, and for medical witnesses, and other expenses of holding inquests; And, Return of the number of Coroners appointed to districts in the several Counties and Counties of Cities in Ireland,

and 1847 are absent. The return includes the payments to coroners, costs for medical witnesses, mileage and other expenses (i.e. storage of the corpse, coffins, burial, etc.) and the number of inquests held. Additional commentary includes vacant positions for coroner, how some coroners exercised their right to hold inquests on prisoners at the county or city jail and irregularities including where coroners' records were not available. This indicates that the implementation of the law, or lack thereof, by grand juries varied by county and city. Overall, the public reporting and under-reporting of inquests reflects a society that was politically polarised and conflicted as to the importance of the investigation of the deaths of the poor and other marginalised groups.

Conclusion

Coroners served a crucial and important function during the Great Famine. The coroner held a conspicuous position in local government, and one that was more widely exposed to public opinion when investigating deaths during a time of humanitarian crisis. The inquests taken during the Famine that were published in local and national newspapers revealed how the legislation imposed by both Peel and Russell's administrations combined with delays to implementing relief measures, and local mismanagement, contributed directly to the death of many of society's poorest members. Although the Irish coroners shared a common sphere of activity, the results of their investigations varied depending on the geographic location, the political composition of the local elite and inquest participants. Verdicts of 'death due to starvation' published in local and national newspapers were selective as to which inquests and stories of Famine death they chose to cover. While some verdicts named Lord John Russell and the administration, others exposed pervasive ideologies relating to the poor that blamed the victims for their poverty and the circumstances surrounding their death. The coroners also differed in their performance when executing their duties based on the inclinations and abilities of each man serving in the role. Some coroners announced their temporary refusal to conduct inquests in cases of 'obvious' starvation so as not to impose unnecessary costs on the grand jury and ratepayers. Opinions as to the importance of inquests held by the coroner during the Famine varied; while some sought the attendance of the coroner and saw value in capturing evidence of the humanitarian crisis, others stopped requesting the coroners' investigations of death and saw them only as a futile exercise.

pursuant to the provisions of the Act 9&10 Vict. c.37, and at what presenting term such appointments were made respectively"', HOC, 21 Jun. 1855.

7

Recreation and Public Space in Nineteenth-Century Dublin

Julien Clénet

Introduction

The extent to which public space was availed of for recreation in nineteenth-century Dublin was a source of conflict between the middle class who sought to regulate its use and the population who traditionally – and out of necessity – considered it as a legitimate place to play. The moral ascendancy of the middle class grew throughout the nineteenth century and was reinforced by their control of local government, newspapers and school curricula, which in turn contributed to fashioning public opinion. Traditional and popular recreations then became targeted because of their unruly nature and the incapacity of their participants to respect private property or conform to Sabbatarianism. In their stead, rational recreation – the notion that pastimes should have an improving purpose – was promoted and contributed to redefining acceptable modes of behaviour in the public space. Paternalism and respect for the social hierarchy equally transpired in the promotion of mechanics' institutes, workplace sport and the provision of public parks and playgrounds in the city and its suburbs in the second part of the nineteenth century. In these instances, the quasi-anarchical nature of commons or wastelands was replaced by a set of rules meant to advocate middle-class lifestyles and aspirations.

The present chapter argues that middle-class efforts to control recreation in the public space had already begun in Dublin by the late eighteenth century, that the stamping out of folk pastimes from the city's streets and fields went unabated in the nineteenth century, and that efforts at transforming working-class leisure habits met with only moderate success. It builds on the work of Emma Griffin and James Kelly, who have firmly anchored the roots of such conflict in eighteenth-century socio-economic evolutions and have shown that the advent of the middle class as an economic, political and moral force contributed to delegitimising hitherto popular pastimes.[1] In turn, the creation of public parks and playgrounds from the 1870s in Dublin stemmed from this decline in the popular world of play. It was an integral part of a larger concern for sanitary reform both at individual and systemic levels and yet furthered the regulation of public space according to middle-class values and standards of behaviour. By the mid-nineteenth century, large and unorganised recreational gatherings had disappeared from Dublin. This was both the result of legal and moral opposition and of the advent of a bureaucratic and consumerist society that had begun to transform folk pastimes into codified sports taking place in dedicated grounds. However, such a reforming agenda failed to curb deeply anchored leisure habits, and the politicisation of Irish society from the 1870s brought a renewed interest in the control and use of public space.

The delegitimisation of traditional pastimes

In the late eighteenth and early nineteenth centuries, the streets, squares, fields and commons within Dublin and its immediate vicinity were considered as legitimate spaces for recreation and socialisation by the population. Bullbaits, such as the ones that took place in Grangegorman in 1777, or in Clonskeagh in 1795, attracted hundreds of spectators.[2] Handball, a pastime that neatly fitted the urban fabric, was played in the vicinity of St Patrick's Cathedral and against the walls of the Custom House.[3] Fields in yet-undeveloped areas on Drumcondra Road, Merrion Square, Holles Street, in the Phoenix Park or in the nearby common of Crumlin were used by footballers and hurlers.[4] In wrestling, Dubliners mixed with rural dwellers from the adjacent countryside; informal inter-county competition regularly took place on Sundays near Foster's aqueduct in Broadstone;[5] and in the Phoenix Park, crowds of thousands cheered on their local champions.[6] If the enclosed St Stephen's Green was only accessible to a few, its railings made for an ideal running track.[7] Children and

1 James Kelly, *Sport in Ireland* (Dublin, 2014), *passim*; Emma Griffin, *England's revelry: a history of popular sports and pastimes, 1660–1830* (Oxford, 2005).
2 *Saunders's News-Letter* (henceforth cited as *SNL*), 22 Oct. 1777, 10 Aug. 1795.
3 *SNL*, 24 Sept. 1822; *Dublin Correspondent*, 7 Aug. 1823.
4 *Hibernian Journal*, 23 May 1774; *SNL*, 18 Apr. 1874, 13 Sep. 1776, 4 Aug. 1779, 27 Sep. 1780; *Dublin Evening Post*, 20 Jul. 1779, 16 Dec. 1780.
5 *SNL*, 19 Jun. 1811.
6 *Freeman's Journal* (henceforth cited as *FJ*), 11 Apr. 1827; *Dublin Warder and Weekly Mail*, 14 Jun. 1834.
7 *SNL*, 30 Jun. 1832; *Dublin Observer* (henceforth cited as *DO*), 1 Sep. 1832; *Weekly Freeman's Journal*, 24 Sep. 1842.

adults swam in the Tolka River and in the Royal and Grand Canals.[8] Pitch and toss, that ubiquitous gambling game, was part of street lore.[9]

This public world of play was rapidly declining, however, as a new sporting world, centred on clubs and privately owned grounds and pavilions, slowly emerged. This was partly the result of Dublin's geographical expansion and growth from 140,000 inhabitants in 1760 to over 230,000 by 1831.[10] Open fields southeast of St Stephen's Green were built on and Oxmantown Green, a place long associated with revelries, became steadily encroached on until the Blue Coat Hospital (later renamed King's Hospital) was constructed on its last remains in the 1780s.[11] Successive private Acts of Parliament in 1818 and 1821 precipitated the enclosure of over 2,791 acres of common and waste land in the parishes of Clondalkin, Crumlin, Kilmainham, Kilsallaghan, Lusk, Newcastle, Rathcoole and Tallaght.[12] Previously, these had all been places to play.

More significant to the decline of folk pastimes was the development of modern capitalism and centralised states in eighteenth-century Britain and Ireland, which resulted in a more complex social stratification and the emergence of the middle class.[13] This upwardly mobile group was by no means monolithic, nor did all its members share the same living conditions and aspirations, but it had a few distinctive marks: it was prosperous and sought to widen the social gap with the lower orders while narrowing it with the aristocracy, whom they looked at with both envy and opprobrium.[14] Its wealth essentially stemmed from industrial and commercial expansion and was legitimised by new economic thoughts regarding the primacy of private property, the concentration of capital and the commercialisation of society. At the same time, new modes of behaviour in the public space began to emerge. The younger and more urban outlook of the rapidly increasing population worried the rising middle class and parts of the elite, who feared a breakdown of old-established social ties. The growing commercial activity and higher wages made possible by the First Industrial Revolution were a further source of concern, as licentiousness and 'luxury' spending were facilitated. The loss

8 *FJ*, 2 Jun. 1840, 8 Aug. 1840, 1 Aug. 1843.
9 *FJ*, 23 May 1837, 9 Aug. 1838, 17 Aug. 1838, 16 Jul. 1842.
10 Mary E. Daly, *Dublin, the deposed capital: a social and economic history 1860–1914* (Cork, 1985), p. 3.
11 Colm Lennon & John Montague, *John Rocque's Dublin: a guide to the Georgian city* (Dublin, 2010), pp 4–5.
12 58 Geo. III c. 28 [U.K.]; 1&2 Geo. IV c. 21 [U.K.].
13 Hugh Cunningham, *Time, work and leisure: life changes in England since 1700* (Manchester, 2014), p. 7.
14 Dennis Brailsford, *British sport: a social history* (Cambridge, 1992), pp 88–90; F.M.L. Thompson, *The rise of respectable society: a social history of Victorian Britain 1830–1900* (London, 1988), pp 256–7; John Golby & A.W. Purdue, *The civilisation of the crowd: popular culture in England 1750–1900* (London, 1984), p. 84.

of American colonies in 1783 merely added to the general feeling of crisis in Britain and calls for moral regeneration became more vocal from the 1780s.[15]

One answer was the rise of a cult of sensibility, which promoted humanitarian feelings and compassion.[16] Old forms of entertainment that involved blood sports, but also boisterous gatherings, heavy betting or drinking and more generally working-class participation, became suspect and resented by the middle classes.[17] Sensibility and humanitarianism were hence deeply embedded in the class structure of early nineteenth-century Britain and Ireland, and used to affirm one's position both on the social ladder and at the vanguard of cultural evolution. Emma Griffin has thus convincingly explained that cruelty *per se* was not the justification for the set of legislative measures passed in the first part of the nineteenth century to curtail blood sports. Instead, it was rooted in the reforming and progressive image that middle-class Victorians legislators had of themselves.[18] The Cruelty to Animals Act 1835 (extended to Ireland in 1837), considered to be the centrepiece of the legislation against bull baiting and dog- and cockfighting, was indeed a cultural stamp, since bull baiting was almost extinct and cockfighting in severe decline on both sides of the Irish Sea in the decades before the bill came into law.

From this middle-class ideology emanated the denigration of folk recreations and opposition to the boisterousness of the gentry and peasantry, although many within the bourgeoisie refused to live a frugal and religious life and sought a conspicuous lifestyle. Conversely, the reforming agenda progressively made inroads within the upper and lower classes, not least in the temperance movement at the turn of the 1840s in Munster.[19] As old communal ties weakened, the concept of private property became firmly established.[20] Newly built gardens in Mountjoy and Merrion squares were reserved for the sole use of residents, and landowners in Eccles Street or Drumcondra became more reluctant to leave their fields at the disposition of the population.[21] The lack of accountability for damage done to private property only added to the class aspect of such restrictions. Public authorities

15 M.J.D. Roberts, *Making English morals: voluntary association and moral reform in England, 1787–1886* (Cambridge, 2004), pp 24–33.

16 Paul Langford, *A polite and commercial people: England 1727–1783* (Oxford, 1992), chap. 10 and esp. pp 498–505.

17 Kelly, *Sport in Ireland*, pp 157–74, 198–203, and 218–33.

18 Ibid., pp 232–3; Emma Griffin, *Blood sport, hunting in Britain since 1066* (London, 2007), pp 145–51; Griffin, *England's revelry*, pp 224–34.

19 P.A. Townsend, *Father Mathew, temperance and Irish identity* (Dublin, 2002), pp 11, 55–9.

20 Hugh Cunningham, *Leisure in the Industrial Revolution: c.1780–c.1880* (Oxford, 1980), pp 80–2.

21 *SNL*, 18 Apr. 1774; *Hibernian Journal*, 23 May 1774, 10 Apr. 1780.

progressively adopted a utilitarian and business-friendly conception of the streets and public spaces, and withdrew their consent to the use of urban public space for recreational purposes. For Emma Griffin, this 'was symptomatic of a progressive narrowing of the cultural space provided by streets and squares in the eighteenth-century town, a breakdown of consensus concerning the right of the poor to appropriate the streets for activities of their choice at the time of their choosing'.[22] The shift in attitude observed in Britain was equally clear in Ireland, as hurlers and footballers were summoned to court for trespassing or playing on Sundays in County Tipperary.[23] In Dublin, judges also asserted the new civic order: children 'might hurl as much as they pleased in the fields, but ... in the streets they should not'.[24] Parents were especially urged to prevent them 'from hurling in the streets, as the practice is very dangerous both to the eyes of the passengers and the windows of the inhabitants'.[25]

Regulating the use of public space went hand in hand with a restructuring of the police. The ineffective parish-based watchmen were replaced by a professional force in 1786, but it was only from 1836 onwards and the creation of the Dublin Metropolitan Police that policing the city became more effective.[26] The ancillary fear of the mob had reached new heights in Dublin in the 1780s and 1790s, fuelled by the French Revolution, continental warfare and insurrections in 1798 and 1803. This had already resulted in the prohibition of horse racing meetings of more than twelve people within nine miles of the city in 1791.[27] The suspicion that sporting crowds were a decoy for riots and subversion remained deeply ingrained among the city's authorities and often resurfaced when political agitation loomed. Concerns were thus raised at the sudden blooming of rifle shooting clubs throughout the country in the months preceding the 1848 Young Ireland rebellion, despite it being more an expression of virile sociability among young men than a real commitment to insurrection.[28] More pervasive perhaps were recurrent episodes of recreational

22 Griffin, *England's revelry*, p. 82.
23 Pat Bracken, *The growth and development of sport in County Tipperary, 1840–1880* (Cork, 2018), pp 200–5.
24 *FJ*, 9 Nov. 1841.
25 Ibid., 28 Oct. 1843.
26 Anastasia Dukova, *A history of the Dublin Metropolitan Police and its colonial legacy* (London, 2016), pp 57–61. Brian Griffin, *The Bulkies: police and crime in Belfast, 1800–1865* (Dublin, 1998).
27 Kelly, *Sport in Ireland*, pp 97–101.
28 *Dublin Weekly Nation*, 8 Apr. 1848, 29 Apr. 1848; *Evening Packet*, 6 Jul. 1848; Gary Owens, 'Popular mobilisation and the rising of 1848: the clubs of the Irish Confederation' in L.M. Geary (ed.), *Rebellion and remembrance in modern Ireland* (Dublin, 2001), pp 60–2.

violence, which witnessed their heyday in the eighteenth century and then lingered on for decades at wrestling matches.[29]

Thus, in the first part of the nineteenth century a picture emerges of slowly shifting mores and opinions on what was tolerable or not in society. Moral and social reform, urged by a profusion of societies and lobbies, steadily became a matter of public concern and forced authorities to legislate in Britain and Ireland alike.[30] The class aspect was difficult to ignore as traditional recreations bore the brunt of the restrictions.[31] Their association with Sunday, drinking, sexual promiscuity or gambling especially clashed with the new gospel of respectability, which ironically still tolerated some of the aristocracy's extravagances. The 1853 Betting House Act, for example, prohibited businesses from taking bets from all-comers but allowed private bets to take place within clubs.[32] Likewise bull baiting, cockfighting and pugilism ran against the humanitarian underpinnings of such movements and sustained a prolonged campaign for their abolition, which culminated in 1835. The Society for the Prevention of Cruelty to Animals, created in 1824 (with a Dublin branch since 1840), was instrumental in canvassing for stricter legislation but refused to campaign against the excesses of shooting or hunting, partly out of class deference and partly because prominent hunters were subscribers to the society.[33] Leonard Morrough, the Master of the Ward Hunt, and Lady Ardilaun whose husband, Sir Arthur Guinness, owned extensive shooting ranges at Ashford Castle in County Galway, were indeed firm supporters of the society in subsequent decades.[34] The high moral stance held by many within the middle class was crucial in legitimising their social rise:

> By casting the perpetrators of cruelty as ignorant and unenlightened, Victorian reformers inevitably defined themselves as in the vanguard of progress and civilisation; this was a way for the middle classes to reaffirm their status as humane and enlightened individuals. The ignorant masses needed to be saved from their wickedness, but

29 *Warder and Dublin Weekly Mail*, 14 Jun. 1834; *FJ*, 16 Jul. 1834; *DO*, 9 May 1835; Gunning, 'Hardy Fingallians, Kildare trippers and "the Divil Ye'll Rise" scufflers, wrestling in modern Ireland' in *Sport in Society*, xix, no. 1 (2016), p. 122.

30 Bailey, *Leisure and class in Victorian England: rational recreation and the contest for control, 1830–1885* (London, 1978), pp 30–4; Golby & Purdue, *The civilisation of the crowd*, p. 85; the 1842 Dublin Police Act reiterated the legislation on animal-baiting, gambling and inappropriate use of thoroughfares and entrusted the Dublin Metropolitan Police to enforce it, see 5 & 6 Vict. C. 24 [U.K.] (31 May 1842).

31 Paul Rouse, *Sport and Ireland: a history* (Oxford, 2015), p. 90.

32 Carl Chinn, *Better betting with a decent feller: a social history of bookmaking* (2nd ed., London, 2004), pp 65–7.

33 Griffin, *Blood sport*, p. 150.

34 *FJ*, 4 May 1875; *Daily Express* (henceforth cited as *DE*), 15 Nov. 1884.

> fortunately there was a well-meaning middle class, willing and able to do the saving.[35]

The reforming agenda was also crucial in establishing a hierarchy of cultures whereby folk traditions were deemed inferior by virtue of their lack of sophistication as against the 'scientificity' of new pastimes.[36]

Municipal endorsement reflected this hierarchisation. In 1828 the regatta committee had its headquarters in the Mansion House and the Kingstown races received £25 in stakes from the local authorities' treasurer.[37] The Phoenix Cricket Club also benefited from public largesse as the Commissioner of Woods and Forests allowed them to enclose a piece of ground in the Phoenix Park for their own private use. In 1846, a remodelling of the park led the Board of Works to pay the £73 necessary to relocate them to their present-day ground.[38] In early nineteenth-century Dublin, official encouragement was given to horse owners, yachtsmen and cricketers, while parties of wrestlers, hurlers or footballers could be broken up. Devoid of civic or aristocratic patronage, the traditional world of leisure, whose very legitimacy was questioned by the middle class, was disappearing fast by 1850. Instead, it was being replaced by the commercial world of entertainment, in the likes of music halls, gin palaces, exhibitions halls and sport grounds and stadiums.[39] Meanwhile, recreation taking place in the public space was being increasingly redirected towards public parks and playgrounds.

Middle-class recreation, sanitary reform and the park movement

In the new moral order advocated by social reformers, leisure had to be justified and purposeful rather than enjoyed *per se*. Concurrently with the legal and moral onslaught on popular recreations, a wealth of initiatives were promoted independently by the elite and middle class and became known as rational recreation.[40] It drew on humanitarian feelings to provide the population with recreational outlets, yet was essentially driven by growing concerns over public

35 Griffin, *Blood sport*, p. 150.

36 D.A. Fleming, 'Diversions of the people: sociability among the orders of early eighteenth-century Ireland' in *Eighteenth-Century Ireland/Iris an Dá Chultúr*, xvii (2002), p. 102. See also Griffin, *England's revelry*, p. 3.

37 *FJ*, 5 Jul. 1828, 21 Mar. 1834.

38 John Lawrence, *Handbook of cricket in Ireland, 1865–6* (Dublin, 1866), p. 5; W.P. Hone, *Cricket in Ireland* (Tralee, 1956), pp 8–9.

39 Bailey, *Leisure and class*, pp 154–7; Rouse, *Sport and Ireland*, pp 98–112.

40 Cunningham, *Leisure in the Industrial Revolution*, p. 76.

health and order and the desire to promote polite behaviours. For temperance campaigner William B. Allen:

> Public play ground[s] should be provided, in which the people could amuse themselves at gymnastics and otherwise. Mechanics' Institutes should be provided, with well stored libraries; a constant supply of lectures on the science should be procured; schools should be established; and above all, large and extensive reading rooms opened in connection with such Institutes, well supplied with newspapers and periodicals, and every work calculated to instruct and amuse. Public gardens, wherever they are established, should be thrown open to the sober and well conducted, and wherever a charge becomes necessary, it should be so low that the poorest would not be precluded from participating in the benefits to be derived from such Institutions.[41]

Libraries, zoological or botanic gardens as well as workingmen's institutes thus became symbols of a movement that forced the imposition of middle-class ideals on working-class leisure.[42]

The creation of the City of Dublin Workingmen's Cricket Club in 1883 highlighted some of the paternalistic resorts of the rational recreation movement.[43] The new club was uncharacteristically granted a private playing pitch by the Board of Work in the Phoenix Park, and its first president was Granby Burke, a former prominent rugby player with Dublin University and son of the Master of the Court of Common Pleas. Unlike traditional pastimes, formally organised sport, which had developed rapidly since the 1830s in Dublin, reflected the rationalisation of industrial societies.[44] The codification and integration of sport in bureaucratic and hierarchical structures as well as the development of privately owned grounds and pavilions also suited middle-class socio-economic aspirations. Crucially, modern sport was imbued with their own cultural ideals of muscular Christianity, respectability and control over body and mind. Such rhetoric was powerful and largely contributed to differentiating newly codified sports from older traditional pastimes and therefore legitimising middle class

41 *Dublin Weekly Herald*, 8 Aug. 1840.

42 Cunningham, *Leisure in the Industrial Revolution*, pp 151–8. A minority within the working class also adhered to such reforming programmes and within this working-class reforming strand, a form of autonomy subsisted free of middle-class interference. See Brad Beaven, *Leisure, citizenship and working-class men in Britain, 1850–1945* (Manchester, 2005), pp 16–27.

43 *Sport*, 21 Apr. 1883.

44 See Allen Guttman's definition of modern sport in that regard: Allen Guttman, *From ritual to record: the nature of modern sports* (New York, 1978), pp 15–55.

leisure. For instance, cricket pitches and pavilions were among the first dedicated sporting facilities built in Dublin from the 1860s and often doubled as promenades or athletics tracks.[45] They became part of the suburban fabric and helped convey the image of suburbs as wealthy, modern and wholesome places, as well as creating a community of values between the Irish and British middle classes. More prosaically, modern sport was also used as a recruiting tool for reforming institutions. The adoption of soccer by the Boys' Brigade (an urban religious youth movement) in the 1890s was as much a nod to the Corinthian ideals as a means of attracting new members.[46] Two decades earlier, the Young Men's Christian Association and the Temperance League in Dublin had already begun playing cricket and organised athletics on excursion days, while mechanics' clubs began to be fitted with billiard tables and offered dancing classes.[47]

Because popular leisure was taking place on public space, it became equally significant for the middle class to assert their dominance over it. In the 1830s and 1840s, British reform groups and societies started to advocate the transformation of open space into public parks.[48] In Dublin as in other British cities, they were the antidote to rapidly urbanising and industrialising societies. Public parks provided the population with open air, promoted moral reform, disciplined working-class children and were subtle reminders of the imperial context in Ireland and other British colonies.[49] Thoughtfully arranged, they were often located in the growing middle-class suburbs and contributed both to answering the aesthetic and pastoral needs of local residents and crucially to increasing the value of nearby housing.[50] Initially mooted by societies and lobbies, the public park movement found in the ongoing municipal devolution a fertile ground to expand.[51] In that regard, policy makers in Dublin clearly imitated developments that were then taking

45 *DE*, 21 Aug. 1866.

46 Brendan Power, 'The functions of association football in the Boys' Brigade in Ireland, 1888–1914' in Leeann Lane & William Murphy (eds), *Leisure and the Irish in the nineteenth century* (Liverpool, 2016), pp 45–6, 51–2.

47 *FJ*, 23 Jun. 1874, 9 Jun. 1875, 6 Jun. 1876, 6 Aug. 1878; *DE*, 22 May 1877; *Irishman*, 4 Dec. 1880.

48 Hazel Conway, *People's parks, the design and development of Victorian parks in Britain* (Cambridge, 1991), pp 39–55.

49 Vanessa Rutherford, 'Muscles and morals: children's playground culture in Ireland, 1836–1918' in Lane & Murphy, *Leisure and the Irish*, pp 78–9; Joanna Brück, 'Landscapes of desire: parks, colonialism, and identity in Victorian and Edwardian Ireland' in *International Journal of Archaeology*, xvii, no 1 (2013), pp 214–17; N.H. Dreher, 'Public parks in urban Britain, 1870–1920: creating a new public culture' (PhD thesis, University of Pennsylvania, 1993), pp 30–7.

50 Dreher, 'Public parks in urban Britain', pp 38–43.

51 Séamas Ó Maitiú, *Dublin's suburban towns 1834–1930* (Dublin, 2003), pp 169–73.

place in Britain.[52] This was especially visible in the independent suburban townships of Kingstown, Rathmines, Blackrock, Dalkey, Pembroke, Killiney and Clontarf, where municipal politics came to reflect the middle-class, Protestant and unionist ideology of their residents.[53] There, local authorities were keen to display their philanthropic credentials and sought to increase their attractiveness, bolster civic pride and arouse the envy of neighbouring townships.[54]

The proceedings of the Bray township, a seaside resort south of Dublin City, offer an insight into the suburban acquisition of land and its transformation into a highly regulated open space. The building of a train station in 1854 fuelled the development of a town whose municipal authorities sought to develop its touristic appeal. In 1858, a sub-committee looked into the feasibility of transforming the shoreline into a pleasure ground and found that 'it would add very much to the attraction of this locality, enhance the value of property in the neighbourhood and tend materially to improve the town'.[55] Contact was immediately made with the landowning Earl of Meath, and control over the esplanade was finally rested in the town commissioners' hands in August 1861.[56] Meanwhile they had also retained ten acres of Bray common in 1860 to lay out a public park while the rest of the common was sold piecemeal following the passing of the Bray Common Inclosure Act in 1859.[57] Formal control over the ground was obtained in March 1867 and the park was open during daytime to the public in May 1867.[58] Both the esplanade and the public park were a highly normative environment. Grazing rights were limited in the park, horses were banned from the esplanade and preaching was forbidden there too.[59] The concept of private property was enshrined. Damaging the shrubs and railings (or even drying clothes on them) could lead to prosecution.[60] Sabbatarianism ruled and popular recreations were proscribed on Sundays that resulted in furthering the religious divide at a time of increasing political unrest. Footballers and wrestlers were repeatedly told so, and Gaelic Athletic Association clubs had to ask permission to use

52 Nathan Booth, David Churchill, Anna Barker & Adam Crawford, 'Spaces apart: public parks and the differentiation of space in Leeds, 1850–1914' in *Urban History*, xlviii (2021), pp 556–68.

53 Ó Maitiú, *Dublin's suburban towns*, pp 19–46; Daly, *The deposed capital*, pp 168–71.

54 *Irish Society* (henceforth cited as *IS*), 11 Oct. 1890; *Irish Daily Independent* (henceforth cited as *IDI*), 26 Jul. 1898.

55 Minutes of the Bray Township Commissioners (henceforth cited as BTC), 12 Jul. 1858 (Wicklow County Archives).

56 Ibid., 7 Aug. 1861.

57 *Dublin Evening Mail*, 5 Sep. 1860.

58 BTC, 4 Mar. 1867, 20 May 1867.

59 Ibid., 22 Mar. 1868, 17 May 1875, 20 Sep. 1875, 6 Sep. 1876, 9 Sep. 1880.

60 Ibid., 18 Nov. 1867, 19 Nov. 1877, 21 Jan. 1889.

the park.[61] Pitch and toss and card players were to be brought to the attention of the police.[62] Such dispositions were by no means singular to Bray and were equally observed in Kingstown's people's park, where two caretakers were employed 'to keep order at the place'.[63] In Blackrock's People's Park, meetings were altogether proscribed and football was forbidden on Sundays.[64]

The opening of Harold's Cross Park in 1894 further illustrated how common land, long associated with May Day festivities and used by the population at large, came to be appropriated by local authorities and redesigned to promote middle-class values. A charitable society, the Harold's Cross Improvement Association, was created in June 1891 and canvassed local residents with a view to transform 'the present unsightly common' into a public park.[65] Eventually rights of commonage were waived by the Irish Land Commission and ownership of the ground was sold to the parsimonious Rathmines Town Commissioners for a nominal five shillings.[66] The subscription fund set up for the occasion included prominent Rathmines residents, a few well-wishing professionals from the city, the drink industry (a reliable contributor to nineteenth-century charitable projects) and Sir John Talbot Power.[67] The nationalist *Freeman's Journal* advocated a utilitarian design to enhance playing facilities for children, yet also rejoiced that 'the scheme proposed would better the approach to the several religious institutions in the district, and would prevent people having occasion to visit the well-ordered Mount Jerome Cemetery from observing the dilapidated and unsightly condition of things at present existing'.[68]

Eventually, the park was opened in May 1894 amidst self-congratulatory speeches and patronising claims that 'it was for the working classes the park had been opened' and that 'they may recreate themselves under circumstances calculated to afford them thorough and sincere enjoyment'.[69] Yet children's recreation largely gave way to aesthetic imperatives, which included flower beds, rockeries, brick shelters, grassy mounds, public toilets and a lake.[70] Few dissenting voices were heard. Among them, however, was Thomas Myles, the larger-than-life vice-president of the Royal College of Surgeons, who declared that 'such places are absolutely useless for children who want places where they

61 Ibid., 1 May 1876, 20 Jan. 1879, 5 Sep. 1887, 17 Jul. 1893.
62 Ibid., 1 Aug. 1887.
63 *Evening Herald* (henceforth cited as *EH*) 3 Jul. 1897.
64 *DE*, 7 Feb. 1885, 30 Mar. 1899; *EH*, 1 Mar. 1899.
65 *EH*, 7 Jan. 1892.
66 *FJ*, 7 Apr. 1892.
67 *IDI*, 2 Jul. 1892.
68 *FJ*, 9 Apr. 1892, 6 May 1892.
69 *IDI*, 2 May 1894.
70 *IS*, 5 May 1894.

can knock about and amuse themselves generally, and not places where they are warned off the grass at every hand's turn'.[71] Myles was right, and despite high-flown ambitions, the public parks created in middle-class Dublin suburbs in the second part of the nineteenth century did not provide the population with adequate recreation facilities.

Municipal authorities had by the turn of the twentieth century appropriated for themselves common land and open spaces that had not yet been privatised, and transformed them into public parks in accordance with contemporary conceptions of physical and moral needs.[72] By doing so, they actually regulated and reduced the playing time and space of the population. Moving from the suburbs to the city, different socio-economic and political dynamics ensured a different pattern in the development of public playgrounds, yet middle-class controlling and fashioning of working-class leisure was equally observable.

The density of urban fabric, more pressing sanitary concerns, chronic financial difficulties and the relieving presence of the Phoenix Park meant that Dublin Corporation lagged behind suburban townships in the creation of large public parks. Instead, a multitude of small parks and playgrounds were built after the passing of the Open Spaces Act in 1887 that facilitated the conversion of disused burial grounds into public venues.[73] By and large, the impetus came from philanthropic societies such as the Kyrle Society, whose Dublin branch was founded in 1885, and the Open Space Association (1887), modelled on the Earl of Meath's similar initiative in London.[74] Assistance of municipal authorities was then sought to bring projects to completion. Focus was brought to the disaffected neighbourhood of the Liberties and the north inner-city centre as playgrounds were opened in Pimlico, New Row South, Queen's Street, Hill Street, Green Street and at the Blessington Basin.[75] Churchyards near St Mary's, St Audeon's and Christchurch were also transformed into playgrounds at the turn of the 1890s.[76] In marked contrast to the unionist flavour of suburban parks, city developments were wrapped in a nationalist rhetoric that reflected the political allegiance of Dublin Corporation.[77] Yet similar conceptions of recreation and respectability applied in the city and townships alike. The Pimlico and New Row South playgrounds

71 *Daily Nation* (henceforth cited as *DN*), 1 Oct. 1898.

72 Alvaro Sevilla-Buitrago, 'Central Park against the streets: the enclosure of public space cultures in mid-nineteenth century New York' in *Social and Cultural Geography*, xv, no. 2 (2015), pp 164–5; Brück, 'Landscapes of desire', pp 206–10.

73 The act was the extension of the Open Space Act (1877) and Open Space Act (1881) from London to the rest of Britain and Ireland, see *DE*, 22 May 1886; *IT*, 3 Sep. 1887.

74 *DE*, 22 Jul. 1885, 16 Mar. 1887.

75 *DE*, 5 Sep. 1887, 4 Mar. 1889; *FJ*, 23 Dec. 1898.

76 *FJ*, 23 Dec. 1898.

77 Brück, 'Landscapes of desire', pp 217–19.

were only open from 2pm to 6pm on Sundays and caretakers were hired 'to see that no injury [was] done to the grounds and that no accidents occur[ed]'.[78]

Motivations behind the creation of playgrounds were multiple. For the Earl of Meath, it was about increasing 'the health and the strength of the population living in the large towns' and to 'throw a little happiness into the lives of those whose existence is often exceedingly monotonous.'[79] Sanitary reform and social paternalism permeated such considerations and were expressed by leading physicians, such as Charles Cameron and Thomas Myles. Both deplored the cramped housing and lack of means of many families, which prevented them from taking a trip to the sea or affording public baths.[80] Myles (a nationalist in politics) also denounced the 'lack of personal cleanliness' and drunkenness to prove that 'the personal element is largely responsible' in the destitution of many families.[81] This was a point of view widely shared by the Dublin middle class, who grew increasingly concerned at the risk of contagious diseases. Such discourse also transcended the religious and political spectrum.

The nationalist and Catholic *Irishman*, for example, was an active proponent of opening St Stephen's Green to the public. In 1863, the newspaper asked for it to be 'open to all classes, upon the simple restriction that they be sober, well conducted and decently dressed. That no assemblages of boys, for the purpose of racing, cricket, foot-ball, hocky, prison-bar or any other game be allowed.'[82] The need for playgrounds in the city was also embedded in a utilitarian discourse, which perceived the streets as dangerous places for children and where they should not wander. The unionist *Irish Times* reasoned that 'the alternative, therefore, lies between the manifest danger on the streets and the safe, cleanly, and healthy playground, with perhaps a sward, or even a bare flagging'.[83] In 1875, an employer whose van driver ran over a girl playing outside St Stephen's Green's railings was fined £200. The case elicited comments on 'the hard conditions such verdicts impose on traders, and declares that street accidents are unavoidable as long as parents in the humbler classes are allowed to send their children out into the streets to play, instead of keeping them at home'.[84] Rather than seeing the incident as a matter of personal responsibility, the nationalist *Nation* suggested the blame be attributed to the structural economic conditions of the working class and pressed for the creation of

78 *DE*, 5 Sep. 1887.
79 *DE*, 5 Sep. 1887.
80 *DN*, 1 Oct. 1898; *FJ*, 23 Dec. 1898.
81 *DN*, 1 Oct. 1898.
82 *Irishman*, 3 Oct. 1863. St Stephen's Green was eventually opened to the population in 1880, thanks largely to the efforts and money of brewer and philanthropist Arthur Guinness.
83 *IT*, 8 Sep. 1874.
84 *Weekly Nation*, 27 Feb. 1875.

playgrounds to offset the negatives of cramped housing.[85] Crucially, the paper also agreed that 'it was inside the locked gates of St Stephen's-green and not outside in the crowded roadway, that the poor child ought to have been at play, whose misfortune entailed on our respected fellow-citizen the severe verdict of the jury'.[86] The belief that streets were not made for recreation was thus rooted in the class structure of nineteenth-century Dublin and the fault line within the middle class was not whether play should be condoned on the streets, but whether it should be dissuaded by harsh punishment or by active municipal action towards providing alternative recreation space.

Public space and popular recreation in late nineteenth-century Dublin

The conflict between the middle class, for whom the streets should be orderly and facilitate transit, and the working class, who considered them a legitimate recreational space, remained prevalent throughout the nineteenth century. The dispute was thus essentially between those who often lived in suburban terraced housing and resorted to private sport grounds and commercial leisure outlets for socialising and those who lived in cramped tenements and used public space for their social interactions. Attempts by local authorities and charitable societies to alleviate the need for playing space in working-class neighbourhoods were simply not sufficient and the regulation of public space according to middle-class values remained only partly achieved by the turn of the twentieth century. Meanwhile, preserving public rights and access to public space grew on the Dublin political agenda from the 1880s as the Irish Parliamentary Party became the voice of nationalist Ireland and the country at large convulsed around the question of land ownership.

Public authorities never succeeded in preventing children from using streets, and stamping out all forms of recreational activity proved impossible.[87] Children made the streets their playgrounds and were reprimanded for doing so.[88] Teenagers and adults went to jail. In 1860, twenty-one people aged fourteen and over were incarcerated in Richmond prison for playing ball, pitch and toss, cards or hopscotch in the street.[89] In 1900, seventeen people, all

85 Ibid.

86 Ibid.

87 Chinn, *Better betting*, pp 85–93; Mark Clapson, *A bit of a flutter: popular gambling and English society, c. 1823–1961* (Manchester, 1992), pp 79–84.

88 *Evening Freeman*, 28 Mar. 1864 (hurling); *Dublin Evening Mail*, 7 Feb. 1876 (hurling); *FJ*, 24 May 1883 ('road cricket'); *DE*, 29 Jan. 1895 (tip-cat and peg-top); *EH*, 16 Apr. 1896 (football); *Dublin Daily Nation*, 29 Apr. 1899 (cricket).

89 Dublin – Bridewell (Richmond) Prison general register 1859–1860 (National Archives of Ireland (N.A.I.)/PRIS/1/13/13).

over sixteen years of age, spent time at Mountjoy prison for similar offences.[90] Available data remain insufficient to evaluate trends in street games, and prison records fail to translate the level of leniency shown by judges or policemen in dealing with such offences. What was clear, however, was that streets were used throughout the century for casual recreation, and not only by children. Among thirty-two men whose occupation was identifiable, one was a soldier, five were skilled workers and twenty-six were unskilled workers. Those were precisely the people who lived in overcrowded tenement housing and who were unable to pay the fine imposed by the judge. Conclusions from prison records remain nevertheless limited in scope and further research must be undertaken to assess whether participation in street games and petty gambling was affected by religion, class and gender.

Preserving public order and the tranquillity of residents remained the primary reasons to prosecute infringements. Increasingly though, a social and cultural layer was added that had its origin in the greater wish for social segregation and in the feeling that betting had become pervasive among the working class.[91] Trotting on the Howth Road was recurrent in the 1880s, but became especially resented when it took place on Sunday. Clontarf residents then objected to the degradation of the middle-class character of the township by 'a motley assemblage of cars, bookmakers, and the class of men frequenting races'.[92] Playing in the streets was bad, but betting was worse, and occurrences were 'viewed as symptoms of a wider crisis of morality among the youth expressed in disobedience of the law'.[93] Fear was propagated by the conservative *Daily Express,* which saw in young pitch and toss players mere 'corner-boys' eager to assault the policemen who arrested them.[94] The widening gulf between middle- and working-class interpretations of the law was nowhere made clearer than by a case that took place at the Kingstown police courts in 1895:

> Two young lads ... were charged with playing pitch and toss on [a] public thoroughfare at Albert road on the 2nd inst. The father of one of the boys stated that the game was being carried on in an old laneway which was not a public thoroughfare, about 150 yards from the road. His Worship asked severely if he desired to bring up the boys as gamblers, and imposed a fine of 1s each, with the option of 4 ½ hours' imprisonment.[95]

90 Mountjoy Prison male general register 1899–1901 (N.A.I./PRIS/1/43/1).

91 Ross McKibbin, 'Working-class gambling in Britain, 1880–1939' in *Past & Present,* no. 82 (1979), pp 149–50.

92 *IT,* 31 Oct. 1889; *Sport,* 2 Nov. 1889. The popular *Sport* however believed that 'the proceedings passed off in the most orderly manner'.

93 Clapson, *A bit of a flutter,* p. 81.

94 *DE,* 8 Apr. 1884, 1 Aug. 1890, 30 Jan. 1894.

95 *DE,* 21 Jun. 1895.

Other attempts at controlling behaviours reflected the ambitions of a reforming strand within the middle classes, their ability to get attention from courts and ultimately their limited powers to curb popular practices. Gambling prosecutions and the refusal to grant licences to sell alcohol were mere statements of intent that highlighted a pious wish to regulate society in line with virtuous and middle-class values. They were no deterrent for the population, who enjoyed betting within racecourses and socialising around sporting events, especially Gaelic games, which took place on Sundays. In Inchicore, there was 'ball-playing, football and handball on the public road, and far worse on Sundays than week days'.[96] Thus, by the 1880s, the fight for Sabbatarianism was truly lost in 'Catholic' Ireland, and streets remained a privileged space of working-class leisure.

Concurrently with the repression of play on public thoroughfares began a debate on the appropriation of public land by private interest. Stemming from the emergence of a popular press, a class of populist politicians, and the growing schism between the Irish population and its elite, this debate largely espoused contemporary political lines and echoed the land agitation observed throughout rural Ireland. The enclosing and privatisation of commons became hotly resented. In October 1885, the *Freeman's Journal* wondered 'what has become of Dalkey common?' and set out to demonstrate how a few local residents – including the Catholic barrister, justice of the peace and town commissioner James Milo Burke – had steadily been building walls and gates on the common so that access to the seashore was being denied.[97] In subsequent weeks, the case was ventilated in the columns of the newspaper and attracted the attention of the Dalkey branch of the Irish National League.[98] The town commissioners were eventually left with no choice but to have Burke destroy his wall. His motivation had been 'that a stop should be put to the immoral conduct constantly seen from higher ground' and by preventing locals from reaching the seashore, he would have ensured his peace of mind.[99] Plain land grabbing was wrapped in a social and cultural rhetoric. Two years later the Dalkey town commissioners proudly decided to enshrine the public nature of the ground and to transform it into a public park.[100]

Though of limited scale, this was an unmitigated victory for Dublin middle-class nationalists who had successfully contested a plot of land illegally held by a member of the upper middle class and could boast its contribution to the broader effort to transfer land ownership from landlords to the Irish

96 *IT*, 24 Jul. 1889.
97 *FJ*, 9 Oct. 1885.
98 Ibid., 19 Oct. 1885, 20 Oct. 1885, 21 Oct. 1885.
99 Ibid., 27 Oct. 1885.
100 Ibid., 10 Oct. 1887.

people. Was it a victory for the local working class? Rightful and free access to the ground was restored, yet it had become aligned with the same middle-class conception of respectability and sobriety as Harold's Cross Park. Such episodes also revealed the evolving position of the law (when called upon) towards the public nature of space and a move towards preserving the right of the people, albeit conditioned to appropriate behaviour. This trend was already observed in the late 1870s when the building of a new quay at the East Wall, according to the dispositions of the Dublin Port and Docks Act 1879, threatened a local spot, known as the Smoothing Iron, and free bathing more generally. Attention was brought to the committee of the House of Commons by Corporation member Granville Somerset and nationalist MP Edmund D. Gray and resulted in the insertion of a clause 'binding the board not to remove or interfere with the existing bathing places until bathing places and approaches were constructed in lieu of them, to be maintained in good repair afterwards'.[101] Similarly, when negotiations regarding rights of way in Howth between distiller and unionist politician Andrew Jameson and the Committee of the Howth and Sutton Rights of Way Association failed in 1894, the matter was brought to court and largely settled against Jameson.[102] He had purchased a large tract of land in Howth in 1892 that included four rights of way – one being a popular and scenic cliff walk – and sought to extinguish such rights. Opposition to his project was this time fuelled by nationalist MPs Timothy M. Healy and John J. Clancy and eventually resulted in the preservation of these public rights.[103]

Lack of playing space in the city was relieved by the nearby Phoenix Park. Access to one of the largest recreation grounds in Europe was free, within commuting distance of the city, and thousands of players and spectators could gather at once. Yet the attribution of grounds between 1838 and 1884 by the Board of Works to the Phoenix, Civil Service, Garrison, Workingmen's and Constabulary cricket clubs, as well as to the All-Ireland Polo Club, was contested.[104] Over the years these clubs enjoyed the right to enclose their grounds, to build sheds, pavilions and stands rent-free in easily accessible portions of a public park. While ownership remained in the hands of Dublin Corporation, these clubs could warn off trespassers and eventually prosecute.[105] Their clear association with the establishment, rather than their size, was the crux of the matter. As with Dalkey common and Sutton rights of way, such moves were understood by nationalist historian John P. Prendergast

101 *IT*, 7 Jul. 1879.

102 *Flag of Ireland*, 24 Nov. 1894; *FJ*, 26 Dec. 1894, *Evening Telegraph*, 9 Mar. 1896.

103 *IDI*, 22 May 1897.

104 *Irish Sportsman*, 19 Jun. 1880; *IT*, 12 May 1881; *IDI*, 29 May 1894. The Board of Works had been managing the park since 1860.

105 *Evening Telegraph*, 10 May 1894.

and politicians Timothy and Maurice Healy as part of the annexation of public land by an elite that was both unrepresentative and estranged from its people.[106] Such semi-privatisation of grounds was, however, offset by a non-partisan approach by the Board of Works as a public cricket ground (able to host four simultaneous games) was laid out in 1894 and over thirty public football pitches had been built by 1907.[107]

Conclusion

Cultural attempts at shaping recreational behaviours in the public space in late nineteenth-century Dublin met with multiple contradictions. Legislation that had favoured the enclosure of commons and privatised land from the mid-eighteenth century was completed by incentives for public authorities to create public parks and playgrounds from the mid-nineteenth century. These were availed of and both township commissioners in the suburbs and Dublin Corporation in the city presented a limited yet real track record in the provision of public parks and playgrounds. Such efforts were borne out of philanthropic and sanitary concerns to provide poor urban dwellers with open space and free leisure facilities but were also entangled in a mesh of egotistic interests. Ornamental parks contributed to fashioning civic pride in middle-class suburbs and came to reflect the status and taste of its residents. By providing an alternative to street games, they further permitted their stamping out and delegitimisation. By enacting rules and codes of behaviours, they also attempted to convert the population to contemporary middle-class mores. Such endeavours were met with internal paradoxes, and bathing perhaps best encapsulated the limits and hypocrisy of the reforming agenda. Bathing, aside from its recreational aspect, was a hygienic necessity and was therefore ardently promoted across the political and religious divide. The Baths and Washhouses Act (1846) was the legislative cornerstone that permitted British and Irish municipalities to build public swimming pools and derive considerable civic pride from it from the 1870s.[108] Belfast, for instance, boasted four such establishments by the 1890s.[109] In Dublin, financial considerations and lack of goodwill postponed the opening of the first public swimming

106 *Hansard 3*, ccxcvii (17 Apr. 1885); *Hansard 3*, ccxcix (20 Jul. 1885); *Hansard 4*, xxv (5 Jun. 1894); *Hansard 4*, li (9 Jul. 1897); *IT*, 27 Jul. 1885, 12 Aug. 1886.

107 *EH*, 6 Jun. 1894; *DE*, 10 Feb. 1903; Neal Garnham, *Association football and society in pre-partition Ireland* (Belfast, 2004), p. 12.

108 Christopher Love, 'Local aquatic empires: the municipal provision of swimming pools in England, 1828–1918' in *International Journal of the History of Sport*, xxiv, no. 5 (2007), pp 626–8.

109 *IT*, 19 May 1900.

pool and washhouses in Tara Street until 1885.[110] The inefficiency of Dublin Corporation and townships municipal authorities in providing affordable bathing places to the population was offset by the free use of canals and open sea by the population at large. This, however, was equally met with contempt from middle-class reformers who could not reconcile their own conception of chastity and modesty with the public display of the body and the absence of sexual segregation. At times, how one indulged in physical recreation was more important than the moral or healthy rhetoric that underpinned it, and Thomas Lenehan, a twenty-one-year-old labourer, was accordingly sent to jail in 1900 for 'bathing within public view'.[111]

The reforming agenda thus largely failed to make significant sways into working-class attitudes by the late nineteenth century. Streets were used for recreational purposes by children and adults alike, both out of necessity and because it was positively embedded in working-class leisure in both Britain and Ireland.[112] Betting went on unabated. Teetotalism was undermined by the rise of music halls and gin palaces as popular and commercialised forms of entertainment. Sunday likewise remained the privileged day of leisure for the greatest part of the population. Middle-class endeavours to shape recreational habits largely failed because they meant to transform popular leisure, and not solely to provide space for recreation. However, further research is needed to bring focus on Dublin working-class attitudes. It should determine whether such resistance deliberately challenged social paternalism, the extent to which middle-class initiatives were welcome yet insufficient, and whether the gospel of respectability was slowly gaining currency among the population. In an Irish context, can the conflict over the use of public space for recreation from the late 1870s in Dublin and its suburbs be tied to the ongoing political and land agitation witnessed in the country at large? And, from an international perspective, how did such a strongly ingrained popular conception of the right to use public space and the ensuing defiance of the law and the police contribute to fashioning urban, masculine and working-class identities?

110 *FJ*, 18 Apr. 1884, 13 Jul. 1886; *DE*, 20 Mar. 1885, 4 Jun. 1885; *IT*, 13 May 1897.
111 Mountjoy Prison general male register 1899–1901 (N.A.I./PRIS/1/43/1), 23 Jul. 1900.
112 David Churchill, *Crime control and everyday life in the Victorian city* (Oxford, 2018), pp 109–10.

Warfare

8

'More Irish than the Irish Themselves': Conflict, Discipline and the Image of the Irish militia during the Nineteenth Century

William Butler

Introduction

In their introduction to the seminal work *A Military History of Ireland,* Thomas Bartlett and Keith Jeffery observed that throughout Irish life, beset by centuries of conflict, there has been a persistent military flavour, which made military service seem normal. Moreover, the presence, over many centuries, of the British army and the auxiliary forces in Ireland – not to mention the existence of the Royal Irish Constabulary as an armed police force – demonstrates the interwoven nature of civil and military power.[1] Sometimes that military presence was reassuring, often it was intimidating, and always it was a reminder that the potential for conflict was never far away. More recently, in his study of Irish military elites, Loughlin Sweeney has argued that the army of the late nineteenth and early twentieth century 'was not just a foreign imposition on Ireland but rather a longstanding and deeply rooted institution within society.[2] As the primary locally raised force linking the army to society, the militia is, therefore, fundamental to this notion.

The Irish militia materialised as one small part of what historians have defined as an Irish military tradition, operating within the framework and becoming an integral part of a burgeoning official military culture.[3] British

1 Thomas Bartlett & Keith Jeffery, 'An Irish Military Tradition?' in idem (eds), *A military history of Ireland* (Cambridge 1996), pp 7–8.

2 Loughlin Sweeney, *Irish military elites, nation and empire, 1870–1925: identity and authority* (Switzerland, 2019), pp 28–37.

3 For more on an Irish military tradition see Timothy Bowman, 'Irish military cultures in the British army, c.1775–1992' in Kevin Linch & Matthew Lord (eds), *Redcoats to*

perceptions of the Irish as simultaneously possessing the martial qualities to be 'good' soldiers, while also being ill-disciplined and prone to rebellion, extended to the militia.[4] These notions, as Catriona Kennedy has observed, certainly had their antecedents in the participation of Irish soldiers in the British army of the eighteenth century.[5] Indeed, the view that 'the Irish' had a propensity to rebellion perhaps accounted for the disproportionate number of artillery regiments in Ireland following the Napoleonic Wars. Though apocryphal, the 1906 observation that it was safer to give forty Irishmen one big gun between them, rather than a musket each, clearly still resonated with the authorities and became a catalyst for tension.[6]

Using the Crimean War and other political 'flashpoints' as its backdrop, this chapter will focus on three areas of friction relating to the Irish militia. First, it will reflect on tensions between the Irish militia and civilian populations in both Britain and Ireland. Second, it will explore the discord often felt between Irish militia regiments and regular British forces throughout the United Kingdom. Third, it will discuss the, perhaps more abstract, clashes between the Irish militia and its political masters in both Dublin and London. In so doing, it will be argued that the perception of the militia in Ireland depended largely on factors beyond the militia's control, particularly the domestic political situation, but that occasionally, the actions of individual regiments did little to help its cause either. It will be demonstrated that any trust afforded to it by the British authorities was always conditional, often prompted by national crises during times of war, and that loyalty to the Crown (or questions pertaining to it) became a defining feature for much of the Irish militia's existence.

Tommies; the experience of the British soldier from the eighteenth century (Woodbridge, 2021); William Butler, *The Irish Amateur Military Tradition in the British Army, 1854–1992* (Manchester, 2016); Bartlett & Jeffery, *A military history of Ireland*; Keith Jeffery, 'The Irish military tradition and the British Empire' in idem (ed.), *'An Irish Empire'?: aspects of Ireland and the British empire* (Manchester, 1996).

4 For more on the perception of Irish indiscipline see Timothy Bowman, *The Irish regiments in the Great War; discipline and morale* (Manchester, 2008).

5 Caitriona Kennedy, '"True Brittons and real Irish": Irish Catholics in the British army during the Revolutionary and Napoleonic Wars' in Caitriona Kennedy & Matthew McCormack (eds), *Soldiering in Britain and Ireland, 1750–1850* (Basingstoke, 2012).

6 Parliamentary (Parl.) Debates (Debs) (House of Lords (HL)), vol. 154, cols 6–50, 19 Mar. 1906.

The Irish militia in context

At any given time during the period under consideration, the Irish militia constituted anywhere between twenty and thirty thousand men.[7] This was not an insignificant number of what, at times of training and periods of embodiment, were armed and trained individuals. As such, it is not possible to discuss its use and continued existence without considering the political situation in Ireland during the latter half of the nineteenth century. The situation, whether it be a fear of Fenian infiltration into the armed forces, the Land Wars or war with a foreign power, also dictated what strategic role the militia would or could carry out, and whether it could even exist in the first place. Its image in the eye of the authorities and the public (both positive and negative) also depended on these factors, particularly because these influences often made its position in Parliament at Westminster a difficult one.

Whether justified or not, distrust emerged from outside Ireland, and this had a significant effect on the position of the force. As Charles Townshend has observed in his work on politics and violence in Ireland, the study of Anglo-Irish relations at this time often leaves the impression of English government and Irish resistance locked in a seemingly endless embrace.[8] Under the political control of the English government, and simultaneously viewed as an outlet for Irish resistance, the Irish militia was caught somewhere in the middle.

This distrust endured for much of the nineteenth century but was not a new phenomenon. The Irish militia had played a significant role during the Napoleonic period, and this has resulted in a great deal of historical scrutiny – particularly regarding the political sensitivities surrounding its use.[9] Once re-established in the mid-nineteenth century, it continued to hold a prominent role in Irish society, particularly in towns in which regiments were headquartered. During times of annual training, regiments were a regular feature in town life, often taking part in public spectacles, including parades

7 'Militia regiments. Return showing the establishment of each regiment of militia in the United Kingdom; and the numbers present, absent, and wanting to complete, 1885' [C.4675], *1890* [C.6261], *1895* [C.7939], *1900* [Cd.579], H.C 1885–1900.

8 Charles Townshend, *Political violence in Ireland; government and resistance since 1848* (Oxford, 1983), p. 406.

9 Ciarán McDonnell, '"Zeal and patriotism": forging identity in the Irish militia. 1793–1802' in *Journal for Eighteenth-Century Studies*, xlii, no. 2 (2019), pp 211–28; Neal Garnham, *The Militia in eighteenth-century Ireland: in defence of the Protestant interest* (Woodbridge, 2012); I.F. Nelson, *The Irish militia 1793–1802: Ireland's forgotten army* (Dublin, 2007); J.E. Cookson, 'Service without politics? Army, militia and volunteers in Britain during the American and French revolutionary wars' in *War in history*, x (2003), pp 381–97; idem, *The British armed nation 1793–1815* (Oxford, 1997); Henry McAnally, *The Irish militia 1793–1816* (Dublin, 1949).

and musical performances.[10] Prominent members of Irish society also gave service to the militia, particularly as officers. For example, John Redmond's brother, William, joined the Wexford Militia in 1879, while Charles Stewart Parnell was an officer in the Wicklow Rifles. As Roy Foster stated in his biography of Parnell, the latter joined the regiment 'as befitted a Wicklow landowner', and it was even remarked that he was proud of this service, hating the idea that his uniform might be mistaken for that of a Fenian.[11]

A key theme to think about in the context of the Irish militia during this time is loyalty to British rule. Even before the militia in Ireland had been reconstituted, questions were asked about perceived disloyalty, simply because it had not been resurrected in 1852 alongside its English and Welsh counterparts. In early 1854, Lord Palmerston, at the time the Home Secretary, was forced to state in Parliament that this was not due to any doubts over its reliability. The *Freeman's Journal* reported that 'Lord Palmerston then passed a lofty eulogy on the loyalty and patriotism of Irishmen and attributed the omission to the simple fact that they were not wanted just at that time to guard their native shores from invasion!'[12] The force in Scotland was also not afforded that opportunity, but this was to change later in the year when both countries were instructed to begin enrolment of their respective forces. In Ireland, provision was made for the voluntary enrolment of thirty thousand militiamen, each committing to service of five years, with an obligation to serve anywhere in the United Kingdom.[13]

Immediately, the force came to hold immense strategic value. The primary role intended by the authorities for the militia, and particularly the Irish militia, was to furnish recruits to the regular army to reinforce its ranks.[14] The despatching of recruits to the Line, often after the visits of recruiting parties, was a regular occurrence throughout all of the embodiment periods, and none more so than during the Crimean War. Regiments were also moved around both Ireland and the rest of Great Britain, to perform their secondary role on garrison duties. This brought units into close contact with different communities in Ireland and elsewhere. Tensions were not uncommon.

Domestically, the Irish militia, like the rest of the militia, was used in isolation as an aid to the civil power. Usually the Permanent Staff of officers was used, rather than the entire battalion, or at most small pickets of men

10 For examples of this see Butler, *The Irish amateur military tradition*, pp 101–2.
11 R.F. Foster, *Charles Stewart Parnell: the man and his family* (London, 1976), p. 93 and p. 116.
12 *Freeman's Journal* (henceforth cited as *FJ*), 8 Feb. 1854.
13 'Militia (Ireland). A bill (as amended in committee) to amend the laws relating to the militia in Ireland' [250], 1854.
14 I.F.W. Beckett, *The amateur military tradition, 1558–1945* (Manchester, 1991), p. 153.

were detached to guard against any civil unrest. For example, in May 1855, the Cavan and Monaghan Militias were used to 'preserve the peace' at the execution of some convicts in their localities. In August 1855, 140 men of the South Tipperary Artillery (Militia) were required for the suppression of a riot in Clonmel.[15] This role, however, was fraught with difficulties for all militia units – though particularly those in Ireland. Local sympathies, it was felt, could often influence interventions negatively. Consequently, the decision was soon taken to transfer most Irish militia units to the British mainland.

Riots, mutinies, and disturbances

During the Crimean War, several riots, mutinies and disturbances involving the Irish militia took place; both at home and in Great Britain, their scale much larger than in the militia as a whole. The most famous example is the mutiny of the 2nd or North Tipperary Militia while stationed at Nenagh, County Tipperary, in July 1856.[16] Paul Huddie has covered this incident in detail, including in his work on Ireland and the Crimean War, but it is worth outlining here.[17] Having returned to its locality for disembodiment, the men, who had been treated poorly and left in an appalling condition, decided to imprison their officers and take over the town. After a day's rioting, elements of the 41st Regiment of Foot arrived to restore order, resulting in three fatalities: two among the mutineers and one from the regular battalion. Dubbed the 'Battle of the Breeches' by the local press on account of the militiamen's refusal to return their uniforms until their enlistment bounty was paid in full, the resulting enquiry found the officers largely to blame for the incident. Still, ninety members of the unit were tried by courts martial.[18] The individual identified to have killed the soldier of the 41st Regiment of Foot, Private

15 Returns of military parties assigned in aid of the civil power, 1837–1870 (N.L.I., MS 1226).

16 When in existence in the late eighteenth and early nineteenth centuries, the Irish militia was also involved in several similar incidents, which may have contributed to the history of distrust by the authorities. See Thomas Bartlett, 'An end of moral economy: the Irish militia disturbances of 1793' in *Past & Present*, no. 99 (1983), pp 41–64; idem, 'Defence, counter-insurgency and rebellion: Ireland, 1793–1803' in Bartlett & Jeffery, *A military history of Ireland*.

17 For a closer look, see Paul Huddie, 'The Nenagh mutiny of 7–8 July 1856: a re-appraisal' in *British Journal for Military History*, xi, no. 1 (2020), pp 5–20; idem, *The Crimean War and Irish society* (Liverpool, 2015), pp 147–9; Butler, *Irish amateur military tradition*, p. 117; David Murphy, *Ireland and the Crimean War* (Dublin, 2002), pp 197–204.

18 Memorandum by the Under-Secretary of Ireland, regarding the Nenagh Mutiny, 10 Jul. 1856 (N.L.I., MS 1056); *Times*, 10 & 11 Jul. 1856.

Stephen Burns, was sentenced to transportation.[19] The greatest sympathy was expressed towards the men of the regiment, particularly in Ireland, but this feeling could also be found in Parliament. It did, however, very little to show that the Irish militia could be trusted in the eyes of the authorities.

Though not necessarily resulting in mutiny, there are other examples that equally highlight the militia's poor disciplinary record and often brought it into conflict. The Limerick County Militia appear to have been quite prolific in this regard. Between 1856 and 1860, newspapers recorded no fewer than three incidents of varying degrees of severity. The first was a riot in 1856, which also involved the Royal Marines in Plymouth. Having been stationed in the area, it was said that the Limerick men wished to give the Marines a 'bating' as a parting gift before heading back to Ireland.[20] In 1857, while assembled in their own county, a quarrel arose between a policeman and a member of the regiment, resulting in an attack on the police barracks by a hundred men of that regiment.[21] While, in October 1859, when the regiment was once again on garrison duty in England, the *Hampshire Advertiser and Salisbury Guardian* reported that over the course of a week, clashes had occurred between inhabitants of the town of Portsea, members of the navy and soldiers of the militia. Nevertheless, according to the newspaper report, much of the trouble had originated in hostility from some of the town's inhabitants towards the Irishmen, a not uncommon reaction to the presence of Irish soldiers in British towns.[22]

Clashes with the inhabitants of towns in which militia regiments were stationed were not unusual occurrences, and the actions of individual regiments did little to endear the Irish militia to the civilian population. In August 1859, four men of the Louth Rifles had been charged with assaulting several civilians when they were stationed in the county of Suffolk.[23] Earlier that year, a 'considerable disturbance' was reported in Berwick, caused by 'violent proceedings by parties of the Roscommon Militia' who had commenced attacks on the local inhabitants.[24]

The most significant example of this type of conflict, however, was the so-called Kinsale Riot, occurring in July 1859, a disturbance so serious that

19 Confidential memorandum on the Nenagh Munity, 5 Aug. 1856 (N.L.I., MS 1056); Letter from General Lord Seaton, to Major-General Sir Charles Yorke, 11 Aug. 1856 (N.L.I., MS 1239); Memorandum detailing the sentences given to those convicted in the North Tipperary Militia, 1 Sept. 1856 (N.L.I., MS 1056).

20 *Dundee Courier* (henceforth cited as *DC*), 11 Jun. 1856.

21 *FJ*, 23 Sept. 1857; *Saunders's Newsletter*, 23 Sept. 1857; *Lloyd's Weekly Newspaper* (henceforth cited as *LWN*), 27 Sept. 1857; Police Report on the Limerick County Militia, Buttevant, 29 Sept. 1857 (N.L.I., MS 1056).

22 *Hampshire Advertiser and Salisbury Guardian*, 22 Oct. 1859. For additional examples of clashes with civilians see *FJ*, 23 Sept. 1857; *LWN*, 27 Sept. 1857; *Birmingham Daily Post*, 26 Jun. 1861.

23 *The Bury and Norwich Post, and Suffolk Herald*, 2 Aug. 1859.

24 *Cheshire Observer* (henceforth cited as CO), 26 Jan. 1856.

it resulted in a parliamentary inquiry.[25] It was felt that this clash between members of the Antrim Artillery (Militia) and locals in Kinsale, County Cork was the result of sectarian feeling, partly because it had taken place on 12 July.[26] The nationalist press described that 'the Orange rabies had been manifesting itself among the rabble who compose the Antrim Militia for many days', and that those in Kinsale had given the 'Orange Militia such a drubbing as they will recollect'.[27] Rumours regarding the disturbance circulated and many were even reported in Parliament, with blame placed on both sides. One account described an attack on a Roman Catholic chapel, while another claimed that the attack on the regiment was premeditated by the local population.[28] The Parliamentary Inquiry concluded that the inexperience of the officers had contributed to the lack of discipline amongst the soldiers, but that before the disturbance, the conduct of the regiment had been 'creditable and soldier-like'. It stressed that any attacks on the militiamen may have awakened some party feeling amongst some of the men, but that this was largely absent prior to the disturbance.[29] It was stated that the violence had originated when a Kinsale resident had taken exception to the fact that his sister had been seen with a militiaman.[30] Though party feeling does not seem to have been the cause, *The Times* reported that a song entitled 'The Battle of Kinsale; or, the Defeat of the Antrim Orangeman' had been written, which it described as 'truly diabolical, the tone most virulent, the rhyming is wretched, and the language in every way detestable and blackguardly'.[31]

These examples go some way towards explaining why the Irish militia found itself in a challenging position when faced with the distrust of the authorities. It was usually poorly trained, partly because it lacked experienced officers capable of extinguishing any flames of discontent, and it also dealt with a high turnover of trained personnel.[32] As the above demonstrates, this often led to clashes with a variety of groups. While this paints a negative picture on some occasions, individual militia regiments were viewed much more positively.

25 Kinsale Riots. Copies of the official reports made by the civil and by the military authorities, who held investigations regarding the recent rioting at Kinsale, between some of the soldiers of the Antrim Militia Artillery and some of the inhabitants of Kinsale, 1860, H.C. [19].

26 Letter from James Colborne, to the Under-Secretary of Ireland, 16 Jul. 1859 (N.L.I., MS 1057).

27 *Nation*, 16 Jul. 1859.

28 Parl. Debs (HL), vol. 154, cols 1280–1, 15 Jul. 1859.

29 Kinsale Riots, 1860, H.C. [19].

30 *Belfast Newsletter* (henceforth cited as *BN*), 25 Jul. 1859; *Times*, 27 Jul. 1859.

31 *Times*, 3 Feb. 1860.

32 When the Irish militia was reconstituted in 1854, it relied on the appointment of many officers with no previous military experience, while the continued recruitment of more experienced personnel into the regular army did little to help the situation.

The Irish militia positively received

In contrast to its neighbouring regiment, the South Tipperary Artillery (Militia) had managed to cultivate a positive image in the eyes of both the public and the authorities. The North Tipperary Militia had, of course, taken part in the Nenagh Mutiny, and those from South Tipperary felt the full effect of that mutiny when the regiment arrived in Clonmel in the days after it had taken place. Local magistrates had applied for extra protection for the town and, as noted in the regiment's digest of service (essentially its daily diary for the period), this was because 'they knew the men of the two regiments were the same and they did not sufficiently appreciate what discipline had done for the Corps at hand'.[33]

Along with other militia regiments across the United Kingdom, two years after its original reconstitution, in 1856, the South Tipperary Artillery (Militia) was disembodied. Continued demands on military manpower in the wake of the Indian Rebellion in 1857, meant that selected regiments of militia were re-embodied in 1858, tasked with the garrison of areas of strategic importance across the United Kingdom. Those in the South Tipperary Artillery (Militia) were ordered to leave for England towards the end of the year and were 'surrounded by the friends and relatives of the men who came in crowds to see them off'.[34] Its primary responsibility was to garrison the artillery forts along the south coast of England: Gosport in Hampshire being its first location for this duty, one that it carried out until the summer of 1860. While in the area, one of the responsibilities given to the regiment was to guard Queen Victoria while she was on holiday on the Isle of Wight. This resulted in a change in perception of the regiment: from one that could not be trusted to one that had demonstrated the highest degree of loyalty. One newspaper reporting on the event stated:

> Some dozen years ago, London would have been in a panic had it been informed that the Queen was at her seaside home, protected solely by some hundreds of Irishmen, all freshly arrived from Tipperary whose name was supposed to be synonymous with lawless violence. Now the case is different, and Tipperary turns out, not a body of wild rebels, thirsting for Saxon blood, and practicing for landlord shooting, but an orderly soldier-like body of men, such as few localities in our own Country can boast of.[35]

33 Digest of Service of the South Tipperary Artillery (Militia) (T.N.A., WO 68/88).

34 Ibid.; *Standard*, 2 Nov. 1858.

35 *Globe Newspaper*, 29 Aug. 1860; also quoted in Digest of Service of the South Tipperary Artillery (Militia) (T.N.A., WO 68/88).

The regiment found itself written about in the press days later when it was reported that, on the instigation of its officers, the men were to visit the Crystal Palace in London.[36] Further demonstrating the positive image that the regiment had built for itself, the announcement was made in both local and national newspapers, and was celebrated by those in Ireland.[37] In London, *The Times* reported on the occasion in great detail. In describing the events of the day, as well as the appearance of members of the regiment, it stated,

> here were several hundred young men in the flower of youth and masculine comeliness, clean, orderly, intelligent, and sober to a marvel, now admiring a statue, now a flower, now gazing in wonder on the hollowed trunk of the great tree, now playing innocently on the terraces or in the toy gallery with the little children who accompanied the regiment. Here was Tipperary! – not Tipperary of old- drinking, quarrelling, bloodletting, but Tipperary paid, trusted and disciplined.[38]

In addition, *The Standard* reaffirmed this positivity and revealed how Irish militia units could be viewed as 'loyal' under the right conditions. It stated that

> The Whigs deem it inadvisable to arm the Irish at home, and when the sons of the Green Isle who follow an absurd crusade abroad show no merit of the soldier beyond a love of fighting, it is refreshing to see that 'the might which slumbers in a giants arms', is still to be found in the sister country whenever it is deemed necessary to awake it for our own military purposes, to develop it by kind treatment and good pay, and to organise it by training and discipline. These remarks are called forth by the appearance and demeanour of the Tipperary Artillery Regiment at the Crystal Palace.[39]

Having greeted the occasion in a celebratory manner, the Irish press reportage of the visit continued along similar lines. The *Freeman's Journal* reported that 'never was there such a thoroughly Irish day at the Crystal Palace'.[40] In a more understated celebratory fashion akin to the London press reportage, the *Belfast Newsletter* wrote that: 'Monday was a day of many attractions at the Crystal Palace. Some went to see the pigeons and rabbits, others the poultry and the hollyhocks, great numbers of Irish went down to

36 *BN*, 30 Aug. 1860; *FJ*, 31 Aug. 1860.
37 Ibid.
38 *Times*, 30 Aug. 1860.
39 *Standard*, 30 Aug. 1860.
40 *FJ*, 1 Sept. 1860.

see a regiment ... more Irish than the Irish themselves, a corps collected from the heart of once lawless Tipperary.'[41]

During the day, all seven hundred members of the regiment present visited the grounds and, towards the end of the day, were hosted at a dinner. At the great central hall, after dinner, 'an immense audience assembled to hear the regimental band play "largely Irish airs"'.[42] Finally, a spontaneous cheer, said to have come from both the English and Irish crowd, greeted the regiment as it left to resume its duties.[43] The *Freeman's Journal* once again praised the regiment by paying tribute to the appearance of 'the finest and most soldier-like looking men in her Majesty's service', and to the 'self-respecting, orderly, and even most polite conduct on the part of those who, though but peasants, respect themselves and their country'.[44]

Partly because of its high profile, the Secretary of State for War, Sidney Herbert, controversially began the process of converting the regiment into a permanent brigade of the Royal Artillery in late 1860. It was proposed that most of the initial recruits would come directly from the Tipperary Artillery (Militia), and that it would recruit exclusively from County Tipperary. In essence, as was remarked in the regiment's digest of service, it would become an Irish Artillery Brigade.[45] The corps was created immediately but within two weeks it became clear that the idea had met with some disapprobation. The conflict had played out in the pages of various newspapers, especially *The Times*, where the editorial columns were very quickly filled with a campaign designed to undermine efforts, while the War Office was bombarded with letters of protest.[46] As *The Times* put it, the 'utterly untenable' plan had been abandoned by January 1861. The main contention was that officers of a militia regiment would be promoted ahead of those already in the Royal Artillery, an arm that already had slower rates of promotion.[47] Elements of the nationalist press also reacted with satisfaction arguing that the officers of the regiment had treated their men like cattle being taken to market, and that they had been tricked into joining the new brigade.[48] The fact that the idea was even suggested by military officials, though, was a rare but clear vote of confidence in the loyalty and abilities of Irish soldiers.

Despite dabbling in controversy, the South Tipperary (Artillery) Militia returned to Clonmel in March 1861, where it was afforded the singular

41 *BN*, 4 Sept. 1860.
42 Digest of Service of the South Tipperary Artillery (Militia) (T.N.A., WO 68/88).
43 *Standard*, 30 Aug. 1860.
44 *FJ*, 1 Sept. 1860.
45 Digest of Service of the Tipperary Artillery (Militia) (T.N.A., WO 68/88).
46 *Times*, 8 Dec. 1860. For more details on the plan see Butler, *Irish amateur military tradition*, pp 17–18.
47 *Times*, 19 Dec. 1860.
48 *Nation*, 19 Jan. 1861.

privilege of marching through the town under arms. Its image had evidently come full circle. Circumstances had been kind and allowed the unit to demonstrate its loyalty and re-establish that all important trust with the local inhabitants before its lengthy period of embodiment had come to an end.[49]

Fenianism and the South African War

Positive expressions exhibited by the public notwithstanding, from the 1860s onwards, the Irish militia's political masters were clearly still mistrustful – not least owing to the emerging threat of Fenian infiltration into the armed forces.[50] Thus, the Irish militia took part in a different type of conflict, one in which it became stymied by the authorities and that it could do very little to remedy.

It had been reported in the autumn of 1865 that Fenian agents had achieved great success in their attempts to infiltrate the Irish militia, taking advantage of that year's annual training when large numbers of individuals were gathered in one place over a longer period. The *Irish Times* reported that Fenians were 'eager aspirants for enlistment in the militia', for when the militia was called out for training their drill was perfect, and members of a variety of regiments performed their duties nearly as skilfully as soldiers of the Line. After years of what it labelled as 'deficient' training, this change was put down to the fact that many men were being illegally drilled late at night or early in the morning by Fenian agents sent from America.[51]

Though, perhaps sounding like an exaggeration, *The Times* had reported in early September 1865 that a corporal of the Louth Rifles had been caught and charged with illegally drilling 120 men. A witness had claimed that they had seen the corporal forming men into sections and marching them along a road while calling out phrases closely associated with drill such as: 'close up', 'double up', and 'fall into fours in the front'.[52] Additionally, a non-commissioned officer in the North Down Militia had attempted to convince several of his fellow militiamen to join the Fenian Brotherhood.

49 Letter from E.A. Whitmore, to the Under-Secretary of Ireland, 12 Mar. 1861 (N.L.I. MS. 1057). Enthusiastic scenes were also noted upon the return of the Armagh Light Infantry to their locality. *The historical record of the 3rd Battalion (Princess Victoria's) Royal Irish Fusiliers* (RIF Museum).

50 For more on the Fenian infiltration of the British army see E. Ó Cathaoir, *Soldiers of liberty: a study of Fenianism 1858–1908* (Dublin, 2018), pp 118–38; Virgina Crossman, *Politics, law and order in 19th century Ireland* (Basingstoke, 1996); A.J. Semple, 'The Fenian infiltration of the British army' in *Journal of the Society for Army Historical Research*, lii, no. 211 (1964), pp 133–60.

51 *Irish Times*, 5 Sept. 1865; *Standard*, 6 Sept. 1865; *DC*, 6 Sept. 1865; *CO*, 9 Sept. 1865.

52 *Times*, 5 Sept. 1865.

This continued into 1866 when members of the Antrim Militia were arrested for a similar offence.[53] Eight men of the Kilkenny Fusiliers were also prosecuted for their role in similar activities during February of that year.[54] In response to these events, the annual training of the Irish militia was suspended during that summer. The Chief Secretary to the Treasury, Chichester Fortescue stating in Parliament that

> it would be unfair to the militia to call them together in large masses at a time when all the barracks in Ireland which usually received them were filled by detachments of troops, and to expose them to the attempts and to the machinations of Fenian agents, who, the Government knew, from information they had received, had directed their endeavours especially ... to the corruption of the Irish Militia.[55]

He went on to say that 'the Irish militia must inevitably be more or less affected by the spirit of Fenianism, as the class from which they are mainly recruited was unfortunately more or less tainted with it', and that 'without meaning to cast an imputation on the fidelity and loyalty of the militia as a body, it was impossible for them to escape from the infection'.[56] Throughout the 1870s, suspicion lingered as arrests of militiamen continued to be made. With no annual training, Fenianism was exhibited in a different way, namely through the theft of arms from military barracks. For example, two non-commissioned officers from the South Cork Militia were charged and imprisoned for organising and carrying out a theft of eight firearms at the barracks in Cork.[57] Cork appears to have been a hotspot for this type of activity. In Mallow, where the North Cork Rifles' barracks was situated, 120 firearms were stolen in 1871. Suspicion for the act fell on those on guard duty at the time, who, it was deemed, had allowed it to take place.[58] A similar theft took place at the same barracks six years later, although, on this occasion, the regiment was absolved of any involvement.[59]

For the British authorities, the potential for Fenian infiltration into the Irish militia was not the only perceived threat. Though training had been reinstituted for all units in 1872, the Land War in the latter years of the decade had resulted in its suspension once more in 1880. It was remarked that

53 *Nation*, 12 Aug. 1865; *BN*, 20 Oct. 1865; *Times*, 23 Feb. 1866; *Times*, 27 Feb. 1866.
54 *Morning Post*, 26 Feb. 1866; *Bristol Mercury*, 3 Mar. 1866. There were also several arrests made into 1867, including that of three men of the North Mayo Rifles, see *Times*, 17 May 1867.
55 Parl. Debs (House of Commons (HC)), vol. 183, cols 177–80, 30 Apr. 1866.
56 Ibid.
57 *FJ*, 18 Jul. 1873; Parl. Debs (HC), vol. 217, cols 970–1, 25 Jul. 1873.
58 *FJ*, 20 Jun. 1871.
59 Ibid., 28 Jun. 1877.

the decision had been taken because of 'a system of lawless terrorism which prevails over many parts of Ireland'.[60] It was even specifically noted that, for those serving in the Kerry Militia, 'nearly all are members of the Land League'.[61] It is not difficult to conclude that those serving in other militia regiments were also members. The decision to suspend training also had wider implications, particularly on the number of men enlisting or re-enlisting in the force, and it soon found itself nearly a third down on its establishment.[62] Annual training was seen as such a significant draw for recruits – especially those considering a transfer to the regular army – and that continued mistrust on behalf of the authorities could only result in a reduction in numbers.[63]

The inability to recruit enough men was a long-term result of the continued suspension of annual training. It also had consequences for the number of recruits from Ireland joining the regular army, and affected the strategic utility of the Irish militia in the broader context of home defence.[64] Questions about its loyalty also persisted and, by the mid-1880s, it was clear that, in the event of a conflict, most Irish regiments (both regular and militia) would be removed from Ireland as soon as was feasibly possible. In plans drawn up in late 1886, it had been decided that all Irish militia regiments, except six that were 'well known to be loyal', would be moved to England in order to carry out garrison duties there.[65] Those deemed to be 'loyal' were the four battalions of the Royal Irish Rifles, the former North Downshire Militia, Antrim Militia, Royal South Down Light Infantry, and the Louth Rifles (by this stage the county titles had been replaced so as to integrate the militia more closely with the regular army, and these regiments were known respectively as the 3rd, 4th, 5th

60 Letter from the Earl of Donoughmore to Mr Forster on the State of Ireland, 8 Oct. 1880 (T.N.A., CAB 37/3/68).

61 Letter from the Adjutant of the Kerry Militia, to the Under-Secretary at Dublin Castle, 8 Jan. 1881 (N.L.I., MS 1304).

62 Militia regiments. Return showing the establishment of each regiment of militia in the United Kingdom; and the numbers present, absent, and wanting to complete 1885 [C.4675].

63 For more on the draw of annual training see the evidence presented by militia officers in the following: Report of the committee appointed to enquire into certain questions that have arisen with respect to the militia, together with minutes of evidence and appendices, 1890 [C.5922]; Royal Commission on the Militia and Volunteers. Appendices to the minutes of evidence taken before the Royal Commission on the Militia and Volunteers, 1904 [Cd.2064].

64 The percentage of Irishmen in the British army steadily declined throughout the latter nineteenth century. The inability of the militia to hold annual training was clearly a factor in this, but was one of many other factors influencing this downward trend, not least because of the decreasing pool of available manpower because of the Famine and emigration. See H.J. Hanham, 'Religion and nationality in the mid-Victorian army' in M.R.D. Foot (ed), *War and society: historical essays in honour of J.R. Western* (London, 1973).

65 Reports of a Committee on Army Mobilisation, Dec. 1886 (T.N.A., WO 147/33).

and 6th Battalion, Royal Irish Rifles[66]), as well as the 4th and 5th Battalions of the Royal Inniskilling Fusiliers. It is no coincidence that these regiments drew recruits predominantly from the Protestant population in Ulster who, by this time, were deemed to be more trustworthy than their Catholic counterparts.

By the 1890s, those battalions of the Royal Inniskilling Fusiliers were no longer deemed loyal, and neither was the 6th Battalion, Royal Irish Rifles, leaving only the three battalions of the latter regiment in line for service in Ireland in the event of war.[67] This latter recommendation can largely be attributed to the Commander-in-Chief of Forces in Ireland, Sir Garnet Wolseley, whose views were endorsed by the War Office, and broadly involved removing all 'dangerous' elements from the area upon the outbreak of hostilities. When asked for an opinion on the use of Irish forces in Ireland, Wolseley stated:

> I am influenced by the conviction based upon my knowledge of Ireland and Irish ways that you draw the teeth from the elements of possible internal disturbance whenever you remove from Ireland all regular Irish regiments, all the Army Reserve and all the militia regiments except the Antrim, Mid-Ulster and Londonderry Artillery, and the 3rd, 4th, and 5th Royal Irish Rifles, and the 3rd Royal Irish Fusiliers.[68]

Subsequently added to the list of 'loyal' battalions, at the outbreak of the South African War, were the 8th Battalion, King's Royal Rifle Corps, recruited in County Carlow, and the 3rd Battalion, Royal Irish Fusiliers, which had been allocated for garrison duties in Dublin. The damage, however, was already done – it was clear that the authorities viewed the militia in Ireland, particularly those units of a predominantly Catholic composition, negatively. Once again, it took another major conflict to alter this view as the British government scrambled to assemble sufficient forces to subdue the Boer Republics. Yet again, it was only the specific circumstance, namely that the British government had no other option but to trust the Irish militia in this time of war, that caused it to change its attitudes towards a force it had deemed to be largely disloyal for nearly half a century.

It is estimated that 28,000 Irishmen fought in South Africa, and approximately 4,000 did so while serving in the militia. In all, the 3rd Battalion, Royal Munster Fusiliers, 3rd Battalion, Leinster Regiment, 4th and 5th Battalions,

66 For more on the localisation of British auxiliary forces see David French, *Military identities; the regimental system, the British army, and the British people c.1870–2000* (Oxford, 2005), pp 203–31.

67 Irish militia battalions allotted to defended ports in Ireland, 1887–1908 (T.N.A., WO 32/7081).

68 Ibid. Extract from a letter to the War Office from Lord Wolseley, 31 Mar. 1895; Letter from Sir Neville Lyttelton to Lord Wolseley, 25 Apr. 1895.

Royal Dublin Fusiliers, 5th Battalion, Royal Irish Rifles and 9th Battalion, King's Royal Rifle Corps served as whole units in South Africa. In addition, companies of the 3rd and 5th Battalions, Royal Irish Rifles also served there, while detachments of two artillery regiments, the Antrim Royal Garrison Artillery (Militia) and Donegal Royal Garrison Artillery (Militia), united as the Brigade Division Irish Militia Artillery, served in both South Africa and St Helena, and the 5th Battalion, Royal Munster Fusiliers performed garrison duties on Malta and Gozo. This was, however, only a small portion of the total number of militia regiments serving abroad at this time. A total of fifty-nine battalions from across the United Kingdom saw service in South Africa over the course of the war, while other amateur forces, such as the Imperial Yeomanry, were also utilised.[69] Other regiments were also embodied for service at home, and some even refused service abroad when given the option.

Confined largely to a supporting role on garrison duty, transporting supplies or guarding prisoners, these forces, as they had done in the 1850s, performed crucial work in support of the British fighting forces. Many were publicly recognised for this work in the regiments' localities when lavish parties and banquets were often put on for leaving or returning soldiers, while war relief funds were also setup in several areas, especially those directly connected to those serving abroad.[70]

Conclusion

Not long after the conflict in South Africa, and partly because of the poor performance of British armed forces in the field, the militia across the whole United Kingdom was disbanded. In England, Wales and Scotland, a series of reforms resulted in the establishment of the Territorial Force in 1906. In Ireland though, no such force came into being. A mounted force of yeomanry (the North and South Irish Horse) was permitted to exist, as well as Special Reserve battalions. The militia appeared to have lost its final battle with the authorities in Westminster. As the threat of a European war re-emerged on the horizon, Sir Neville Lyttelton, by now the General Officer Commanding Forces in Ireland, declared to the War Office in 1909 that 'the time has now come when the Irish soldiers can safely be entrusted with the local defence of Ireland'.[71] Necessity, seemingly, once more dictated that Irish amateur

69 Butler, *Irish amateur military tradition*, p. 145; Keith Jeffery, 'The Irish soldier in the Boer War' in John Gooch (ed), *The Boer War: direction, experience and image* (London, 2013), p. 142.

70 See *Pall Mall Gazette*, 20 Feb. 1900; *Morning Post*, 23 Feb. 1900; Digest of Service of the North Cork Rifles (T.N.A., WO 68/306).

71 Letter from Sir Neville Lyttelton to the War Office, 14 Sept. 1909 (T.N.A., WO 32/7081).

forces could be trusted at home, at least in the short term, though manpower shortages and the increasingly challenging political situation in Ireland before 1914 meant that this was never fully realised.

As with the majority of the nineteenth century though, it was only the advent of war and necessity for manpower that had brought this situation about. The Crimean War and Indian Rebellion had permitted the Irish militia to demonstrate its loyalty when called into existence in the late 1850s when soldiers were required for garrison duties and for the line, both roles of which the militia in Ireland could perform. Following significant years of distrust thereafter, on account of Fenianism and the Land Wars, the South African War afforded the militia in Ireland another opportunity to demonstrate its loyalty.

The period, however, was dominated by conflict between the Irish militia and various external actors, which did much to harm its reputation. The political backdrop mentioned above, meant that the militia in Ireland often clashed with its political masters in Dublin and London. This conflict demonstrated that trust was often conditional and resulted in continued questions about its reliability, though was often made worse by the actions, including rioting and disorder, of individual regiments. The Irish militia also came into physical conflict with both British and Irish citizens, especially during periods of training and embodiment when the two groups often clashed. Sometimes this was the result of a hostility held by civilians towards the militia, at other times the militia clearly held responsibility. Similarly, and occasionally with a more deadly outcome, the militia came into conflict with other British regular forces. Most incidents resulted in a damaged reputation for Irish soldiers, partly because sometimes the fault lay with the militia.

There were, of course, occasional bright spots – the Tipperary Artillery (Militia)'s responsibility in guarding Queen Victoria, its visit to the Crystal Palace and even the Irish militia's role during the South African War being obvious examples, but they just go to show the conditional nature of this perception. A particular set of circumstances, namely that usually a crisis or emergency leaving the government in Westminster with few other options, had to exist to inspire loyalty. Without that, conflict with a variety of different groups became the dominant feature of the militia's existence in the nineteenth century.

9

Sir Hugh Gough's Press Wars, 1843–49

Gerry O'Keeffe

Introduction

On 21 February 1880, the thirty-first anniversary of the Battle of Gujrat (fought in the Punjab of northern India), an equestrian statue by John Henry Foley was unveiled in honour of Field Marshal Viscount Hugh Gough in Dublin's Phoenix Park. The monument depicted an eighty-three-year-old Gough as an all-conquering imperial soldier dressed in full military regalia.[1] The representation later attracted the odium of militant Irish republicans who considered it a valorisation of British imperialism and, from December 1944, the monument was repeatedly vandalised until it was eventually bombed off its plinth in July 1957.[2] An extract from the inscription on the pedestal reads as follows: 'In honour of Field Marshal Viscount Gough [...] an illustrious Irishman whose achievements in the Peninsular War, in China, in India have added to the lustre of the military glory of the country which he faithfully served [...] this statue [...] was erected by his Friends and Admirers.' Following its unveiling, the military band present struck up 'St Patrick's Day'.[3] The mid-twentieth-century controversies surrounding the equestrian effigy's symbolism renewed a polemical discourse that centred on Gough himself one hundred years earlier. This paper will examine the response of the O'Connellite press to intense British criticism of Gough in the first quarter of 1849 and the light that this sheds on nationalist Ireland's unstable relationship with empire at this time.[4]

1 *Freeman's Journal* (henceforth cited as *FJ*), 23 Feb. 1880; *Illustrated London News*, 6 Mar. 1880.

2 *Irish Press*, 25 Dec. 1944, 11 Apr. 1945; *Irish Times*, 6 Nov. 1956, 31 Jul. 1957, 18 Dec. 1961, 29 Dec. 2018. The restored equestrian of Gough is presently located on the grounds of Chillingham Castle in Northumberland.

3 *Illustrated London News*, 6 Mar. 1880.

4 For the reaction of the nineteenth-century Irish radical nationalist press to Gough see

Gough in India

In 1843, when Gough assumed the role of commander-in-chief, India, the future of Britain's empire on the subcontinent hung in the balance. Indeed, British anxieties surrounding the humiliating loss of military prestige following the First Anglo-Afghan War (1838–42), which famously witnessed the destruction of Elphinstone's army and provided the context for the entirety of Gough's tenure, as the East India Company sought to consolidate its grip on India. The province of Sindh was annexed in the spring of 1843.[5] In December of the same year a rebellion in the centrally located territory of Gwalior was suppressed, and two wars involving the Company's armies and the Sikh Empire were fought in the Punjab, between 1845 and 1849.[6] By far the most serious threat to British power in India was the encounter with the Sikhs. However, in all three wars that directly involved Gough (Gwalior and the First and Second Anglo-Sikh Wars), the opposing native armies comprised sophisticated forces, schooled to varying degrees in European military tactics.[7] Moreover, these native armies possessed large, skilfully handled artillery components capable of outmatching those of their Company antagonists. Consequently, the Gwalior and Sikh Wars featured uncharacteristically high casualty rates (totalling 10,331 men killed or wounded), especially among the Company's European regiments.[8] These figures shocked a British metropolitan public, accustomed to often facile victories, and Gough was severely censured for his tactics. Colonel George Bruce Malleson (1825–98) damningly noted of Gough: 'few men braver than the soldier who commanded the British army have ever lived; not one who was less of a strategist or a tactician … [u]nder

G.J. O'Keeffe, '"Bravery deserving of a better cause": the British East India Company's Irish soldiers, 1830–60' (unpublished PhD Thesis, Maynooth University, 2022).

5 See W.F.P. Napier, *The conquest of Scinde with some introductory passages in the life of Major-General Sir Charles James Napier* (2nd ed., London, 1845). For First Anglo-Afghan War see for example Antoinette Burton (ed.), *The First Anglo-Afghan Wars: a reader* (Durham, 2014); Michael Barthorp, *Afghan Wars and the North-West Frontier 1839–1947* (London, 1982).

6 Christopher Brice, *Brave as a lion: the life and times of Field Marshal Hugh Gough, 1st Viscount Gough* (Solihull, 2017), pp 223–51, 261–498; Robert Rait, *The life and campaigns of Hugh first Viscount Gough* (2 vols, Westminster, 1903), i, pp 301–41, ii, pp 1–287.

7 J.C. Pollock, *Way to glory: the life of Havelock of Lucknow* (London, 1957), p. 101; G.B. Malleson, *The decisive battles of India: from 1746 to 1849 inclusive* (4th ed., London, 1914), pp 345–6; Harry Smith, *The autobiography of Lieutenant-General Sir Harry Smith* (2 vols, London, 1902), ii, pp 125–6.

8 Rait, *The life and campaigns*, ii, pp 75–8, i, pp 331–2; R.G. Burton, *The First and Second Sikh Wars: an official British Army history* (Yardley, Pennsylvania, 2008), pp 135–9, 145–8; Charles Gough & Arthur Innes, *The Sikhs and the Sikh wars: the rise conquest and annexation of the Punjab state* (London, 1897), pp 131–8.

the excitement of battle he forgot all his plans'.[9] These views were echoed in the critique of Gough carried by the contemporary British newspapers, which likewise denounced his lack of tactical sophistication, his alleged lax implementation of military discipline and his Irish temperament, which supposedly rendered him unfit for command in India.[10]

Most aspects of these debates have been thoroughly treated.[11] However, a striking press war that erupted between the British and Irish newspapers has been all but neglected.[12] Critique of Gough's leadership carried in the British press, which conflated his Irishness with his alleged military incompetence, prompting a robust response from a variety of O'Connellite Irish newspapers. The ensuing public discourse, and the historical context within which it played out (the Great Irish Famine), serve to highlight the fault lines and inequalities that beset the imperial metropole at this time. That this was not merely a knee-jerk response on the part of the O'Connellite press is evident in the extent to which the stereotypical tropes deployed against Gough by the British press continued to exercise the Irish nationalist press (moderate and radical) throughout the ensuing decade where, now inverted, the same tropes were employed to highlight the British establishment's underappreciation of its Irish imperial soldiers.[13]

Gough and the British press

Like Gough – who viewed the press as a 'pest upon all military occasions' – British military figures, generally, had no great love of newspapers and their informants. Indeed, the Duke of Wellington labelled as a 'system of croaking', the tendency whereby disgruntled army officers anonymously used the press either to air private grievances publicly or settle scores with peers and superiors.[14] Moreover, the problem of 'croaking' was deemed so damaging to the Indian army's reputation in July 1835 that a General Order forbidding

9 Malleson, *The decisive battles of India*, p. 356.

10 *Daily News*, 22 Jun. 1846; *Times*, 5 Mar. 1849; *London Morning Herald* (henceforth cited as *LMH*), 5 Mar. 1849; *Morning Post* (henceforth cited as *MP*), 5 Mar. 1849; *Sun* (London), 5 Mar. 1849; *Liverpool Mercury* (henceforth cited as *LM*), 6 Mar. 1849; Rait, *The life and campaigns*, i, p. 333; Brice, *Brave as a lion*, pp 235–50.

11 For Gough's tactical capabilities see Brice, *Brave as a lion*, pp 261–498; Gough & Innes, *The Sikhs and the Sikh wars*; Rait, *The life and campaigns*, ii, pp 1–287; Malleson, *The decisive battles of India*, pp 335–438.

12 Brice touches on this question from a British press perspective only: *Brave as a lion*, pp 235–50.

13 For example: *Nation*, 25 Sep. 1852, 12 Dec. 1857, 26 Dec. 1857.

14 'Gough to Fitzroy Somerset, 3 July 1846' (N.L.I., Gough Papers, MS 50, 120/2/130); *Asiatic Journal*, xxxi (Jan.–Apr., 1840), part 1, pp 2–3.

the practice – on pain of dishonourable discharge – originally issued by the commander-in-chief, India, in June 1822, had to be recirculated.[15] Although it is unsurprising, therefore, that Gough too should find himself targeted by the Indian and British press, the vitriolic and stereotypically Hibernophobic framing of the opprobrium directed against him is striking.

The anti-Gough 'croaking', based on camp gossip, appears to have emanated from sources within Gough's officer corps. For a variety of reasons, a finger of suspicion points to Henry Havelock, who was later a celebrated hero of the Indian Rebellion (1857–59), or his wife Hannah, née Marshman.[16] From 1843 onwards, Havelock became increasingly critical of Goughs's decisions and tactics, even claiming that had his own plan been adopted by Gough at the decisive Battle of Sobraon (10 February 1846), victory would have been secured with one-third of the eventual British casualties. Havelock was a confidante of Lieutenant General Sir Henry Hardinge, the Governor General of India at this time, and stated that Hardinge approved of his battle plan for Sobraon, which Gough had rejected.[17] Havelock was also frustrated with the slow pace of his career trajectory and claimed that a number of his successive superiors, including Gough, had 'picked [his] brains and elevated themselves on [his] exertions'.[18] Additionally, Havelock lost two close friends (Sale and Broadfoot) during the First Sikh War, and lost his older brother, William, at the Battle of Ramnagar during the Second Sikh War. Motives aside, Havelock also had the means to broadcast his displeasure with Gough through his close connection to the Indian press. His brother-in-law, John Clark Marshman, was the proprietor of the *Friend of India* newspaper, one of Gough's most outspoken critics on the subcontinent.[19] Indeed, the *Friend of India* on a number of occasions published Havelock's private critique of Gough's decisions and tactical capabilities almost verbatim.[20] Moreover, according to his biographer, Havelock, had recourse to the term 'Tipperary tactics' in his private correspondence.[21] This phrase was a recurring trope deployed by Gough's most ardent critics.[22] For their part, both Gough and his wife suspected Havelock's involvement in the press leaks, though the latter's

15 *Asiatic Journal*, xix (Jan.–Apr. 1836), part 2, p. 134. See also pp 108, 282–4 of the same issue.

16 Pollock, *Way to glory*, pp 98–114. For Havelock as a celebrated hero, see David Saul, *The Indian Mutiny 1857* (London, 2002), pp 309–31.

17 Pollock, *Way to glory*, pp 108, 110–12; John Clarke Marshman, *The memoirs of Major General Sir Henry Havelock K.C.B.* (3rd ed., London, 1867), pp 152, 157.

18 Pollock, *Way to glory*, pp 98, 103. Pollock reproduced this quote based on his reading of Havelock's private papers.

19 Ibid., pp 16, 114; Saul, *The Indian Mutiny 1857*, p. 240.

20 Pollock, *Way to glory*, pp 104, 112, 114.

21 Ibid., p. 114.

22 *Times*, 5 Mar. 1849; *LMH*, 5 Mar. 1849; *MP*, 5 Mar. 1849; *Sun* (London), 5 Mar. 1849.

biographer denied his complicity in the affair.[23] These considerations, together with his own frustrated career ambitions, probably coloured Havelock's harsh critique of the commander-in-chief's leadership style, providing him, or his wife Hannah, with the motive, opportunity and means to undermine Gough.[24] However, Havelock was far from the only officer in India having an axe to grind with Gough.

Gough's newspaper woes began in the aftermath of the Battle of Maharajpore, during the Gwalior Campaign of December 1843, which witnessed high casualty rates among his European regiments.[25] The Indian and British press reported that the Company's army had brought an insufficient compliment of lower-calibre 'popguns' to the fight.[26] The *Spectator* and other British journals laid the blame for this supposed oversight at Gough's feet, a charge he strenuously denied.[27] Unsurprisingly, these press reports and the camp gossip that informed them irritated Gough, and from this point forward Robert Rait, Gough's hagiographer, noted that a state of war existed between the commander-in-chief and the Indian press.[28]

Criticism of Gough intensified during the Anglo-Sikh Wars, and his national identity became the hook upon which all disapproval of his tactics was hung.[29] Despite defeating the Sikh armies in every battlefield encounter during the First Sikh War, the press lampooned Gough's battlefield nous and regimental control with the terms 'Tipperary tactics' and 'Donnybrook discipline'. In the words of the mid-nineteenth-century commentator, Beaver Henry Blacker, Donnybrook Fair was 'for generations a perfect prodigy of moral horrors, a concentration of disgrace upon, not Ireland alone, but civilized Europe'.[30] Further, under the 1847 Coercion Act, Tipperary (Gough's then home county) was listed among the proclaimed districts.[31] To the contemporary British mind,

23 Pollock, *Way to glory*, p. 112.

24 Marshman, *The memoirs of Major General Sir Henry Havelock*, pp 154–5, 174–8; Pollock, *Way to glory*, pp 112–14; Richard Holms, *Sahib: the British soldier in India* (London, 2005), pp 360, 369.

25 Rait, *The life and campaigns*, i, pp 338–40; Brice, *Brave as a lion*, p. 249; *Times*, 8 Mar. 1844; *Glasgow Citizen*, 23 Mar. 1844; Rait, *The life and campaigns Gough*, i, p. 331.

26 *Times*, 8 Mar. 1844; *Kentish Independent*, 16 Mar. 1844; *Reading Mercury*, 16 Mar. 1844 (citing the *Calcutta Englishman*, *Delhi Gazette*, *Agra Ukhbar*); *Glasgow Citizen*, 23 Mar. 1844.

27 Rait, *The life and campaigns*, i, pp 333–40. For discussion on the Gwalior campaign see Brice, *Brave as a lion*, pp 235–50.

28 Rait, *The life and campaigns*, i, pp 338–40.

29 For critique of Gough's tactics during the two Anglo-Sikh Wars see Brice, *Brave as a lion*, pp 263–497.

30 Beaver H. Blacker, *Brief sketches of the parishes of Booterstown and Donnybrook in the County of Dublin* (Dublin, 1860), pp 13–14, 44–8.

31 *Daily News* (henceforth cited as *DN*), 25 Dec. 1847; *Nation*, 24 Dec. 1847. Under the 1847 Crime and Outrage (Ireland) Act, the inhabitants of proclaimed districts were

therefore, these terms conjured up images of chaotic and crude *Irish* martial attributes that were devoid of *British* science, finesse and discipline.[32]

For example, in June 1846 the *Daily News* stated that 'The *Tipperary tactics* of Sir H. Gough in the recent campaign [First Sikh War] have furnished a fertile theme of discussion and satire to our newspapers for the last fortnight', going on to say that

> they who were at first inclined to condemn the Governor-General [Hardinge], now admit, that to him, and to the bull-dog courage of the troops, do we owe our successes and the averting of fearful disasters. The Commander-in-Chief's Tipperary tactics do not form the only subject of condemnation; his Donnybrook discipline has been severely commented on.[33]

This newspaper's attempt to attribute the successful outcome (from a British perspective) of the First Sikh War to Hardinge and the troops' 'bull-dog' courage is problematic, however. First, the term 'bull-dog' failed to acknowledge the ethnic diversity of Gough's troops (both Indian and European). The Indian army was an overwhelmingly native affair with Company Sepoys outnumbering European soldiers by a factor of five to six, notwithstanding that the strength of the Company's own European regiments was augmented by Crown troops. For example, in 1852, of 288,000 troops serving in India, 239,000 were native Sepoys, 21,000 were Company Europeans and 28,000 comprised Crown forces.[34] Within its European cohort, Irishmen comprised the largest ethnic demographic of the Company's soldiers at this time, as well as a significant proportion within the contemporary Crown army.[35] Indeed,

obliged to hand in all weapons held privately, only firearms licenced by stipendiary magistrates could be retained. See also Enda Delaney, *The curse of reason: the Great Irish Famine* (Dublin, 2012), pp 180, 182.

32 *DN*, 22 Jun. 1846.

33 Ibid.

34 'Report of the commissioners appointed to inquire into the organization of the Indian army; together with the minutes of evidence and appendix 1859 session 1', pp 1–603, H.C. 1859 [2515], v, 21, Appendix 15. This parliamentary paper includes Indian Army returns for the period 1852–57.

35 'Registers of Bengal Army European Soldiers, 1840–1850, A–K' (British Library, IOR/L/MIL/10/124); 'Registers of Bengal Army, 1840–1850, L–Z' (BL, IOR/L/MIL/10/125); 'Bengal Muster Rolls, 31 August 1842 to 1 September 1843' (BL, IOR/L/MIL/10/164); 'Madras Muster Rolls and Casualty Reports for 1850' (BL, IOR/L/MIL/11/157); 'General Annual Return of British Army: 1880', pp 1–102, H.C. 1881 (C.3083), lviii, pp 65–6; 'Return of the number of English, Scotch, and Irish non-commissioned officers and privates in the British army, in each of the years on the 1st day of January 1830 and 1840', pp 1–2, H.C. 1841 (307), xiv; 'Census of Ireland, 1841, Report of the commissioners appointed to take the census of Ireland for the year

since the early nineteenth century, the Company had consistently recruited more Irishmen than Englishmen.[36] This pattern was particularly marked during the Great Irish Famine, and the only period that witnessed more Englishmen than Irish enlisting with the Company coincided with the final three years of its existence (1858–60), in the context of the Indian Rebellion. However, this was a temporary phenomenon that did not alter the overall Irish complexion of the Company's European regiments in India.[37]

Second, far from 'averting disasters', Hardinge's interventions during the First Sikh War tended to undermine Gough's authority as commander-in-chief.[38] Indeed, the language critiquing Gough that later appeared in British newspapers such as *The Times*, the *Daily News* and the *Morning Herald*, among others, suggests that they may have picked up on the contents of confidential letters, written by Hardinge (who had lost confidence in his commander-in-chief) to the then prime minister Sir Robert Peel, and Lord Ripon, president of the Board of Control for India, in December 1845. The Board of Control had been established under the India Act of 1784 and from its inception, it was empowered to 'superintend, direct, and controul [*sic*], all acts, operation and concerns, which in any wise relate to the civil or military government or revenues of the British territorial possessions in the East Indies'.[39] Though the Board of Control – which comprised a secretary of state, the Chancellor of the Exchequer and four other members of the Privy Council – could exercise considerable control over the activities of the Company and the Court of Directors, the day-to-day relationship between the Court and the Board was typically collaborative and discreet.[40]

At the time of writing, Hardinge sought to have Gough superseded by Sir Charles Napier, and though it was within his right, as Governor General, to set in motion the supersession process, his letters did not place the London authorities in possession of the full circumstances surrounding the conduct of

1841', x [504], H.C. 1843, xxiv; E.M. Spiers, 'Army organisation and society in the nineteenth century' in Thomas Bartlett & Keith Jeffery (eds) *A military history of Ireland* (Cambridge, 1996), p. 337.

36 Thomas Bartlett, 'The Irish Soldier in India, 1750–1947' in Michael Holmes & Denis Holmes (eds), *Ireland and India: connections, comparisons, contrasts* (Dublin, 1997), pp 18–19; Joel Mokyr & Cormac Ó Gráda, 'Height and health in the United Kingdom 1815–1860: evidence from the East India Company' in *Explorations in economic history*, xxxiii, no. 2 (1996), pp 141–68.

37 O'Keeffe, 'Bravery deserving of a better cause', pp 280–1, 292–3.

38 Brice, *Brave as a lion*, pp xx, 276–7, 280–1, 284, 286–96, 306–20. Hardinge was sent to India because the London political establishment and Company directors viewed him as less 'hawkish' than his brother-in-law, Ellenborough, and he assiduously followed the directions given to him by his political masters.

39 Quoted in Ian Barrow, *The East India Company, 1600–1858: a short history with documents* (Cambridge, 2017), p. 63.

40 J.M. Bourne, 'The civil and military patronage of the East India Company, 1784–1858' (unpublished PhD Thesis, University of Leicester, 1977), pp 14–15, 25, 30–5.

the war in India up to that point.[41] In his letter to Peel, Hardinge acknowledged Gough's courage, but accused him of having 'no capacity for administration ... at outposts wonderfully active ... but the more important points ... of framing proper orders and looking to their execution, are very much neglected'.[42] Hardinge's letter to Lord Ripon was written in a similar vein.[43]

The immediate aftermath of the Battle of Ferozeshah, a two-day affair fought on 21 and 22 December 1845, provided the context for Hardinge's letters. Sheer good fortune had secured British success at Ferozeshah, and after the first day of battle Hardinge was said to have remarked to Havelock that 'another such action will shake the empire'. Furthermore, Hardinge so despaired of victory that he issued orders for his state papers to be burned.[44] Gough, however, was unaware that these letters had been sent and, therefore, had no opportunity to defend himself against the allegations contained in them.[45] For the time being, however, this matter was not pursued further and rather than being superseded, Gough's was instead rewarded with a viscountcy.[46]

With the outbreak of the Second Anglo-Sikh War in December 1848, newspaper attacks on Gough were given renewed impetus and vigour, especially following the Battle of Chillianwalla (13 January 1849). This was a particularly bloody affair, characterised by confusion and heavy losses of European troops.[47] Gough, in a letter to Lord Fitzroy Somerset (Crown Army Military Secretary), confessed to being utterly baffled by the actions of some of his brigade and cavalry commanders on the day. The outcome at Chillianwalla was really a stalemate, which Gough claimed as a victory based on the Sikh Army being first to retire from the field.[48] Within a month of Chillianwalla, Gough decisively defeated the Sikh Army at Gujrat in the Punjab (21 February 1849), effectively ending the Sikh Wars.[49]

41 See Brice, *Brave as a lion*, pp 347–57 for the political machinations in India and London following the Battle of Ferozeshah but prior to news of the victory at Sobraon (10 Feb. 1846) reaching London. For Harding's letter to Peel, see Rait, *The life and campaigns*, ii, pp 88–94.

42 Rait, *The life and campaigns*, ii, p. 34.

43 In this role, Ripon provided Government oversight of the Company along with the Court of Directors. See Brice, *Brave as a lion*, pp 350–7 for a discussion on the ramifications and government response to this letter.

44 Marshman, *The memoirs of Major General Sir Henry Havelock*, p. 152; Pollock, *Way to glory*, p. 108; Brice, *Brave as a lion*, pp 326–7; Rait, *The life and campaigns*, ii, pp 88–94.

45 Rait, *The life and campaigns*, ii, pp 34, 88–94.

46 Brice, *Brave as a lion*, pp 356–7.

47 The British casualty return from the Battle of Chillianwalla totalled 2,357 of whom 602 were killed and 104 missing. See Brice, *Brave as a lion*, p. 461.

48 'Gough to Fitzroy Somerset, Headquarters Camp Chillianwalla, 17 January 1849' (N.L.I., Gough Papers, MS 50, 120/2/136).

49 'Gough to Fitzroy Somerset, camp before Goojrat, 1 March 1849' (N.L.I., Gough Papers, MS 50, 120/2/136).

Unofficial reports of Chillianwalla reached Britain from India in early March 1849, ahead of official despatches. These were greeted with universal dismay in the British newspapers, which excoriated Gough for the ensuing month. News of Gujrat did not arrive until April. But even prior to Chillianwalla, some London newspapers were already calling for Gough's supersession. In January 1849, the *Standard* carried a lengthy article lamenting a decade of British decline in India. 'Never was [there] a time', the article proclaimed, when 'our Indian Empire [was] in greater peril'.[50] While lauding Gough's 'mere bull-dog bravery', the article denigrated his command ability stating 'there must be a head to direct as well as the arm to execute'. The *Standard* concluded that one name would 'resound' throughout British India as a replacement for Gough: 'Napier'.[51] The three themes expressed here – Gough's command incompetence, his undoubted courage and who his successor should be – aligned closely with the *Daily News* article of two-and-a-half years earlier and, especially, with the views expressed in Hardinge's letters of December 1845, all of which combined to present a damning indictment of the Irish general.[52]

From 3 March 1849 onwards, unofficial casualty returns and reports following Chillianwalla, derived from the Indian press and private letters, began to circulate in Britain. The early editions of the London papers on 5 March railed against Gough.[53] The *Morning Herald* infantilised him as having 'the hot impulsive brain of a boy' and being 'a thoughtless, impetuous, Hibernian fighting man ... no more able to restrain himself than a child', before continuing 'Good God! are our troops to be mown by thousands because the Irish blood of a hair-brained commander cannot stand a stray shot or two from the enemy's guns?' The paper claimed that Gough's 'Irish blood' had been provoked into precipitously initiating the battle when a stray Sikh artillery round landed close to him.[54] The *Morning Post* declared Gough's actions to be those of 'a vulgar gladiator', further stating that his duty was to be 'the head that thinks rather than the arm that strikes', reiterating the sentiments expressed in the *Standard* a month earlier.[55] The *Daily News* announced '[h]ere are Englishmen and an English army ... making war in the same savage way as the first barbarians that clothed themselves in skins ... ordered to conquer by

50 *Standard*, 29 Jan. 1849.
51 *Standard*, 29 Jan. 1849; *FJ*, 5 Mar. 1859.
52 *Standard*, 29 Jan. 1849; *DN*, 22 Jun. 1846; Rait, *The life and campaigns*, ii, pp 88–94.
53 *Sun* (London), 5 Mar. 1849, carried extracts from the morning editions of the *Times*, *Chronicle*, *Morning Herald*, *Morning Post*, and *Daily News* under the headline 'SPIRIT of the PUBLIC JOURNALS' on that day.
54 *Evening Sun* (London), 5 Mar. 1849.
55 *Sun* (London), 5 Mar. 1849; *Standard*, 29 Jan. 1849.

brute force, and met by barbarians, who showed far more skill and coolness'.[56] This article pointedly went on to remind its readers that 'the General [Gough] was known by the whole empire to be incapable ... and none can so fully tell his merits as Lord Hardinge'.[57] Analogies were drawn between Chillianwalla and Elphinstone's disastrous retreat from Kabul in January 1842, and it was claimed that Wellington had warned the Company of Gough's incompetence in 1848 and had advised the Court of Directors to appoint Charles Napier as commander-in-chief, rather than extend Gough's tenure.[58]

The *Times* proclaimed that 'Leadenhall-street [the Court of Directors] must remember that the Indian empire is not a *personal* affair' and that the very name of Napier was worth five thousand men, enough to strike terror into the Sikhs.[59] The *Times* also published unsubstantiated reports from letters penned by a variety of unnamed informants in India, which were solely based on camp gossip.[60] It was stated that Gough, had planned to fight the battle on 14 January but was provoked into 'a passion' that could not be reasoned with when Sikh artillery shots had landed close to him on the afternoon of 13 January. The 'Tipperary tactics' he subsequently employed, it was stated, resulted in an utterly uncoordinated attack that led to battlefield confusion. Gough allegedly 'swore to drive the *Sakes* from the face of the earth' and on this basis committed his army to battle with 'every general and brigadier [sent] on his own way, receiving no orders – the same way as you imagine the Sikhs doing'.[61] An unnamed army surgeon was reported as saying:

> I hear on all sides it would be a wise and prudent measure on the part of the governor-general [Dalhousie] to recall Lord Gough from the Punjab ... His lordship fancied himself at Donnybrook Fair, and was in the thick of it, in the *melee*, and lost to sight ... I hear on all sides his troops have lost confidence in him.[62]

These reports were disseminated verbatim in the British provincial press over the ensuing days.[63] The *Spectator*, in its reportage on Chillianwalla went so far as to suggest that Gough's perceived incompetence evinced sinister intents.[64] This bizarre allegation was made in the context of two articles: one

56 *Sun* (London), 5 Mar. 1849.
57 Ibid.
58 Ibid.
59 *Times*, 5 Mar. 1849; *FJ*, 6 Mar. 1849.
60 *Times*, 5 Mar. 1849; *LM*, 6 Mar. 1849; *FJ*, 5 Mar. 1849.
61 *Times*, 5 Mar. 1849.
62 Ibid.
63 *LM*, 6 Mar. 1849; *Dublin Evening Mail*, 7 Mar. 1849; *Scotsman*, 7 Mar. 1849.
64 *Spectator*, 10 Mar. 1849.

that dismantled Gough's military reputation, and a shorter piece questioning his loyalty. 'Although Lord Gough is as strong and tough in courage as ever', noted the *Spectator* in its first article, 'he … is a commander who inspires confidence only in the enemy … He has been training the Sikh armies into very efficient enemies.'[65] This article was immediately followed by the *Spectator's coup de grâce* for Gough:

> The Irish sympathy with Sikh successes shows, too, that it will not be politic to withdraw the garrison from Ireland and leave that country at the mercy of Shere Singh's Celtic allies … By the by, is not Lord Gough an Irishman? and if so, does not his peculiar kind of victory fall in very curiously with the Irish sympathy for the Sikhs.[66]

In its haste to condemn Gough, the *Spectator* essentially characterised him as a clandestine Irish radical nationalist, sympathetic to the Sikh cause.

The response of the O'Connellite press

The British condemnation of Gough elicited a remarkable response from several of Ireland's O'Connellite newspapers, including the popular *Freeman's Journal*,[67] the *Cork Examiner*, the *Tipperary Vindicator* and the *Galway Vindicator*, among other titles. These newspapers comprised a variety of geographically dispersed provincial and Dublin-based independent liberal organs with widespread circulations, which offered varying perspectives on Gough and his Irish soldiers in imperial service.[68] While their influential proprietors/editors were firmly supportive of Daniel O'Connell's repeal campaign, relations between them and O'Connell had at times been fractious.[69] These sprang to Gough's

65 Ibid.

66 Ibid.

67 Sir John Gray grew the *Freeman's Journal* circulation from about two to three thousand in 1841 to ten thousand in 1875. See Felix M. Larkin, 'The old woman of Prince's Street: *Ulysses* and the *Freeman's Journal*' in *Dublin James Joyce Journal*, no. 4 (2011), pp 14–30; Larkin, *The Freeman's Journal* (www.blog.nli.ie/index.php/2012/08/21/thefreemansjournal/) (accessed 14 May 2023). Reading rooms and public reading could greatly boost these numbers. See R.F. Foster, *Modern Ireland, 1600–1972* (London, 1989), pp 310–17; Marie-Louise Legg, *Newspapers and nationalism: the Irish provincial press, 1850–1892*, pp 58–71.

68 For these papers' circulation areas, see Legg, *Newspapers and nationalism*, pp 67–71, 177–222.

69 These proprietors include Sir John Gray, John Francis Maguire, Maurice Lenihan, J.P. Blake and others. For O'Connell's relationship with the Irish press see Brian Ingles, 'O'Connell and the Irish press, 1800–42' in *Irish historical studies*, viii, no. 29 (Mar. 1952), pp 1–27.

defence, seeking to present a more incisive and nuanced critique of his predicament in India. Three common themes permeated the commentary published in these papers: criticism for British rule, a robust defence of Gough and Britain's dependence on Irish soldiers to man its imperial war machine. As if picking up on the *Standard*'s anxieties from the previous January, the *Cork Examiner* concurred that

> British power in India was never in a more critical situation. Everything of settlement unsettled; millions of men suddenly bursting from bondage ... which seems to portend the not distant downfall of a dominion built up at more cost of blood and gold than any in ancient or modern times ... The Sikhs appear to have fought with a bravery worthy of any troops.[70]

Here the *Examiner* censured imperial Britain's injustice, violence and greed in India while lauding the courage of the Sikhs. This was followed by the *Examiner*'s expression of support for Gough, which contrasted his courage with an allusion to the cowardice shown by two Crown cavalry regiments that reputedly fled the field at Chillianwalla.[71]

> Those who are ready to embrace any excuse for a defeat,... endeavour to lay all the blame of this unsuccessful attack upon Lord Gough's rashness ... We suspect that his lordship's country [Ireland] enters largely into the [good] estimate of his qualifications. So we interpret the allusions to 'Tipperary tactics,' to his pronunciation of 'the *sakes*,' and the expression that during the engagement he seemed to fancy himself at Donnybrook Fair ... though the Commander-in-Chief may retain his native brogue, he is a brave man ... we [Irish] are glad to think that rashness is a fault more excusable than cowardice ...[72]

The *Examiner* concluded by highlighting the Government's immoral fiscal priorities at home, in the context of the Famine crisis, while Irish soldiers fought and died for empire in India:

> Contrast the sums lavished upon the destruction of life abroad with the sums refused to preserve it at home ... there was no distinction of country among those who in this last and terrible carnage shed

70 *Cork Examiner* (henceforth cited as *CE*), 7 Mar. 1849.

71 The cowardice alluded to the disorderly flight of the 9th Lancers and 14th Light Dragoons at Chillianwalla. See Brice, *Brave as a lion*, pp 457–9.

72 *CE*, 7 Mar. 1849.

> their lives to uphold her [England's] sway. Even our own city [Cork] is not without hearths made desolate by the loss of men, who fell fighting with a bravery deserving of a better cause, than the attempt to subjugate a people whose struggle, disfigured by many vices, is yet redeemed by the great and sacred name of freedom.[73]

It is striking that while lauding the misplaced courage of the Irish and British soldiers, caught up in the Punjab conflict, the *Examiner* resisted the impulse to condemn the Sikh struggle, though it was 'disfigured by many vices'. This probably referenced reports that, during the Sikh Wars, wounded Company and Crown soldiers abandoned on the battlefield were routinely mutilated.[74] The *Examiner*'s commentary sought to balance condemnation of British imperial excesses in India with a commensurate obligation to laud the military virtue of Gough and his soldiers, many of whom were not only Irish, but fellow Corkmen.

The *Tipperary Vindicator,* wrestling with similar tensions, offered a different approach to reporting on Gough's difficulties. Its 7 March 1849 edition devoted most of its front page to reproducing the *Morning Chronicle*'s reports on Chillianwalla, published a few days earlier. However, it did not reproduce London's Hibernophobic tirade against Gough. The *Vindicator* chose, rather, to counter these attacks by arguing that placing the blame solely on the Irish general's shoulders for the perceived disaster in India was unfair. Gough was favourably compared with the French marshal, Michel Ney, and lauded as 'bravest of the brave' and 'impetuous as a lion'.[75] Moreover, the *Vindicator*'s London correspondent highlighted Gough's popularity among the troops he commanded.[76] However, in relation to his temperament, it was conceded that the Sikhs – whose military virtues were also extolled – were aware of Gough's impetuosity, and had possibly lured him into a well-prepared trap at Chillianwalla.[77]

The *Galway Vindicator, and Connaught Advertiser* likewise mounted a sympathetic defence of Gough saying:

> English journals have discovered a sufficient cause for the disaster [at Chillianwalla] in the "Irish blood" of the valiant veteran [Gough], at the same time that the *Times* is calling lustily for the reappointment

73 Ibid.

74 Brice, *Brave as a lion*, pp 369–70.

75 *Tipperary Vindicator* (henceforth cited as *TV*), 7 Mar. 1849; *Morning Chronicle*, 3 Mar. 1849.

76 *TV*, 7 Mar. 1849.

77 Ibid.

> of Sir C[harles] Napier, whose Irish blood once did the Government a good service in India [the annexation of Sindh].[78]

This newspaper evidently savoured the 'piquant irony' in *The Times*'s call to appoint Napier as Gough's replacement, given both generals' Irish connections. Napier had been raised in Ireland from the age of three.[79]

Unlike the *Cork Examiner* and the *Tipperary Vindicator* however, the *Limerick and Clare Examiner* expressed antipathy for the Sikhs while simultaneously using the 'Irish blood' motif to highlight empire's dependence on Irish soldiers in India suggesting that 'more British and Irish blood must flow, perhaps in a wider and still deeper current', before the situation on the subcontinent could be stabilised. While supporting the view that Napier should replace Gough, this support was qualified:

> We do not love English rule, but we love Sikh supremacy and slaughter of our [Irish] countrymen infinitely less; and so we shall be glad to hear of Lord Gough's triumph – if he can achieve it. He is infamously, rancorously and specifically assailed because he is an Irishman.[80]

Yet again, the prominent presence of Irish soldiers in India obliged these independent O'Connellite newspapers to temper their odium for British colonial rule at home with praise for the military virtue of the Irish involved in upholding colonial rule abroad.

Meanwhile, the *Freeman*'s response to the British newspapers' slight on the value of 'Irish blood' to empire was even more expansive and laden with sarcasm than the other O'Connellite organs:

> England and her empire has already suffered too much from the prevalence of Irish blood in the veins of her generals, her admirals, her fleets and her armies! That 'Irish blood' of old Garret Wellesley flowing in the veins of Arthur at Plassey [*sic*] and Talavera, Vittoria and Waterloo, was a national calamity. Sir Charles Napier, at Meannee and Hyderabad, had villainous Irish blood in his veins, and triumphed there with his old 'Tipperary boys'. We shall not enumerate all the misfortunes which have befallen England from this 'Irish blood' calamity ...[81]

78 *Galway Vindicator, and Connaught Advertiser*, 7 Mar. 1849.

79 Robert Hamilton Vetch, 'Napier, Charles James (1782–1853)' in Leslie Stephen and Sidney Lee (eds), *Dictionary of National Biography* (63 vols, London, 1885–1900), xl, pp 45–54. See page 45.

80 *Limerick and Clare Examiner*, 7 Mar. 1849.

81 *FJ*, 6 Mar. 1849.

The 'Tipperary boys' fighting at the Battle of Miani (7 February 1843) referenced by the *Freeman* alluded to the ethnic composition of the 22nd (Cheshire) Regiment of Foot, which Sir Charles Napier claimed as 'Irish'. Here the *Freeman*'s rebuttal of the London establishment's attacks on Gough drew on an imperfect military history lesson to highlight the contributions of Irish soldiers to imperial expansion in the first half of the nineteenth century.[82] The *Freeman* further censured the *Herald* and *Times* for using camp gossip to

> condemn and ruin an absent man – a gallant veteran who had so well stood to England in her greatest need – without a particle of evidence beyond the private accounts of persons who may have themselves contributed to the loss of the field ascribed to their commander.[83]

Crucially again, at no point throughout this polemical discourse was any attempt made by these O'Connellite newspapers to condemn either Gough or his Irish soldiers outright for their participation in the imperial state's oppressive apparatus in India. Nor should we find it surprising that this was the case when, for two decades to come, the evolving mainstream nationalist 'political culture' in Ireland followed an O'Connellite model of 'conditional monarchism'.[84] Accordingly, Christine Kinealy has noted how, throughout the nineteenth and into the twentieth centuries, Irish nationalism – depending on its flavour – could vacillate between 'reform and revolution'.[85]

The denouement of Gough's press war

Ultimately, uncertainty regarding the campaign outcome in India in 1849, in addition to the mounting pressures of British public opinion, and an unfolding newspaper frenzy in Britain, unsettled the government in India and resulted in an official request from Governor General Dalhousie seeking Gough's supersession and recall.[86] 'Why', *The Times* asked, 'are the destinies

82 The *Freeman's Journal* had incorrectly placed Arthur Wellesley at the Battle of Plassey (1757), rather than at the Battle of Assaye (1803).

83 *FJ*, 6 Mar. 1849.

84 Christine Kinealy, 'At home with the empire: the example of Ireland' in Catherine Hall & Sonya Rose (eds), *At home with the Empire: metropolitan culture and the imperial world* (Cambridge, 2006), pp 85, 93–4; J.H. Murphy, 'Fashioning the famine queen' in Peter Gray (ed.), *Victoria's Ireland? Irishness and Britishness, 1837–1901* (Dublin, 2004), pp 15–26.

85 Kinealy, 'At home with the empire: the example of Ireland', pp 80, 85.

86 Rait, *The life and campaigns*, ii, pp 290–6; Clarke, *The East India register and directory for 1849* (London, 1849), Bengal, p. 3.

[*sic*] of India, why is so much British blood and treasure, at the mercy of a man whose sole qualification for that trust is mere animal courage?'[87] This article also appealed directly to the Duke of Wellington, Parliament and the Court of Directors to do their duty and remove Gough. London capitulated to the pressure and Charles Napier was selected to supersede Gough with immediate effect.[88] Ironically, on Saint Patrick's Day 1849, a celebratory feast was held in honour of Napier at the London Tavern on the eve of his departure for India.[89]

Unknown to London, Gough had already decisively defeated the Sikh Empire at the Battle of Gujrat in February. The Sikh Wars were, to all intents and purposes, over. Confounding his detractors, Gough produced an almost textbook victory, combining infantry, artillery and cavalry (with relatively few casualties), as a swan-song to his career.[90] The news of the victory arrived in London after Napier's rushed departure. Amid parliamentary blushes, English press vitriol against Gough quickly transformed into popular acclaim.

In Ireland, as news filtered through of Gough's supersession, the *Tipperary Vindicator,* as a counterweight, published an article detailing Gough's achievements over his by then fifty-five-year military career, describing him as a 'gallant soldier'.[91] As the first intimations of Gough's victory at Gujrat reached England ahead of official despatches, the *Vindicator* stood squarely behind Gough reporting that

> [a]t the very time the ruffian press of England were assailing with opprobious [*sic*] epithets, and seeking to tarnish the reputation of our countryman, the brave and gallant Lord GOUGH, that fearless veteran and illustrious Irishman was achieving a glorious victory ... and the entire camp of the enemy fell into the victorious hands of this 'Tipperary man' as the *Times* in derision called him.[92]

Here again it is noteworthy that despite its impulse to side with the Sikhs in their struggle against Britain's imperial forces, the *Tipperary Vindicator* was obliged, for the sake of upholding Irish military virtue, to oscillate between imperial condemnation and imperial accommodation.

Later in April, following the arrival of official despatches from India, votes of thanks to the Indian army and Gough were proposed in the House of

87 *Times*, 5 Mar. 1849.
88 Rait, *The life and campaigns*, ii, pp 290–6.
89 *Times*, 19 Mar. 1849; Brice, *Brave as a lion*, pp 474–5.
90 'Gough to Fitzroy Somerset, camp before Goojrat, 1 March 1849' (N.L.I., Gough Papers, MS 50, 120/2/136); *FJ*, 27 Apr. 1849; Brice, *Brave as a lion*, pp 495, 501.
91 *TV*, 24 Mar. 1849.
92 Ibid., 7 Apr. 1849.

Commons by Sir John Hobhouse,[93] the *Freeman* was not slow to capitalise on the irony.[94] Citing an article from 'the *Press*', the *Freeman* proclaimed:

> 'Tipperary tactics' are, after all, not quite so despicable a commodity as our scientific, strategic, London compeers would have the world imagine, Lord Gough, the 'incompetent old Irish gladiator' – the 'Donnybrook combatant' ... has added a leaf of evergreen to the laurels of the United Kingdom at Goojerat, which our scornful cotemporaries are now no way backward in entwining with their national chaplet. Considering how much of the wreath has been contributed by our [Irish] countrymen, we would humbly remind Britannia that looks of impudence towards either Tipperary or Donnybrook are not quite becoming under brows so decorated.[95]

Yet again, the salient issue here was not that great numbers of Irishmen, drawn from across the socio-economic spectrum, were engaged in defending and expanding the bounds of empire and coercively upholding British colonialism in India. The *Freeman*'s grievance centred rather on the lack of recognition and gratitude extended by the British press and political establishment to Irish soldiers for their contributions to empire building.

Though the *Tipperary Vindicator* lamented the subjugation of the Punjab and 'the fallen freedom of the Sikhs', its praise for Gough, 'the Tipperary man' and 'grey haired warrior Irishman', was fulsome, as was its praise for the 'characteristic gallantry' of Gough's 'fellow- countrymen' who 'rushed to the encounter, and dealt destruction and death among the opposing ranks'.[96] However, a note of caution was also sounded: accommodating empire, as the O'Connellite press, including the *Tipperary Vindicator*, was obliged to do for the time being, was not in Ireland's best interests.

> Yet mark the ingratitude of the nation they serve – look at the condemnation that was heaped on Lord Gough now so strongly falsified, and listen if you can, to the abuses pronounced by the ruffian *Times* and the rancorous *Mail*, against the Irish people who pour out their blood like water in achieving victories for a country hostile to their interests.[97]

93 For Hobhouse's presidency of the India Board at the time see Clarke, *The East India register and directory for 1849* (London, 1849), Bengal, p. xv.

94 *Hansard 3, Military operations in the Punjab–vote of thanks*, civ, 755 (24 Apr. 1849); *Morning Chronicle*, 25 Apr. 1849.

95 *FJ*, 27 Apr. 1849.

96 *TV*, 21 Apr. 1849.

97 Ibid.

As for Gough, he ultimately returned to London as an all-conquering imperial hero and a wealthy man, his share of the prize money and *batta* from the Punjab campaigns, alone, amounted to approximately £21,000 sterling.[98]

Conclusion

Gough's press wars shed light on the nuanced attitudes to the participation of Irishmen in empire emanating from the British print and political establishments and the independent moderate Irish nationalist press at the height of the Great Famine. Though these O'Connellite newspapers generally deplored Britain's imperial policies in India and Ireland, they simultaneously accorded with one another in defending Gough and the Irish soldiers tasked with implementing those policies in India. The polemical discourse centred on Gough, and the Great Famine context within which it played out, exposed the mid-nineteenth-century fault lines and inequalities that beset Britain's imperial core.[99] In Gough's case, these had their basis in anxieties surrounding Ireland's place in and loyalty to empire. That the task of securing a precarious empire in India was in the hands of an army that largely comprised soldiers drawn from two subject territories (India and Ireland), led by an apparently volatile Irishman, was a phenomenon that amplified the sense of vulnerability felt in the imperial metropole.[100] The resultant impulse was to aggressively deploy a range of Hibernophobic canards fixated on Gough's presumed military incompetence in order to rationalise, accelerate and effect his supersession. From a moderate Irish nationalist perspective, the conundrum involved formulating a cogent nationalist response to the same phenomenon – the proliferation of Irishmen serving in imperial armies. While British imperial and colonial endeavour could be legitimately targeted and condemned, the Irish soldiers implicated in that endeavour could not, since to do so would mean aligning with the British political and press establishments in impugning Irish military virtue. Consequently, the O'Connellite press was obliged to oscillate between imperial condemnation and imperial accommodation.

98 'Prize and Batta Rolls Indus, Sutlej and Punjab, 1846–49' (BL, IOR/L/MIL/5/276). This comprised Rs 35,598 in *batta* and Rs 173,610-9*a*-1*p* in prize money. Allowing for inflation, Gough's award would presently equate to approximately £2,700,000. See https://www.bankofengland.co.uk/monetary-policy/inflation/inflation-calculator (accessed 7 Dec. 2020).

99 Kinealy, 'At home with the empire: the example of Ireland', pp 86–8.

100 Linda Colley associates this sense of vulnerability with 'imperial overstretch'. See *Captives: the story of Britain's pursuit of empire and how its soldiers and civilians were held captive by the dream of global supremacy, 1600–1850* (London, 2002), pp 4–12.

10

Glorious Victory? The Visual Spectacle of War in Nineteenth-Century Dublin

Kathryn Milligan

Introduction

In the early decades of the nineteenth century, and in cities across Europe, commercial venues specialising in the exhibition and sale of engravings, art supplies and other luxury paper goods proliferated. These businesses specialised in one-painting exhibitions to supplement their sales of prints, stationery, collectibles and books, with these special events being an opportunity to sell subscriptions for an engraving of the artwork on display. In Dublin, one of the most prominent of these firms was that of Thomas Cranfield, with premises at 23 Westmoreland Street, and after 1849, at 115 Grafton Street, opposite the Provost's House at Trinity College; another important venue was the gallery of Adolphe Lesage, on Sackville Street. The success of businesses like Thomas Cranfield's was driven in part by changes to how visual art could be transported and reproduced as industrialisation progressed. Popular paintings were frequently brought on long tours around Britain and Ireland, visiting key cities in the four nations, facilitated in part by the expansion of the railway network. To further increase the public's knowledge of these artworks, where paintings went the sale of an engraving followed: the chief aim of the touring circuit was to gather subscriptions for the subsequent print. These changes were further supported by an increase in art media: although newspaper accounts were generally anonymous and more generalised than true art criticism, they were copious and detailed; and from 1838, the *Art Journal* provided more specialised reading material for artists, collectors and enthusiasts. In this burgeoning market, Dublin (and other regional cities) took their lead from London publishers, and dealers such as Rudolph Ackermann, Martin Colnaghi, Ernest Gambart, Joseph Dickinson and Henry Graves were notable among the firms responsible for distributing paintings and engravings.[1] As Robert Verhoogt has written, the 'nineteenth-century art world was characterised by a complex assortment of closely related works in the form of repetitions, replicas, reductions and other copies'.[2]

Focusing on Dublin and the business of Thomas Cranfield, this chapter will explore how two nineteenth-century conflicts were represented through the gallery's displays: the Peninsular and Waterloo campaigns during the Napoleonic Wars (1807–14 and 1815, respectively) and the Crimean War (1853–56). Cranfield's exhibitions in this period have been described as having 'a notably conservative and loyal flavour'[3] and as Fintan Cullen has expressed, the display of British artworks in Ireland was tightly bound with engendering support for the imperial project in Ireland, to the extent that 'union and display in nineteenth-century Ireland had become one'.[4] Although other imperial conflicts appear through other works (including the Indian Mutiny through Thomas Jones Barker's *The Relief of Lucknow* (1857, National Portrait Gallery, London) exhibited in 1862) these two conflicts emerge as the most significant and offer an interesting case study. Dublin was by no means the only Irish city in which these types of exhibitions took place: Belfast and Cork were also popular venues, with the firm of Magill's in the former city being particularly active.[5] Additionally, and of importance, it must be noted at the outset that despite the prominence of the Cranfield firm in Dublin at this time, no business records are extant, and so research into its activities relies solely on newspaper accounts and advertisements relating to their activities, as well as the prints, photographs and other publications that they produced. With the exceptions of *The Nation* and the *Freeman's Journal*, the newspapers cited here were generally unionist and conservative in their political leanings, and this undoubtedly colours their coverage of these exhibitions. A final difficulty with this subject is the lack of written responses, whether as attributed reviews, letters, or diary entries, from those who visited the exhibitions. As evidenced from the ephemera and pamphlet collections now in the National Library of Ireland, Jaspar Robert Joly was invited to several of Cranfield's exhibitions, and collected other printed material relating to these: none of his impressions, or indeed, those of his contemporaries, have yet come to light (Figure 3).

1 Robert Verhoogt, *Art in reproduction: nineteenth-century prints after Lawrence Alma-Tadema, Jozef Israëls and Ary Scheffer* (Amsterdam 2007), p. 142.

2 Ibid., p. 35.

3 William Laffan, 'Buying, selling and exhibiting art in Ireland c.1700–c.1900' in Nicola Figgis (ed.), *Art and architecture of Ireland volume ii: painting 1600–1900* (New Haven, 2014), p. 21.

4 Fintan Cullen, *Ireland on show: art, union, and nationhood* (Farnham, 2012), p. 79.

5 See Eileen Black, *Window to an age: a chronicle of art in Belfast 1760–1888* (Belfast, 2016) and Peter Murray, 'Cork Art 1800–1900' in *Illustrated summary catalogue of the Crawford Municipal Art Gallery* (Cork, 1991), pp 185–259.

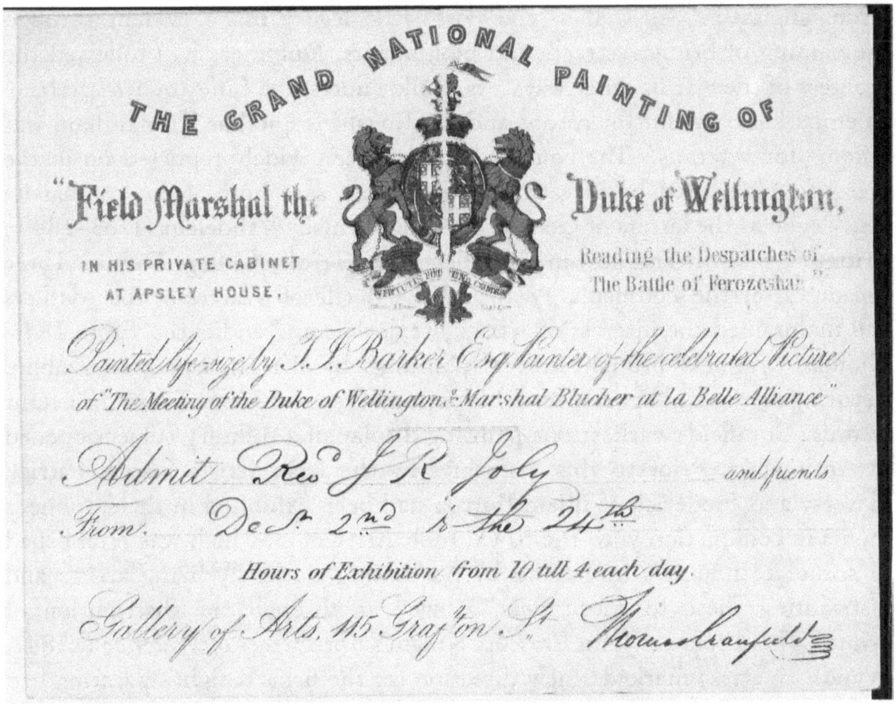
THE GRAND NATIONAL PAINTING OF
"Field Marshal the Duke of Wellington,
IN HIS PRIVATE CABINET
AT APSLEY HOUSE,
Reading the Despatches of
The Battle of Ferozeshah."
Painted life-size by T. J. Barker Esq. Painter of the celebrated Picture
of "The Meeting of the Duke of Wellington & Marshal Blucher at la Belle Alliance"
Admit Revd J R Joly and friends
From Decr 2nd to the 24th
Hours of Exhibition from 10 till 4 each day.
Gallery of Arts, 115 Grafton St. Thomas Cranfield

Figure 3 Invitation to Jasper Joly from Thomas Cranfield to view 'The Grand National painting of: Field Marshall the Duke of Wellington in his private cabinet at Apsley House'. Image courtesy of the National Library of Ireland (NLI EPH A287).

Despite these methodological concerns, the impression of these exhibitions that emerges from the extant records is one of a vibrant appetite in Dublin for visualisations of contemporary conflict abroad rather than at home.

Heroes of Waterloo: Cranfield and the Napoleonic Wars, 1843–54

The memory of Waterloo and other campaigns of the Napoleonic Wars permeated Dublin throughout the early nineteenth century, not least through the naming of parts of the city after the Duke of Wellington and the project to fund and construct the Wellington Testimonial in the Phoenix Park. As Peter Molloy has noted, Irish soldiers formed an important part of Wellington's forces, serving at every rank and coming from a range of social backgrounds: additionally, Irish civilians were 'also caught up by events, both as fascinated domestic spectators and also as military dependents present during the campaign itself'.[6] As well as the post-battle legacy made evident through the naming of bridges, streets and monuments, Dubliners had followed the progress of the war in other ways. As Molloy notes, the Liffey quays had been an embarkation point for troops and the Royal Hospital at Kilmainham was a home for veterans.[7] The conflict had also been widely reported on in the press, supplemented by private correspondence sent home from the battle-fields, such as the letters of General Sir John Ormsby Vandeleur (1763–1849), written to his wife and now in the collection of Trinity College Dublin. Three decades after the Peninsular War and the Battle of Waterloo, the conflicts still maintained the interest of artists, art dealers and audiences. From 1843, Thomas Cranfield brought several paintings by British artists to Dublin, featuring scenes and figures from this period of recent history. From the extant records, Cranfield's earliest one-painting display of a military subject opened in April 1843. Prior to this, paintings by the Irish artists Joseph Patrick Haverty and Frederick William Burton had been exhibited in the stationer's rooms in conjunction with the Royal Irish Art Union, which was established to stimulate fine arts in Ireland by purchasing works by living artists and distributing these to subscribers, as well as through the distribution of prints.[8] The display of John Prescott Knight's *The Heroes of Waterloo* (c.1842, Wyndham Park) marked a new direction for the firm. Knight's painting had been exhibited at the Royal Academy, London in 1842, and subsequently at the Pall Mall print sellers, Messrs Graves & Co. This group portrait depicted thirty-two military figures connected with the battle, including the Duke of Wellington, with the *Warder and Dublin Weekly Mail* noting that the details of the painting were 'well managed and the hussar uniforms afforded a fine relief amidst the mass of scarlet, which it must be observed is treated with exceeding good effect'.[9]

The following year, this painting was exhibited again at Cranfield's, joined by another work by Knight, *The Peninsular Heroes Assembled at the United Services Club* (date and location unknown) which echoed the earlier work in its composition, being portraits of officers who had served in the Peninsular War (1807–14). In an account of the exhibition, *Saunder's News-Letter* noted that 'two pictures together, representing upwards of sixty portraits of the greatest warriors of the present century, form one of the most interesting exhibitions of portrait painting we ever remember to have seen'.[10] Of course, the press

6 Peter Molloy, 'Ireland and the Waterloo campaign of 1815' (MA dissertation, Maynooth University, 2011), pp 5–6.

7 Ibid., p. 7.

8 Eileen Black, 'Practical patriots and true Irishmen: the Royal Irish Art Union 1839–59' in *Irish arts review yearbook*, no. 14 (1998), pp 140–6.

9 *Warder and Dublin Weekly Mail*, 6 May, 1843.

10 *Saunder's News-Letter* (henceforth cited as *SNL*), 1 May, 1844.

was not unanimous in its praise. On 11 May 1844, the editorial of the *Dublin Weekly Nation* (known as the *Nation*) thanked an anonymous letter writer known as 'An Artist' for 'calling our attention to the Peninsular Heroes. It is, as he says, worthy of the pencil which bedaubed the Heroes of Waterloo, and a most contemptible affair.'[11] Although beyond the scope of this chapter, it is worth briefly noting that in the 1840s, the concept of a national school of Irish painting, and the need for a distinctively 'Irish' school of history painting was being heavily promoted, but in vain, by artists and critics in Dublin and beyond. Thomas Davis, writing on the topic in an article originally published in *The Nation*, had lamented how

> [o]ur portrait and landscape painters paint foreign men and scenes; and, at all events, the Irish people do not see, possess, nor receive knowledge from their works. Irish history has supplied no subjects for our great Artists; and though, as we repeat, Ireland possessed a [Samuel] Forde and a [James] Barry, creative painters of the highest order, the pictures of the latter are mostly abroad; those of the former unseen and unknown ... Alas! that they are so few.[12]

Despite *The Nation*'s criticism, the appetite of both Cranfield and his audience for imagery relating to the Battle of Waterloo continued into the 1850s. In December 1851, Thomas Jones Barker's canvas *The Meeting of Field Marshall Blücher and the Duke of Wellington* (date and location unknown) arrived in Dublin and was exhibited until January 1852. Writing about the painting, the *Freeman's Journal* described how Jones Barker had 'been fortunate enough to discover a new subject for his pencil among the apparently exhausted incidents of Waterloo'. Adding societal lustre to the occasion, the press noted that Field Marshal Hugh Gough, 1st Viscount Gough and his family visited Cranfield's to see the painting, with the *Dublin Evening Post* commenting that the 'hero of Aliwal expressed himself in warm terms of the masterly treatment of the subject'.[13] Gough was an Irish officer in the British army, and had served in the 87th (Royal Irish Fusiliers) Regiment of Foot during the Peninsular War and was later Commander-in-Chief of the British Forces in India during the Gwalior campaign, 1843. By convention, and to underpin the respectability of these displays, visits to Cranfield's exhibitions by notable society and military figures were frequently reported in the press, underlining in many ways the connection between these displays and the

11 *Dublin Weekly Nation*, 11 May, 1844.

12 Thomas Davis, 'National Art' in Thomas Davis, *Literary and historical essays* (Dublin, 1846), p. 153.

13 *Dublin Evening Post* (henceforth cited as *DEP*), 1 Jan. 1852.

patronage or taste of figures associated with the British administration in Ireland. The appearance of a figure like Gough at the exhibition of a military painting underlines this, and Cullen's evocation of union, imperial action and display are inextricably intertwined.

Two further exhibitions of paintings relating to Wellington and Waterloo took place in 1853. In January, portraits of the Duke and of Admiral Nelson, both by Barker Jones, were shown for about a month. A report in the *Freeman's Journal* intimates the regional circuit that brought these works to Dublin, and the commercial importance of the sale of engravings. In the case of the portrait of Wellington, the *Journal* noted that Cranfield had 'found some difficulty in getting the picture for private exhibition in Dublin, until after the principal towns in England should be visited'. Because of this, he had made an agreement with the dealers that four hundred copies of the engraving would be set aside for Dublin subscribers, with the benefit being that 'as the prints will be delivered in the order in which they are subscribed for, they will be much more perfect – more distinct in line and brighter in every respect – than those that will be struck off after the plate shall have done a great deal of work in the production of thousands of impressions'.[14] Because of the nature of the printing process, the early prints – including proofs before letters where the lack of a title or other lettering indicates that the 'plate was still in its near pristine condition' – were sought after by collectors, being both the best quality and the highest in price.[15] As the price decreased so did the quality of the print, and the shilling entry to view the painting would have attracted a larger audience than the subsequent subscriptions.

In May, a painting by Edwin Landseer came to Dublin, being, perhaps, the most notable (given its creator and its subject matter) work relating to the Battle of Waterloo to be shown in an Irish city. First exhibited at the Royal Academy, London in 1850, *A Dialogue at Waterloo* (or *Wellington Revisiting the Plains of Waterloo*) shows the elderly Duke visiting the battlefield with his daughter-in-law, the Marchioness of Douro (Figure 4). When it was first exhibited, the London *Evening Mail* noted how it immediately caught the eye of visitors to the Royal Academy: the two central figures are shown on horseback on the right-hand side of the canvas, with an expansive genre scene of a picnic filling the left. A young girl in traditional Flemish dress offers the Duke and his companion a guidebook to the battlefield, with Landseer suggesting that she does not recognise the eminent visitor, although another man, standing next to two large horses, seems to give a knowing glance at the pair. Interest in the painting was further heightened by the fact that the

14 *Freeman's Journal* (henceforth cited as *FJ*), 3 Jan. 1853.

15 Anthony Dyson, *Pictures to print: the nineteenth-century engraving trade* (London, 1984), p. 67.

Figure 4 *A Dialogue at Waterloo*, by Edwin Landseer. Oil on canvas, exhibited 1850. Photo © Tate, CC-BY-NC-ND 3.0 (unported), https://www.tate.org.uk/art/artworks/landseer-a-dialogue-at-waterloo-n00415.

Duke of Wellington visited the Academy exhibition, where he 'lingered with evident satisfaction before the canvas, which seemed to render him twice over a spectator of his own greatness'.[16] The painting had been purchased by Robert Vernon and was destined to be part of the collection he gifted to the British nation even before it was completed. An important patron of the arts, Vernon had made his fortune in the horse trade during the Napoleonic Wars, and from 1847, donated his collection of artworks to the nation, housed between the National Gallery, London, then located in Marlborough House, and the South Kensington Museum.[17] Landseer was a particular favourite of Vernon's and this was among several canvases by the animal and landscape painter in his collection.

Following its exhibition in London, in 1852 and 1853, the painting travelled to several cities in England, including Manchester, Preston, Blackburn, Norwich, Liverpool, Glasgow and York, where it was on display before its sojourn in Dublin. The painting was then returned to London, where, according to the London *Morning Herald*, Landseer '[rendered] it more imposing by increasing its dimensions' before the engraving was prepared by Thomas Lewis Atkinson.[18] The grand canvas arrived in Dublin at an auspicious time, coinciding with the opening month of the Irish Industrial Exhibition on Leinster Lawn. This context was noted by the *Freeman's Journal*, who, in their

16 *Evening Mail*, 6 May 1850.
17 Robin Hamlyn, *Robert Vernon's gift* (London, 1993), pp 9–20.
18 *Morning Herald*, 11 Jul. 1853.

report of Cranfield's exhibition, commented that 'even in the midst of the many objects of attraction which Dublin at this moment embraces', Landseer's painting was 'certainly not the last which should be visited'. Highlighting the importance of the painting, and its place in the Vernon collection, the article also noted that 'Mr. Cranfield has been obliged to insure it for 5,000*l*, while it remains in his possession'. The emotional appeal of this painting was plainly evident: Wellington had died by the time it arrived in Dublin and the author of the *Freeman's* article appealed to the viewers' emotions, commenting that 'We cannot fancy that even [Wellington's] cold heart could have been free from emotion on thus returning to such a scene; but it is in the eye of his beautiful companion, who listens to his description with the deepest interest, and with thoughts turned to the past, that we read some of the most poetic sentiment of the picture.'[19] Visitors to Cranfield's gallery received, or could purchase, a small booklet to accompany their viewing of the painting that set out a short biography of Wellington and the importance of Waterloo, as well as offering a sales pitch for Atkinson's engraving, complete with an order form where subscribers could request a 'proof before letters' (priced at 12*gn*), 'proofs' (10*gn*) or 'first 500, open letters, impressions', for 7*gn*.[20] The prices of these prints suggest that they were aimed at the upper end of the market: proofs and early impressions were sought after by collectors, being both the largest and finest copies available.

By March 1854, the context in which military paintings were shown at Cranfield's had changed. This was made clear by the *Freeman's Journal* when Thomas Jones Barker's *Napoleon at Bassano* (c.1853, Manchester Art Gallery) was exhibited. This was not the first time that a portrait of Napoleon had been exhibited in Ireland: for example, in 1816 and 1817, a full-length portrait by Robert Lefévre (1755–1830) had been shown in Belfast and Dublin, accompanied by the companion portrait of Joséphine Bonaparte.[21] They wrote:

> We are now at war, and war at this moment engages the attention of all the world; so that this new picture of Mr. Barker's – always so successful in his military episodes – comes most opportunely among us; and those who may have the gratification of seeing it in Mr. Cranfield's gallery, where it is on view for a few days, will, when they read by-and-bye of battles in which our gallant countrymen are falling, be able to realise to themselves some of war's sad realities.[22]

19 *FJ*, 31 May 1853.
20 'Sir Edwin Landseer's celebrated picture of Wellington revisiting the Plains of Waterloo' (Dublin, 1853), p. 9.
21 Black, *Window to an age*, p. 19; *SNL*, 17 Mar. 1817.
22 *FJ*, 31 Mar. 1854.

The author of the article was referring to the Crimean War, which had been officially declared by Britain on 28 March 1854, coinciding nearly simultaneously with the arrival of the painting. The painting, the same author recounts, was based on a 'true historic incident' wherein Napoleon, while riding over the battlefield at Bassano, observed 'a dog howling over the body of his dead master, and pointing to the spot, exclaimed to his officers, "There, gentlemen, that dog teaches us a lesson of humanity!"'[23] Although beyond the scope of this chapter, it is worth noting that in the same period, other paintings depicting Napoleon (rather than Wellington) were exhibited in Dublin. At the repository of Adolphe Lesage, 44 Lower Sackville Street, the eponymous proprietor showed several paintings by the French artist Paul Delaroche (1797–1856) including *Napoleon Contemplating his Abdication at Fontainebleau* in 1848, 1849 and 1850, and *Napoleon Crossing the Alps* in 1851 (Figures 5 and 6). Both paintings exist in original and reduced copies, and it is difficult at this time to identify which canvases were exhibited in Dublin. Lesage was something of a champion of Delaroche's work, and in 1850 had exhibited his *Cromwell in front of the Coffin of Charles I* (Nimes, Museum of Fine Arts).[24] In late 1856, Lesage also secured Jones's *Wellington and Lord Raglan Crossing the Pyrenees* (now titled *Wellington at Sorauren, 27 July 1813*, c.1853, National Army Museum, London). An invitation sent to Jaspar Joly notes that this was a 'companion picture to Napoleon Crossing the Alps' by Delaroche, underlining again the continued interest in depictions of this subject by Dublin audiences, and the clever marketing by business owners like Cranfield and Lesage.[25]

23 Ibid.

24 For a discussion on copies and reduced replicas, see Stephen Bann, 'Reassessing repetition in nineteenth-century academic painting: Delaroche, Gérôme, Ingres' in Eik Kahng (ed.), *The repeating image: multiples in French painting from David to Matisse* (New Haven, 2007), pp 27–51.

25 See invitation from Adolphe Lesage to Jasper Joly, National Library of Ireland, EPH A286.

Figures 5 Paul Delaroche, *Napoleon Contemplating his Abdication at Fontainebleau* (31 March 1814) (1846). Oil on canvas. Royal Collection Trust / © His Majesty King Charles III, 2023.

Figures 6 Paul Delaroche, *Bonaparte Crossing the Alps* (1848–50) (1853). Oil on canvas. Royal Collection Trust / © His Majesty King Charles III, 2023.

Martial spectacle: exhibiting the Crimean War in Dublin

As Paul Huddie has noted, in Ireland the 'response to the Crimean War was a mixture of martial and oftentimes imperial enthusiasm, and local or national interest, with a minority strain of criticism, opposition and nationalism'.[26] Further still, he estimates that in 1854 the proportion of Irishmen in the British army stood at over 40 per cent.[27] In terms of its reporting and visualisation, the Crimean War marked a significant change in how the public engaged with the events of the battlefield. As Ulrich Keller has outlined, the proliferation of imagery in the period of the war – from lithographs and press illustrations based on first-hand accounts, to photographs of battle fields and survivors – mean that

> the modalities of contemporary visual appreciation form an integral part of history.... Military display had been around for centuries, but it was innovations such as steam transportation, press reportage, tourism and modern habits of cultural consumption which gave the traditional visual symbolism a new lease on life and helped to construct martial spectacle on an unprecedented, technically enhanced scale.[28]

In the immediate aftermath of the war, Jones Barker again emerged as Cranfield's favoured artist for exhibiting Crimean scenes, building on Dublin audiences' knowledge of the artist's military painting (Figure 7). Cranfield's belief that the works would be popular is evident through his decision to relocate his first major exhibition of a Crimean military scene to a lager venue. In April 1857 he announced that 'Under the Authority of H.R.H the Commander-in-Chief and the General of the Crimean Army', he had 'the satisfaction to announce that he has secured the Grand Original Picture of THE ALLIED GENERALS with the OFFICERS of their STAFFS BEFORE SEBASTOPOL, Painted by T. J. Barker, Esq., and it will be placed with him in the ROYAL INSTITUTION, COLLEGE-STREET, His own Gallery not being sufficiently spacious.'[29] The gallery on College Street, designed by Frederick Darley, had opened in 1829 under the auspices of the Royal Irish Institution, a corporate body funded by subscribers and commercial income whose aim was to encourage and promote the fine arts in Ireland. The rooms of the gallery are clearly laid out in the 1847 Ordnance

26 Paul Huddie, *The Crimean War and Irish society* (Liverpool, 2015), p. 55.

27 Huddie, *The Crimean War*, p. 133.

28 Ulrich Keller, *The ultimate spectacle: a visual history of the Crimean War* (New York, 2001), p. 4; J.W.M. Hichberger, *Images of the army: the military in British art, 1815–1914* (Manchester, 1988), pp 49–58.

29 *SNL*, 29 Apr. 1857.

Figure 7 *The Allied generals with the officers of their respective staffs before Sebastopol*, by Charles George Lewis after Thomas Jones Barker. Mixed media engraving, published 1 November 1859. Royal Collection Trust / © His Majesty King Charles III 2023.

Survey map of the city, and it was described in the *Dublin Penny Journal* as being 'one octagonal gallery, judiciously lighted by a spacious lantern ... This gallery is forty feet long by thirty feet wide, and nineteen feet high to the cove.'[30] Its spacious dimensions had long been used for showing large works, such as Claude-Marie Dubufe's *Adam and Eve* and *Paradise Lost* and Ernest Slingeneyer's *The Death of Nelson* in 1853, which the newspapers noted, measured 23 x 17 feet.[31] Cranfield's exhibition was also not the first time a display of Crimea-related items had been held in the gallery, for example, in June 1855, the 'Patriotic Fund Exhibition' contained a 'gallery of amateur art and museum of the trophies of ward from the Crimea', and in July of the same year, a model of the Sevastopol Peninsula was also exhibited.[32]

The arrival of the painting in Dublin roused excitement in the press: for example, the *Dublin Evening Packet and Correspondent* listed it among the recent movements of society figures[33] and the *Dublin Evening Post* noted its arrival 'under the superintendence of Mr. Cranfield and Mr. James G. Browne of London' and that they had been 'favoured with a sign of it while in the course of being adjusted for exhibition, and we think when it will be seen by

30 *Dublin Penny Journal*, 22 Dec. 1832.

31 *Dublin Evening Packet and Correspondent* (henceforth cited as *DEPC*), 10 Dec. 1853.

32 *Dublin Daily Express* (henceforth cited as *DDE*), 13 Jun. 1855; *Dublin Evening Mail* (henceforth cited as *DEM*) 18 Jul. 1855.

33 *DEPC*, 20 Apr. 1857.

thousands everyone will pronounce it to be a wonder in the fine arts'.[34] Browne was one of the co-commissioners and proprietors of the painting, and it had been made, *Saunder's News-Letter* reported, 'with all the aids that artistic talent, and sketches, and photographs, fresh from the then terrible scenes of action, could supply'.[35] Prior to its exhibition in Dublin, the painting had been shown in London, Edinburgh and Glasgow, and an engraving was well underway, with a proof available for inspection. Furthermore, several of the newspaper accounts of the painting mentioned that following the full print run of the engraving, the steel plate would be destroyed, limiting availability to those who had subscribed in the first instance and thus preserving the value of the limited edition. The paper also noted that Barker had made specific use of photographs taken by Roger Fenton, and here we see a new intersection between commercial photography and the well-established art and print dealers. Thomas Agnew & Sons, a print seller, publisher and art dealer based in Manchester and London, commissioned Fenton to travel to Crimea in 1854, where he took photographs of the leading figures in the allied armies, camp life of the rank and file, landscape scenes around Balaklava and Sebastopol prior to the battle and most famously the aftermath of the Charge of Light Brigade. Although Fenton had left the area before the destruction of Sebastopol, this was captured in contemporary photography by James Robertson.[36] Focusing on Fenton's photographs, we can see another glimpse of Cranfield's expertise in preparing his Dublin audience for the arrival of Barker's painting, as the previous year, he had organised for a collection of Fenton's photographs of Crimea to be exhibited at the Royal Hibernian Academy.[37]

Jones's painting, measuring twenty feet long and ten feet high, contained several hundred figures with about eighty recognisable portraits, including Florence Nightingale, Lord Raglan, Sir Colin Campbell and the Duke of Cambridge, set against the backdrop of the Mamelon Fort, the Malakoff, the Redan and the city and harbour of Sebastopol. Among general scenery, the artist included convivial exchanges between French and English soldiers, as well as more graphic notes designed to evoke pathos in the viewer, such as the 'dying Highlander partaking in the French vivandiere's hospitality', described as 'a chaste emblem of that kindness which suffering invariably produces'.[38] While the press generally indulged in hyperbole in their descriptions of artworks, the reportage on this painting reached new levels, perhaps reflecting the impact that the conflict had wrought on many in Ireland. For example, the

34 *DEP*, 2 May 1857.
35 *SNL*, 5 May 1857.
36 'Fenton Crimean War photographs' (https://www.loc.gov/collections/fenton-crimean-war-photographs/about-this-collection/#Note1) (accessed 4 Mar. 2024).
37 *DEPC*, 24 Jan. 1856.
38 Ibid., 9 May 1857.

Dublin Evening Mail praised Cranfield's decision to exhibit the painting in a bigger venue as it would

> accommodate the crowds who will, no doubt, eagerly press to scan those well marked lineaments, and to read in the faces of the heroes the character that has made their names historical. We can conceive no greater or more elevated source of reflection than to pass from face to face in this illustrious gathering of the best men of England, France, Sardinia, and Turkey, and to recall to our minds the deeds of skill and daring there displayed.[39]

A further Crimean scene by Jones Barker was exhibited at Cranfield's in May 1858: on the first view of the canvas, the *Dublin Evening Packet and Correspondent* noted that the artist's representation of 'General Williams Leaving Kars' (now titled *The Capitulation of Kars*, c.1860, National Army Museum, London) was:

> one of those pictures that charm at once, continue long upon the memory, haunt the mind, prompt us to communicate the fact to others that another fine historical picture been added to the small collection, and to induce the lovers of the fine arts to feast their eyes upon a beautiful production.[40]

This description also appeared in *Saunder's News-Letter*, opening a longer description of the painting, highlighting that it was part of Cranfield's advance publicity. The piece continued to describe the painting in detail, perhaps for the benefit of those who were unable to see it in person, noting the

> [d]elicate women and fearless soldiers ... dogs scratching the dead out of their graves ... thunder and lightning ranging around the devoted victims ... the noble cavalry horses dying by the hundreds – scanty forage, scanty bread, scanty barley; hope, the seraphic light that leaves the soul ... almost extinguished, when, on the 25th of November, General Williams determines to leave Kars with his staff ...[41]

In the production of this painting, Jones again drew on contemporary photographs of the main protagonists, as well as on the recollections of Humphry Sandwith (1822–81), published in 1856. An army physician,

39 *DEM*, 13 May 1857.
40 *DEPC*, 15 May 1858.
41 *SNL*, 15 May 1858.

Sandwith served with Williams at Kars, and survived the siege. A portrait of Sandwith is included in the painting, appearing to the right-hand side of Williams. As with the *Allied Generals*, this painting was commissioned by James G. Browne and Agnew and Sons, and was engraved by Lewis.[42]

In his analysis of Barker Jones's paintings of the Crimean War, Ulrich Keller has drawn attention to the repetitive processes that led from photograph to painting to engraving, highlighting how, despite these new ways of working, there was still prestige attached to seeing historical events translated into paint on canvas. In works like *Allied Generals before Sebastopol*, Keller notes that in the creation of a type of photo montage, the finished painting is more a 'loose assemblage of historical materials ... rather than an interpretive historical account'.[43] In these paintings, Keller finds a strange juncture in the story of history painting: the public's (and particularly the rising middle class's) desire to see historical events represented in oil on canvas meets rapid technological and visual advancement, where accounts and images of contemporary life were suddenly readily available. As Keller notes, the desire of firms like Agnew's to maintain the 'prestigious appearance of history painting' rested on the availability of photographs and press illustrations for the artist to base his work, and even 'before the paint had dried on the canvas the painting began a transformation into an engraving which again was distributed to thousands of customers'.[44] The exhibition and promotion of these images in Dublin suggest that the Irish city and the general public were keen participants in this visual marketplace.

Revisiting Waterloo and Crimea: Exhibiting Elizabeth Southerden Butler in Dublin, 1876–80

The appetite for military or war imagery at Cranfield's gallery did not dissipate, and from the mid-late 1870s through to 1880 further scenes of the Waterloo Campaign and the Crimean War were displayed. There was an added attraction to these works – all were by one artist, Elizabeth Southerden Butler, Lady Butler (1846–1933). The first of Butler's paintings to be exhibited at Cranfield's was *The Roll Call*, or to give its full title, *Calling the Roll After an Engagement, Crimea*, a large painting depicting soldiers from the Grenadier Guards, shown in the snow, and dressed in greatcoats and bearskins (Figure 8). Many are injured, and they are watched by an officer on horseback as a sergeant takes the roll. This was a key painting in Butler's œuvre. After

42 Ibid., p. 3.
43 Keller, *The ultimate spectacle*, p. 230.
44 Ibid.

Figure 8 *The Roll Call*, by Elizabeth Southerden Butler, Lady Butler. Oil on canvas, 1874. Royal Collection Trust / © His Majesty King Charles III 2023.

its highly successful exhibition at the Royal Academy in 1874 it became a national success, being brought from Burlington House to Buckingham Palace so that Queen Victoria could view it privately and to the sickbed of Florence Nightingale, before travelling around Britain on a national tour. The painting was ceded by the original commissioner, the industrialist Charles Galloway, to the monarch, and remains in the Royal Collection today.[45]

When the painting arrived in Dublin in February 1876, the *Dublin Daily Express* noted that it was 'an appropriate possession' of Queen Victoria, 'seeing that the subject is an illustration of the heroism of her soldiers during the Crimean War. In piping times of peace, perhaps, we do not value our soldiers as they deserve.'[46] The author of the column was alive to both the emotional appeal of the painting, and to the fact that it was now being viewed sometime after the conflict itself, commenting that

> What correspondent's description of the fighting around Sebastopol, read at ten thousand breakfast tables twenty years ago, could possibly have given such an idea of the thing to the readers as is compressed into this picture ... It seems as if by some magic power the artist had brought back an actual scene from the past – at all events, she has held

45 Catherine Wynne, *Lady Butler: war artist and traveller, 1846–1933* (Dublin, 2019), p. 60.
46 *DDE*, 3 Feb. 1876.

> up an artist's looking glass to the British solider in action, and he has no reason to be ashamed of the reflection.[47]

Much like the memory of Waterloo and the Peninsular Wars in the 1840s and 1850s, Butler's paintings enabled audiences to look back, sometimes nostalgically, to the events of the Crimean War. Newspaper accounts suggest, however, that unlike say, Jones Barker's heroic historical scenes, Butler's painting was considered a 'genre' painting, more focused on the plight of the foot solider than the general or commander, offering a more popular, emotional appeal. An account in the *Freeman's Journal* emphasises this, noting the fallen soldier and praising the artist's 'truly modern feeling, a touch of pathos', which it likened to the sadness of King Lear or the tragedy of Walter Scott's *Bride of Lammermoor*.[48] The goal of Cranfield's exhibition remained the enrolment of subscribers for the engraving, and towards the end of the run the *Dublin Evening Mail* noted that the list already included 'the names of the most distinguished persons in the country, and shows by its proportions not only a widely diffused love of art in Ireland, but an equally general pride in the gallant achievements of British arms'.[49]

The sensation caused by *The Roll Call* significantly advanced Butler's professional career and while formal recognition from the Academy did not follow, the willingness of various army regiments to work with the artist enabled her to work on several more large and elaborate canvases. It also led to economic success: her next Academy painting, *The 28th Regiment at Quatre Bras*, garnered a much higher price when commissioned, and the artist also benefited from separate copyright sales (Figure 9). As Maria Quirk has outlined, Butler's success at the Royal Academy assisted her in securing 'a series of profitable one women/one picture shows at the Fine Art Society', and that demand for 'engravings and prints of Butler's early military paintings was high, and her Fine Art Society contracts included the rights to her paintings' copyright which, until 1897, could be purchased independently of the artwork itself'.[50] *The 28th Regiment* was exhibited in Dublin the following year, arriving in late January 1877. An advertisement for the exhibition described it as a 'companion picture to the celebrated 'Roll Call', and admission to see the work was priced at one shilling. Based on an account of the battle written by William Siborne, the painting shows the regiment at the Battle of Quatre Bras, which took place just two days before Waterloo, on 16 June 1815. The

47 Ibid.

48 *FJ*, 2 Feb. 1876.

49 *DEM*, 21 Feb. 1876.

50 Maria Quirk, *Women, art and money in late Victorian and Edwardian England: the hustle and the scramble* (London, 2019), p. 121.

Figure 9 *The 28th Regiment at Quatre Bras*, by Elizabeth Southerden Butler, Lady Butler. Oil on canvas, 1875, National Gallery of Victoria, Melbourne. Photo: National Gallery of Victoria, Melbourne.

Irish Times was among those to refer to the artist's gender, commenting that the work exhibited 'such as wealth of power, passion, variety of expression, and terrific wrath, despair, and ruin, as no female painter, within our experience, has ever evinced before'.[51]

In January 1880, the *Dublin Daily Express* announced that four of Butler's paintings were then on display at Cranfield's, with some advance publicity appearing in December 1879.[52] This bumper display included the two works already mentioned, however rather than the original work, a copy of the *Roll Call* by Paul-Léon Jazet (1848–1918) was shown. Although no record of this copy is now extant, the newspaper reports made it clear that the work exhibited was a copy by this artist: it may be that this was conceived as an intermediate work for the information of an engraver, a practice that was common at the time.[53] The other two paintings had not previously been seen in Dublin: *The Remnants of an Army* (1879, Somerset Military Museum) and *Return from Inkerman* (1877, Ferens Art Gallery) based on the First Afghan and Crimean wars respectively. The latter of these offers a similar subject to *The Roll Call*,

51 *Irish Times* (henceforth cited as *IT*), 29 Jan. 1877.
52 *IT*, 17 Dec. 1879; *DDE*, 2 Jan. 1880.
53 Dyson, *Pictures to print*, p. 38.

showing troops returning to their camp after a battle. Columns of men, many of whom are injured, and are supported by their comrades, stream across the canvas and move towards the viewer, immersing the onlooker in the scene. It is worth noting that a third painting by Butler, titled *Balaclava* (1876, Manchester Art Gallery), was also based on the Crimean War, but it does not seem that this was exhibited in Dublin. On 16 January 1880 Cranfield advertised that 'the receipt of admission to view Miss Thompson's celebrated pictures, will, on this day ... be entirely devoted to the fund for the relief of the distress in Ireland'.[54]

The fourth painting in this exhibition, *The Remnants of an Army*, had relevance to contemporary audiences in the early months of 1880: the painting shows William Brydon arriving at the walls of the Afghan city of Jalalabad in January 1842. An assistant surgeon in the East India Company armies, Brydon was long thought to be a sole survivor of the retreat from Kabul during the First Anglo-Afghan War (1838–42). When Butler completed *Remnants of an Army*, the Second Anglo-Afghan War was underway, and place names made familiar in the first conflict – such as Jalalabad – were once again in the news. As with her Crimean scenes, Butler avoided the photomontage style of Barker Jones and instead focused on the pathos-filled heroism of the individual solider, here seeming to swoon with the fatigue of survival, his horse also weary and exhausted as they reach a place of safety. Following their display in Dublin, these four paintings made their way to the rooms of Rodman & Co. in Belfast and later in the same year to the Royal Institution in Mosley Street, Manchester. Although the painting does not seem to have been extensively commented on in the Dublin press on 7 August 1880, the *Weekly Freeman* included a front-page illustration based on Butler's painting, but updated to reflect events of the current war. The title and caption read:

> 'The Remnants of an Army,' Or, History Repeating Itself. Dr. Brydone [*sic*], the survivor of the Khyber Pass, arrived exhausted at the Gates of Jellalabad [*sic*] January 13, 1842. General Burrows, the survivor of [Kusbk-a-Nakhud] arrived exhausted at the gates of Candahar [*sic*], July 23, 1880. Mrs Butler, when painting her celebrated picture, which we take the liberty of reproducing with some slight alterations, little thought she was depicting the future as well as the past.[55]

54 *DDE*, 16 Jan. 1880.
55 *Weekly Freeman and Irish Agriculturalist*, 7 Aug. 1880.

Conclusion

The reimagining of this painting suggests that the editors of the *Freeman* knew its audience would recognise it and understand its relevance to previous and current conflict. The exhibition of military paintings in Cranfield's gallery from the 1840s to the 1880s is an interesting chapter in the history of display in nineteenth century Dublin, with the commercialism often standing in opposition to the more established fine art venues such as the Royal Hibernian Academy, and regularly in political or aesthetic opposition to those attempting to find a more distinctly 'Irish' mode of visual art. However, these moments of display also evidence the enduring appeal of military painting in this period, and its appeal to audiences in Ireland, even if the cost of visiting an exhibition room or subscribing to a print run was limited to the aspiring middle class and unionist establishment. The ever-present nature of British military action, and the Irish soldiers who participated in these conflicts, tied these artworks to contemporary Irish life, bringing, even in an imagined and mediated way, the sights of the battlefields to the exhibition rooms of Dublin.

11

The Irish Republican Brotherhood, 1858–1924: A Case Study of Terrorism and Irregular Warfare

Timothy D. Hoyt

Introduction

According to Audrey Kurth Cronin, a leading scholar of modern terrorism, the median lifespan of a terrorist group is five to nine years.[1] Campaigns end, typically, through leadership elimination, the group transitioning into a legitimate political process, achievement of group aims, implosion or loss of public support, defeat and elimination of the group by brute force, or transition from terrorism to other forms of violence. Looking at modern Irish history, specifically that relating to militant nationalism, one is thus struck by the longevity of the Irish Republican Brotherhood (IRB). Established in 1858, it survived, despite a prolonged counterintelligence and counterinsurgency campaign by the British State, for sixty-five years (until just after the Irish Civil War in 1924). What explains this organisation's remarkable survival? The IRB was a covert organisation, pledged to overthrowing the rule of one of the most powerful empires in history.[2] Many studies of the IRB have focused on particular periods such as 1858–70, when the Fenian rebellion was organised (and failed militarily) or the 1880s, when American assistance and new technologies fuelled terrorist

1 A.K. Cronin, *How terrorism ends: understanding the decline and demise of terrorist campaigns* (Princeton, 2009), pp 7–8, 213.

2 The key source on the IRB in its entirety remains Leon O'Broin, *Revolutionary underground: the story of the Irish Republican Brotherhood 1858–1924* (Totowa, NJ, 1976). A more recent study is Owen McGee, *The IRB: the Irish Republican Brotherhood from the Land League to Sinn Féin* (Dublin, 2005).

campaigns in England.[3] Focusing on the IRB primarily as a military organisation misses the broader interaction between the movement and Irish society, however.[4] In effect, it emphasises form over function, with the function (the overall goal of the IRB – the establishment of an Irish republic) driving multiple lines of effort including but not limited to violent resistance.[5]

Scholars and readers of Ireland's history will be familiar with the contextualised analysis of the IRB through the prisms of the sectarian and agrarian secret society traditions, nationalist politics and the sometimes-perceived inevitable march towards independence from Britain. This chapter will utilise a different framework, derived from modern terrorism and irregular warfare studies, in an effort to add to our understanding. As mentioned above, Cronin's work highlights the short life span of terrorist groups and identifies six patterns in the decline and cessation of terrorist campaigns.[6] She also identifies the linkages between terrorism and other forms of irregular warfare and political violence.[7] David Rapaport, a pre-eminent scholar of terrorism, identified different 'waves' of modern terrorism – an anarchist wave from 1880 to 1920, an anti-colonial wave from 1920 to 1960, a 'New Left' wave from

3 R.V. Comerford, *The Fenians in context: Irish politics and society 1848–1882* (Dublin, 1998) covers both periods. On the IRB as a terrorist group, see Lindsay Clutterbuck, 'The progenitors of terrorism: Russian revolutionaries or extreme Irish republicans' in *Terrorism and political violence*, xvi, no. 1 (2004), pp 154–81; M.L.R. Smith, *Fighting for Ireland? The military strategy of the Irish republican movement* (London, 1995), pp 8–17; Brian Jenkins, *The Fenian problem: insurgency and terrorism in a liberal state, 1858–1874* (Montreal, 2008). Niall Whelehan, in *The Dynamiters: Irish nationalism and political violence in the wider world, 1867–1900* (Cambridge, 2012), also provides insight on the contemporary international system as well as a detailed study of various groups. New studies include Shane Kenna, *The Invincibles: the Phoenix Park assassinations and the conspiracy that shook an empire* (Dublin, 2019) and Julie Kavanagh, *The Irish assassins: conspiracy, revenge, and the Phoenix Park murders that stunned Victorian England* (New York, 2021).

4 On armed groups, see Andrea Dew & Richard Shultz, *Insurgents, terrorists, and militias: the warriors of contemporary combat* (New York, 2006).

5 On form and function, see T.D. Hoyt, 'Adapting to a changing environment – the Irish Republican Army as an armed group' in J.H. Norwitz (ed.), *Armed groups: studies in national security, counterterrorism, and counterinsurgency* (Newport, RI: 2008), pp 47–59 and David Doolin, *Transnational revolutionaries: the Fenian invasion of Canada 1866* (Oxford, 2015).

6 Cronin, *How terrorism ends*. Of the six patterns identified by Cronin as common to the decline of terrorist groups and campaigns, the most applicable to the IRB experience are the group's transitioning to a legitimate political process or its transitioning from terrorism to other forms of violence.

7 Terrorism here is used, reluctantly, to refer to non-state actors using targeted violence to achieve political aims. It is not intended as a condemnatory phrase. For a detailed discussion of this topic, see Richard English, *Does terrorism work? A history* (Oxford, 2016).

1960 to 1990, and an overlapping religions wave from 1979 to the present.[8] The IRB adopted some of the methods of the first wave, but was more ideologically representative of the second wave.

This chapter comprises two parts. Part one is an abbreviated retelling of the IRB narrative, with particular emphasis on the multitude of difficulties it faced; external and internal factors that influenced its organisation and personnel; and policies and plans that it pursued. The second part will analyse these details through the lens of modern terrorism and irregular warfare studies. The purpose of this chapter, set within this uncommon framework, is to illustrate how the IRB's ability to recover from defeat and adapt to changing political circumstances in the nineteenth century helps explain both its exceptional longevity and its successful revival in the early twentieth century. It will do this by answering four questions. First, how did the IRB adapt to the rapid changes of the later nineteenth century? Second, what was the role of the 'American element' in its development, operations and survival, and what were the inherent difficulties in that relationship? Third, how did it adapt to changes and innovate in light of the changing social, economic and political contexts during its existence. Lastly, it will discuss the extent to which all of this influenced both the IRB's role in the Irish Revolution and how resistance movements and organisations were modelled in the later twentieth century.

Origins and first decade: 1858–68

The origins of the IRB can be found in the Irish famine of 1845–52. The British Empire proved either unwilling or unable to cope with the disaster, which devastated the countryside. A radical faction of the Young Ireland movement launched a brief rebellion, but violent resistance was limited and largely ineffective.[9] Faced with desperate choices over the course of the nineteenth century, millions of Irish emigrated to the United States. In 1850, almost one million American residents had been born in Ireland, and in 1900 there were almost five million Americans who had either been born in Ireland or who had Irish parents.[10]

James Stephens and other survivors of the Young Ireland movement founded the Irish Republican Brotherhood in 1858.[11] Within a year, an allied organisation known as the Fenian Brotherhood was formed in the United

8 D.C. Rapoport, 'The four waves of modern terrorism' in A.K. Cronin & J.M. Ludes (eds), *Attacking terrorism: elements of a grand strategy* (Washington, 2004), pp 46–78.

9 Comerford, *The Fenians in context*, pp 17–18.

10 F.M. Carroll, *American opinion and the Irish question, 1910–1923* (Dublin, 1978), pp 3, 208.

11 McGee, *The IRB*, p. 15; James Stephens, *The birth of the Fenian movement: American diary, Brooklyn 1859*, ed. Marta Ramon (Dublin, 2009).

States by John O'Mahony. Both organisations sought to secretly build an army of Irish, recruited on both sides of the Atlantic, to liberate Ireland from British rule.[12] Initially, it was hoped that the IRB would provide the manpower, while the Fenians provided the 'sinews of war' (arms, stores, officers).[13]

These aspirational plans accelerated dramatically owing to the American Civil War (1861–65). With tens of thousands of Irishmen fighting on both sides, the potential pool of arms, stores and trained officers and men in America increased significantly.[14] Efforts by the IRB to infiltrate the British army and recruit Irish soldiers to the republican cause also looked promising.[15] But what appeared to be a close alliance between Irish leaders on both sides of the Atlantic was illusory. Both O'Mahony and Stephens were trying to take sole control of both organisations.[16] In addition, the American side was divided between a faction led by O'Mahony, who sought decision in Ireland, and another, led by William R. Roberts, that sought to invade Canada and attack the British Empire indirectly.[17]

In September 1865, a British raid on the headquarters of the *Irish People* – the IRB's journal – captured most of the IRB leadership, large amounts of funds and incriminating correspondence.[18] Stephens fled to the United States, and, desperate to maintain access to American funds, soon proclaimed 1866 as the year of decision.[19] The IRB, however, was unprepared for a major rising.[20] The capture of much of the IRB leadership undermined mobilisation and planning, and the British army in Ireland dismissed soldiers suspected of nationalist sympathies in early 1866. Habeas Corpus was suspended, and over a thousand potential rebels were arrested over the next eighteen months.[21]

Ambitious plans for a rebellion in Ireland, therefore, collapsed. The inability of the IRB to rebel in a timely manner pushed Irish-American support towards the Canada option, but multiple expeditions failed to achieve

12 Eva O'Cathaoir, *Soldiers of liberty: a study of Fenianism, 1858–1908* (Dublin, 2018).

13 O'Broin, *Revolutionary underground*, pp 2–3.

14 Christopher Klein, *When the Irish invaded Canada: the incredible true story of the Civil War veterans who fought for Ireland's freedom* (New York, 2019).

15 John Devoy, *Recollections of an Irish rebel* (New York, 1921; reprinted Shannon, 1969); O'Cathaoir, *Soldiers of liberty*, pp 118–38.

16 Stephens's preference for micro-managing and unwillingness to relinquish control of any aspect of the movement is captured in the title of an excellent biography: Marta Ramon, *A provisional dictator: James Stephens and the Fenian movement* (Dublin, 2007). See also Comerford, *The Fenians in context*, pp 120–1.

17 This check on O'Mahony's power came at the third Fenian Brotherhood Convention in September 1865. Comerford, *The Fenians in context*, p. 131.

18 McGee, *The IRB*, p. 35.

19 O'Broin, *Revolutionary underground*, p. 3.

20 Comerford, *The Fenians in context*, p. 124.

21 McGee, *The IRB*, pp 34–5.

any meaningful result.[22] At the end of 1866, Stephens met with officers in New York who had committed to supporting an Irish uprising and proposed yet another delay. The officers, led by Thomas J. Kelly, deposed him and committed to an uprising in Ireland in 1867. A raid on Chester Castle in England was planned for February 1867, but the castle was heavily guarded and the assault was called off. Some Fenian groups rebelled in the Dublin area in March and small gatherings elsewhere across the island quickly dissolved.[23] Despite years of preparation, the long-promised Fenian rebellion of 1867 failed owing to inadequate leadership, lack of arms, ad hoc planning and an inability to organise or mobilise members and potential supporters. The IRB leadership sent a 'Message to the Irish People' blaming the fractious American Fenians and announcing a break in relations with them.[24]

Adapting to New Conditions: 1868–78

Thus, some nine years after its establishment, the IRB appeared to be destined for failure, owing mainly to implosion and loss of support, such as that described by Cronin. However, the ability of both its Irish and American wings to adapt rapidly to these challenges ensured it survived beyond the challenges of 1867. In June of that year, in the United States, Jerome Collins formed a new organisation called Clan na Gael, which became the IRB's most important supporter in the coming decades.[25] After his release from prison and emigration to the United States, John Devoy became one of the Clan's leaders in 1874, and his leadership was critical to IRB efforts over the next fifty years.[26]

The IRB also reconstituted. On St Patrick's Day 1873, its leadership held a convention in Dublin to adopt a new constitution that reasserted the IRB's position as the 'sole government of the Irish Republic' and placed effective control of the movement in the hands of a three-man executive: the president, secretary and treasurer of the Supreme Council.[27] This created an effective decision-making apparatus that lasted for the rest of the organisation's existence.[28] The group's leaders also recognised that any successful

22 Comerford, *The Fenians in context*, pp 132–3.
23 Whelehan, *The Dynamiters*, p. 49; Comerford, *The Fenians in context*, pp 138–9; Padraig O'Conchubhair, *'The Fenians were dreadful men': the 1867 rising* (Cork, 2011).
24 O'Broin, *Revolutionary underground*, p. 4.
25 Carroll, *American opinion*, p. 6.
26 Terry Golway, *Irish rebel: John Devoy and America's fight for Irish freedom* (New York, 1998), p. 73.
27 O'Broin, *Revolutionary underground*, pp 6–7.
28 McGee, *The IRB*, pp 50–1.

rebellion would require mass popular support. As a result, Article 3 of the new Constitution read:

> [T]he I.R.B. shall await the decision of the Irish Nation as expressed by a majority of the Irish people as to the fit hour of inaugurating a war against England and shall, pending such an emergency, lend its support to every movement calculated to advance the cause of Irish independence, consistently with the preservation of its own integrity.[29]

This pivot towards cooperation with other nationalist groups opened new areas of activity to the IRB. The British government had likewise adapted in reaction to the 1867 rebellion, instituting police reform and new intelligence and security procedures. Valuable informers were recruited who gained important positions in both the IRB and the Clan.[30] London also began a series of political reforms that lasted throughout the nineteenth century, beginning with the disestablishment of the Church of Ireland.

As early as 1870, the IRB Supreme Council had encouraged its members to run for local office.[31] Another opportunity emerged in 1873 with the formation of the Home Rule League. This alliance of Irish Members of Parliament (MPs) sought to gain a modest level of self-rule for Ireland, while it would remain part of the Empire and Union. It offered, however, an opportunity for the IRB to inject more radicalism into a constitutional nationalist political party. This might take the form of disrupting and obstructing Parliamentary business to highlight Irish nationalist desires, something members of the ruling IRB Supreme Council practised as Home Rule MPs.[32]

Shifting from the physical force approach to support of a constitutional approach crossed, for the first time, two divides that were matters of intense, almost theological, commitment: constitutionalism vs physical force; and republicanism vs other forms of nationalism or political autonomy. As the Home Rule movement grew in stature and commenced more radical activity, there was a real danger that a substantial portion of the IRB membership might lurch towards a constitutional path. Again, such a transition, Cronin states, forms one of the most common ways terrorist groups end.[33] However, IRB members lacked the social standing (and, perhaps, charisma) to make a

29 'Constitution of the I.R.B. (Irish Republican Brotherhood)', Bureau of Military History, Dublin, C.D. 9/3. This is a typescript copy provided by Bulmer Hobson with a signed affidavit of authenticity as the Constitution in force from 1873 until 1920.

30 O'Broin, *Revolutionary underground*, pp 16–17; Peter Edwards, *Delusion: the true story of Victorian superspy Henri Le Caron* (Toronto, 2008).

31 McGee, *The IRB*, pp 43–4.

32 O'Broin, *Revolutionary underground*, p. 12.

33 Cronin, *How terrorism ends*.

powerful impact in political circles and, in 1876–77, its leadership resumed its opposition to members joining the Home Rule movement and expelled four members of the Supreme Council.[34] Charles Kickham remained the President of the IRB from 1873 until his death in 1882, trying to hold together an increasingly fractious and vulnerable organisation.

In the United States, Clan na Gael continued fund-raising, re-established connections with the IRB Supreme Council, carried out a spectacular rescue of prisoners in Australia and formed a Revolutionary Directory in 1876 to coordinate the next uprising.[35] In this period, Jeremiah O'Donovan Rossa began raising money in an ill-defined 'skirmishing fund', seeking to exploit modern explosives and other technology to attack Britain.[36] Clan na Gael worked deliberately to seize control of this funding, and by April 1877 the renamed 'National Fund' was heavily subscribed.[37] The Clan may have been attempting to take control of the transatlantic movement again, as it had under O'Mahony. Devoy and the Clan pressured the IRB Supreme Council into expelling Home Rule League members.[38] The 1878 visit of Dr William Carroll, one of the Clan leaders, helped revitalise the IRB in Connacht, south Ulster and north Leinster.[39]

The Clan and IRB also attempted to capitalise on international tensions over the Balkans, which almost led to war between Russia and Britain in the late 1870s. Clan representatives held talks with the Russian ambassador in Washington DC, seeking possible assistance for an Irish revolt. The Clan even considered kidnapping the Prince of Wales, and the Revolutionary Directory developed a plot to seize Gibraltar (Spain declined the opportunity to help).[40] The Clan also pursued modern technologies, including John Holland's 'Fenian Ram' – a workable submarine design that was eventually adapted for several navies in the late nineteenth century.[41]

34 McGee, *The IRB*, p. 59; T.W. Moody & Leon O'Broin, 'The I.R.B. Supreme Council, 1868–1878' in *Irish Historical Studies*, xix, no. 75 (Mar. 1975), pp 286–333.
35 O'Broin, *Revolutionary underground*, p. 9.
36 Whelehan, *The Dynamiters*, pp 75–81.
37 Comerford, *The Fenians in context*, p. 107, Whelehan, *The Dynamiters*, pp 82–4. Devoy's linguistic sleight of hand moderated the revolutionary tone of the fund and appealed to a much broader range of donors. When the fund was closed down in 1881, it had received over $90,000 in donations. Golway, *Irish rebel*, p. 142.
38 Comerford, *The Fenians in context*, p. 206.
39 Ibid., pp 207, 214.
40 O'Broin, *Revolutionary underground*, pp 15–19.
41 Golway, *Irish rebel*, pp 141, 147–8. The Clan ran out of funds for submarine development, so Holland took his designs on the international market.

Opportunity and Crisis: 1878–85

The release of Michael Davitt from prison in late 1877 created new opportunities for the IRB and the Clan. Davitt was appointed to the IRB supreme council and had a very positive view of the Home Rule movement, then led by Charles Stewart Parnell. The Clan took an interest in Parnell as well, and Carroll met him in both London and Dublin during his protracted 1878 visit.[42] Parnell reportedly told Carroll that he 'supported nothing short of national independence'.[43]

The result was a remarkable about-face by Devoy and the Clan leadership. In October 1878, Devoy contacted Parnell and offered him a 'New Departure', supporting Parnell in return for a declaration of self-government, agitation on the land question, exclusion of sectarianism, opposition to coercive legislation and advocacy for all struggling nationalities in the Empire.[44] Comerford argues that this abrupt rejection of previous policy was opportunistic and reflected Devoy's belief that he and the Clan now had substantial control over the IRB.[45] The proposal of 'General' F.F. Millen, a member of the Clan's Military Board, that all military matters in the IRB be placed under the control of a military officer from the Clan was yet another attempt to have American control over the IRB and operations in Ireland.[46] However, the IRB Supreme Council rejected the 'New Departure' and participation in parliamentary politics.[47] Devoy's control over the IRB (if it ever existed) proved short-lived, but he did agree to a gun running scheme, which would arm the IRB for a future insurrection.[48]

The formation of the Land League in October 1879 changed the trajectories of both the IRB and the Clan. The Land League straddled the conceptual border between organised violence and political protest. From 1879 until 1881, it was actively involved in clandestine violence, drawing resources and manpower away from the IRB, and became 'one of the most formidable popular organisations of the nineteenth century'.[49] The Clan supported the Land League as the closest approximation to a violent rebellion in Ireland at the time. The IRB Supreme Council, on the other hand, sought to distance

42 Comerford, *The Fenians in context*, pp 224–5.
43 Golway, *Irish rebel*, p. 97.
44 Ibid., p. 108.
45 Comerford, *The Fenians in context*, pp 226–9.
46 McGee, *The IRB*, p. 62.
47 O'Broin, *Revolutionary underground*, pp 16–20.
48 Golway, *Irish rebel*, p. 112. Providing weapons, even in small batches, was one proven way to keep IRB members committed to the cause. The Supreme Council reportedly told Devoy 'arms we must have or we have nothing': see McGee, *The IRB*, p. 61.
49 O'Broin, *Revolutionary underground*, p. 21.

itself from the Land League, fearing the Land War was creating violence that could not be controlled and for which the IRB was being blamed.[50]

The darker side of the physical force tradition re-emerged just as Parnell's influence began to grow. On 6 May 1882, Under Secretary Thomas Henry Burke and Chief Secretary Lord Frederick Cavendish were brutally murdered in the Phoenix Park by a group calling themselves the Invincibles.[51] Though made up former IRB men, the Invincibles were an independent group of militants who had become dissatisfied with the passivity of the IRB's existing leadership.[52] Their attack was condemned by all sides of the nationalist movement, however, and in fact allowed Parnell to strengthen his position as the legitimate voice of Irish aspirations.[53]

The Clan also contributed to the undermining of the IRB. Breaching the unwritten agreement that the IRB and Clan would operate only in their own areas, O'Donovan Rossa and his United Irishmen of America began a campaign of bombing in England in 1881. The technology of explosives had developed rapidly, becoming both more portable and more deadly than before. This new campaign prompted an immediate increase in IRB informers, as members sought to distance themselves from terrorism and the British security services infiltrated O'Donovan Rossa's United Irishmen almost immediately.[54]

Devoy resigned his seat in the Clan's Revolutionary Directory in 1881 to begin a new publishing venture. Support for immediate violence became a key discriminator in competing for support in a fragmenting organisation. In 1881, Chicago lawyer Alexander Sullivan was elected head of the Clan, on a platform of 'active work'.[55] The new leadership of Sullivan, Denis C. Feely, and Michael Boland resolved in 1882 to begin a separate bombing campaign in England and carried out a number of attacks between 1883 and 1885.[56] The tactics of the dynamite campaign alienated IRB supporters and was condemned by the IRB Supreme Council, who insisted that the Clan should not be conducting operations in the IRB's territory (Ireland and Britain).[57] Members of the IRB Supreme Council insisted that Sullivan and Boland deceived them on the

50 McGee, *The IRB*, pp 66–102, presents a detailed discussion of the IRB's complicated response to the Land League and the Clan.
51 Kavanagh, *The Irish assassins*; Kenna, *The Invincibles*.
52 O'Broin, *Revolutionary underground*, pp 24–9.
53 McGee, *The IRB*, p. 101.
54 Ibid., p. 83.
55 Golway, *Irish rebel*, p. 142.
56 Whelehan, *The Dynamiters*, p. 85. Sullivan's position on the dynamite campaign remains murky – he appeared to champion it in 1882, but later denied supporting it: see McGee, *The IRB*, p. 98.
57 Whelehan, *The Dynamiters*, pp 87–8. Boland deliberately misled both the IRB and the Clan about the campaign.

Clan's role in the skirmishing campaign.[58] In retaliation, the leadership of the Clan formally dissolved its link with the IRB.[59] The tensions surrounding the dynamite campaign again posed a significant threat to the IRB's continuing existence, severely damaging the cohesion of the transatlantic alliance that had propped up the IRB while encouraging defectors and informants and alienating potential support in Ireland.

The combination of the radical acts of the Land League, the dynamite campaign and the Phoenix Park murders also brought with them new threats to the IRB as they prompted a major re-examination of Britain's security services. From 1882 to 1887, the British government spent as much on secret service work as it did during the war of independence of 1919–21. It also established the Criminal Special Branch at Dublin Castle, which was the first permanent secret service organisation in the Empire and was created for the specific purpose of destroying the IRB.[60]

The disruption of IRB-Clan ties also reflected successful British infiltration of Clan na Gael. Henri Le Caron, a member of the Clan's Military Board, was a key British agent throughout this period.[61] Michael Boland, a member of the 'Triangle' leadership of the Clan, became de facto head in October 1882.[62] Boland and F.F. Millen (a member of the Military Board and British agent) organised the dynamite campaign without consulting Sullivan, Devoy or the IRB Supreme Council.[63] Patrick Sweeney, the treasurer of the Clan's Revolutionary Directory in 1882–83, was almost certainly a British spy, and his actions were instrumental in shutting down the Clan's arms smuggling efforts from London in 1884.[64]

Through manipulation of these and other agents, Britain was able to widen the split between the IRB and the Clan, undermine arms smuggling and other cooperative efforts, and discredit both the IRB and the Clan in the eyes of their potential supporters in Ireland and America.[65] The damage done to the IRB was sufficient to force it to shift its focus to propaganda and education efforts, and avoid any actions that might bring it in conflict with the

58 Ibid., p. 181.

59 Golway, *Irish rebel*, p. 156.

60 McGee, *The IRB*, p. 102.

61 Edwards, *Delusion*. Le Caron, for example, could provide details of the Clan's arms smuggling plans to the British. McGee, *The IRB*, p. 86.

62 Boland appears to have been a British agent – at a minimum his actions played right into the hands of the British secret service: McGee, *The IRB*, pp 124, 179. Whelehan is more enigmatic, arguing that 'some historians have identified him as a likely spy': Whelehan, *The Dynamiters*, p. 136.

63 McGee, *The IRB*, pp 105, 124. Whelehan refers to Millen as a double agent: *The Dynamiters*, p. 128.

64 McGee, *The IRB*, pp 121–2, 131.

65 Ibid., p. 124.

state.[66] With the IRB crushed and turned into a talking society, and the Clan on the brink of a major fracture, Britain's covert war against physical force nationalism on both sides of the Atlantic appeared to be won.

Stagnation 1885–1900

The dynamite campaign ended, rather abruptly, in 1885, at which point infighting in the Clan proved as crippling as it had been among the Fenians in the 1860s.[67] Sullivan left Clan na Gael and became leader of the new National League of America from 1884 to 1886. Devoy and Dr Philip Henry Cronin split the Clan, taking a third of the membership with them in a new organisation called the United Brotherhood, which the IRB recognised as the legitimate successor of Clan na Gael. In 1888, Devoy presented a series of accusations about Sullivan's misuse of Clan funds that humiliated him and discredited his former allies.[68] The energy and resources expended on American infighting, of course, could not be used to try to restore the IRB's fortunes in Ireland.[69]

Such fragmentation naturally led to declining commitment, interest and membership. The Clan's fortunes reached their nadir in 1889, when the Sullivan faction arranged for the murder of Dr Cronin, a key Devoy supporter in the Chicago area. The Clan, which had operated clandestinely for two decades, was suddenly on the front page of a lurid murder trial that reinforced the worst stereotypes of the Irish in America.[70] It took years of patient politicking by Devoy to re-establish the Clan's membership and influence.

According to British intelligence, the factionalism in the Clan was affecting the IRB as well.[71] Efforts at political reform that would undermine radicalism continued. The most dramatic of these were the efforts by Prime Minister William Gladstone, in 1885–86 and 1892–93, to pass a Home Rule bill. The defeat on the Second Home Rule Bill and the death of Parnell fractured the Irish constitutional consensus and marginalised the Irish party for a decade or more. It did not, however, reinvigorate the IRB.[72] Both constitutional and physical force traditions, by 1900, were splintered and in disarray.

66 Ibid., pp 103–36.
67 Whelehan notes that dynamite attacks continued in scattered fashion until 1900: *The Dynamiters*, pp 128–30.
68 Ibid., p. 182.
69 Golway, *Irish rebel*, pp 162–3.
70 Ibid., pp 167–8.
71 O'Broin, *Revolutionary underground*, pp 34–84.
72 McGee, *The IRB*, pp 212–31.

Although the IRB renewed its alliance with Irish America (in the form of Devoy's United Brotherhood), both financial contributions and arms supply efforts were curtailed, which in turn impacted IRB membership.[73] The IRB's keen awareness that changing conditions necessitated adaptation was evident in their adoption of a yet another constitution in 1894. Here, they placed greater emphasis on discipline, enforcement and funding while deleting Article 3 – that which encouraged participation in all forms of nationalist activity.[74] Nevertheless, IRB and former IRB members began joining new cultural and political organisations emerging at the turn of the century. Although the organisation remained secret, its members became increasingly active and influential in political and social circles. The IRB was instrumental in forming the Young Ireland Society in the early 1880s. It became deeply engaged with the Gaelic Athletic Association following its establishment in November 1884, and later branched into the arts, theatre, literature and new political parties.[75] In the early 1900s, current and former IRB members migrated to many of these organisations, recruiting a new generation of advanced nationalists untouched by the infighting of previous decades, infusing them with radical nationalist ideas and laying the groundwork for what would later become widespread resistance in the war of 1919–21.[76]

Why didn't the IRB collapse?

Given its turbulent history, one is faced with the question of how and why the IRB survived for so long. Applying alternative frameworks to the IRB helps provide us with an answer. While the organisation did not achieve its aims in the nineteenth century – indeed it was nearly extinct, with numbers dropping from around forty thousand in the early 1870s to just a few hundred active members by the close of the century – it survived and positioned itself to radicalise Irish nationalism as a political and social force. By 1910, the IRB had adapted to become a smaller, more covert and more coherent organisation,

73 Ibid., p. 220.

74 A copy of the 1894 Constitution can be found in H.B.C. Pollard, *The secret societies of Ireland: their rise and progress*, reprinted version (Kilkenny, 1998), *Appendix* I, pp 219–27. It is different in layout, style, and content from its 1873 predecessor (and from later versions in the twentieth century).

75 See W.F. Mandle, *The Gaelic Athletic Association & Irish nationalist politics, 1884–1924* (Dublin, 1987).

76 O'Cathaoir, *Soldiers of liberty*, pp 304–34. See also Senia Pašeta, 'Nationalist Responses to Two Royal Visits to Ireland, 1900 and 1903' in *Irish Historical Studies*, xxxi, no. 124 (1999), pp 495–6.

and one capable of capitalising on a range of new opportunities more than fifty years after its formation.

Re-examining Cronin's model for the ending of terrorist organisations, clearly neither achievement of aims nor transition to other forms of non-political violence applied to the IRB. It was not close, in 1900, to achieving its aims of establishing an independent Irish republic; it was also too established and too traditional to move into criminal behaviour or even, as seen in the 1880s, emerging forms of terrorism.

The IRB was, however, vulnerable to the other forms of organisational defeat. Implosion and loss of political support – identified as critical for achieving the IRB's goals – was a reality by 1900. The IRB had dallied with transition to legitimate politics, but ultimately rejected them. In that process, it lost substantial numbers of members to political movements (Land League and Home Rule). While the British were unable or unwilling to physically eliminate the IRB's membership, their infiltration of spies, constant monitoring through informers, and creation of new security forces and legislation severely limited the ability of the IRB to grow. Finally, the IRB managed to survive leadership turnover in the 1860s, the 1880s and the 1890s as well as takeover attempts from American leadership, and still recover in the early twentieth century.

It is this last point that begins to hint at the unique characteristics of the IRB. Many groups do not survive leadership transition – indeed, leadership 'decapitation' is a frequent strategy in counterterrorism efforts. The IRB, however, benefited from two important factors. The first was that it was a quasi-democratic organisation. Each constitution provided a method of electing a supreme council, from which the executive was chosen. Regular elections allowed both for leadership turnover (in the event of failed policies, age or disaffection) and leadership continuity. The IRB was remarkable in its ability to survive multiple leadership shifts. Stephens, Kickham, O'Leary and later Fred Allan and John Daly kept the movement functioning and viable, despite a lack of resources and a rapidly changing political, social and military context.

The second factor was the republican tradition, which predated constitutional politics and Catholic Emancipation. Physical force nationalism had a unique place in Irish history, with both the United Irishmen and Robert Emmet representing a pre-Union spirit of independence. Constitutional politics offered increased influence and autonomy for the Irish people, but always within the British Empire. The IRB, however frail, offered nationalists an alternative vision of self-determination, embedded in a tradition of episodic violent resistance. Ex-IRB members could be found everywhere along the nationalist spectrum, from the Home Rule Party to Sinn Féin, and in the early 1900s the IRB leadership encouraged participation in the widest possible range of organisations as a mobilisation and recruitment tool. The IRB recognised its inability to co-opt constitutional parties, but broadened the acceptance of radical nationalism in Irish society through its political and cultural outreach.[77] In effect, it played a 'long game', seeking to maintain and expand influence at the margins while waiting for conditions to change.

Re-assessing the IRB

The conservatism of the IRB's leadership allowed it to both continue existing and to adapt to the changing character of irregular warfare and political struggle over the course of its existence.[78] Rebellions in the early nineteenth century often began as a coup de main, usually aimed at the capital city as a centre of gravity.[79] This demonstration of revolutionary power would mobilise the people, creating both popular armies and partisan forces that would supplement the main revolutionary effort.[80] Terrorists, starting with the Russian revolutionary group Narodnaya Volya, sought a similar mobilising effect through the 'propaganda of the deed' – a symbolic assassination that would unite the masses in rejection of tyranny.[81]

The IRB leadership rejected both options in the late nineteenth century. Terrorism was seen as a self-defeating action – public revulsion at the Phoenix Park murders in 1882 harmed the IRB, and the bombing campaign was immediately condemned by IRB leadership. Small risings in both Dublin and the countryside had failed in 1803, 1848 and 1867. The constitution of 1873 recognised the need for mass support, but the IRB lacked the ability to co-opt either Home Rule or the Land League. It turned, instead, to using social, cultural and political trends as a venue for gradual radicalisation of the Irish public. In so doing, the IRB began to make the transition between nineteenth- and twentieth-century models of national resistance. As the nineteenth century progressed, the ability to raise massed revolutionary armies that could compete with conventional militaries declined – new military technologies,

77 As early as 1887, police estimated that twenty-three out of eighty-three Parnellite MPs had been Fenians before adopting constitutional politics. See Whelehan, *The Dynamiters*, p. 161.

78 T.D. Hoyt, 'The Easter Rising and the changing character of irregular warfare' in Enrico Dal Lago, Roisin Healy & Gearoid. Barry (eds), *1916 in global context: an anti-imperial movement* (New York, 2018), pp 18–28.

79 See Carl von Clausewitz, *On War*, indexed edition, ed. and transl. by M.A. Howard & Peter Paret (Princeton, 1989), pp 595–6.

80 The role of partisans and irregular forces in the American and French revolutions was discussed by nineteenth-century military theorists, see *Clausewitz on small wars*, ed. and transl. by Christopher Daase & J.W. Davis, with an introduction by J.W. Davis (Oxford, 2015).

81 Whelehan discusses changes in revolutionary approaches to violence in the nineteenth century, moving from insurrection to terrorism: see *The Dynamiters*, pp 27–69.

conscription and military professionalism widened the gap between regulars and ill-trained popular forces. In addition, the Famine created a demographic deficit for Ireland – in 1840, it had approximately one-third of the population of the United Kingdom; by 1900, it was less than one-tenth. A new strategy was necessary.

The difficulties that guerrilla warfare and broad national resistance might cause for imperial rule were recognised both by British military authorities and some IRB leaders in the nineteenth century.[82] Successful twentieth-century rebellions relied on a broader effort including regional or national mobilisation, international alliance, public defiance and guerrilla warfare. At the beginning of the twentieth century, an emerging new generation of IRB leaders, led by Bulmer Hobson, was beginning to move towards this type of strategy. The Boer War demonstrated the ability of a unified people to carry out protracted resistance in the face of enemy occupation and IRB leaders did look towards that conflict as an example of national resistance. Yet the IRB did struggle to mobilise and consolidate public support in Ireland and to develop effective means of combating the ruling state. This was a difficulty of guerilla warfare and national resistance that Mao Zedong later recognised and discussed in his writings.[83] Mao's theories of irregular warfare included careful consideration of the problems of weak revolutionary movements and strong governments. His theory of phases included, over time, a consideration of the notion of 'strategic retreat' – the ability, if necessary, to adapt to circumstances by switching back from a higher phase to a lower one, to protract the war and re-establish political support.[84] While the IRB's efforts do not perfectly mimic Mao's theories – relatively few revolutionary movements do – one can identify similar patterns in the IRB's activity throughout the nineteenth century as they adapted to changing political and social contexts.

82 Colonel C.E. Callwell, *Small wars: some principles and practices* (3rd ed., London, 1906), pp 31–2, 125–49. Bulmer Hobson identified the need for national mobilisation in *Defensive warfare* (Belfast, 1909), but also drew on earlier works of James Fintan Lalor, who argued for a 'moral insurrection' during the Famine and created a secret society dedicated to Republicanism and the physical force tradition that served as a model for the IRB. Ramon, *A provisional dictator*, pp 16–17, 53–7.

83 The first stage is one of strategic retreat and mobilisation, where the movement conserves its strength and attempts to mobilise political support. The second stage is equilibrium or strategic stalemate, when the movement controls territory and wages guerrilla warfare. The third stage is the strategic offensive, when the movement fields conventional forces and defeats the state's forces in the field. Mao Zedung, *Mao Tse-Tung on guerrilla warfare* (transl. by S.B. Griffith II) (2nd ed., Baltimore, 1992), p. 18.

84 Mao wrestles with these problems in 'Problems of strategy in China's revolutionary war' (1936), 'On guerrilla warfare' (1937) and 'On protracted war' (1938), reflecting the collapse of the Chinese Communist Party fortunes leading to the Long March, and the need to husband strength in a long war against Japan and eventually the Chinese government.

The American connection was also critical to this evolution. Overcoming severe leadership struggles in the 1880s, Devoy forged deep connections that gave him influence among both moderates and radicals in the Irish-American community. Both the IRB and the Clan faced problems attracting support from elites with resources – they drew their main initial support from the 'men of no property'.[85] In the early twentieth century, however, Devoy was able to make connections among Irish-American political elites. The American element of the movement could initiate or publicise new policies more effectively than the Irish leadership because of the lack of press restrictions and censorship in the United States. The Clan also arranged speaking tours for IRB and radical leaders, exposing an increasingly affluent and politically minded Irish-American middle class to the ideas of radical nationalism. That the American connection allowed the IRB to stay solvent and relevant was vital for generating international support and providing a sanctuary for exiles, and developed a new cadre of capable transnational activists including Thomas Clarke, Patrick McCartan and Diarmuid Lynch.[86]

The Third Home Rule Bill and the European crisis created new conditions for the IRB leadership to exploit in 1914. The unionist and Tory response undermined constitutional politics and the promise of Home Rule, particularly as the Unionists opted for creating paramilitary organisations to resist the law. The formation of the Irish Volunteers in response gifted the IRB leadership and Clan na Gael with an opportunity. For the first time since the seventeenth century, an organised military force was forming to defend Irish national goals. The IRB was well positioned to co-opt the new Volunteer organisation by infiltrating its ranks. The focus of the IRB, from 1913 onward, was to ensure that it exerted maximum control over the Volunteer force. It could use the military leadership of the Volunteer organisation as a means of radicalising nationalist sympathies away from Home Rule and towards separatism and a republic. The IRB's infiltration of the Volunteers, and Sinn Féin after the Rising, was accompanied by Clan na Gael coopting the leadership of the Friends of Irish Freedom in 1916, creating a formidable transatlantic alliance that coordinated the Easter Rising and cooperated in the war of independence. The Easter Rising was, in many respects, one of the last of the nineteenth

85 Attracting elite support is critical in irregular warfare – elites provide crucial political, military, economic, and intelligence support. See Jacqueline Hazelton, *Bullets not ballots: success in counterinsurgency warfare* (Ithaca, NY, 2021).

86 International linkages have always been critical for revolutionary and terrorist groups. Mao discusses international support in 'On protracted war'; Rapaport emphasises transnational ideological and diaspora connections in 'The four waves of modern terrorism'; and one of the leading volumes on terrorism identifies ethno-national, ideological and state-sponsored linkages as major factors in longevity and relative success. Bruce Hoffman, *Inside terrorism* (3rd ed., New York, 2017).

century-style insurrections, and the war of independence (1919–21) was a prototype for the irregular wars of the twentieth century.[87] The IRB, effectively, was formed in 1858 to fight one kind of rebellion – which failed in the 1860s – but adapted to help lead a very different one in 1919–21. Indeed, the IRB, and the combination of Sinn Féin and the Irish Volunteers that emerged in 1919, would become a model for future national liberation struggles.

Conclusion

Why did the IRB survive and even re-emerge in the twentieth century? The IRB (and Clan) demonstrated three important characteristics of successful revolutionary movements: persistence, adaptability and resilience. As Mao's theories of guerrilla war suggest, protraction is at the heart of revolutionary success. The longer a revolutionary organisation lasts, the weaker the state against which it struggles appears. Sun Tzu says 'no state has ever benefited from a protracted war' – Mao's theory exploits this dilemma, which is why protraction is so important in current revolutionary struggles.[88]

The IRB, despite significant challenges, managed to sustain itself and remain relevant throughout the nineteenth century. Faced with rising interest in constitutional politics, strong competition from the Land League for membership, conflict with Irish-Americans over control of the movement and policy, infiltration by the British intelligence services, and growing British reform movements in response to Irish unrest, the IRB persisted. Accepting that many members would resign over time and join other groups and causes, the IRB maintained a minimal military capacity as it turned itself into a radicalising instrument.[89] Although it entered the twentieth century as a diminished entity, it still possessed the reputation as the keeper of the republican flame and re-emerged leaner but more effective in the 1908–16 period.[90] The Clan also recovered, funding the Easter Rising and becoming a critical interlocutor with yet *another* foreign ally – in this case, acting as a coordinator for planning and resources between the Irish and the Germans from 1914 to 1916.

87 T.D. Hoyt, 'Military innovation in Ireland' in *Defence Forces review 2016* (Dublin, 2016), pp 9–19.

88 Sun Tzu (Sun Zi), *The art of war*, transl. and with an introduction by S.B. Griffith (Oxford, 1963), book ii, verse 7, p. 73.

89 See J.N. Shapiro, *The terrorist's dilemma: managing violent covert organisations* (Princeton, 2013) for an extensive examination of the managerial practices of over one hundred historical case studies.

90 Diarmuid Lynch, *The I.R.B. and the 1916 insurrection*, ed. Florence O'Donoghue (Cork, 1957).

The IRB also adapted to changing circumstances. It overcame failure and successfully reassessed what would be necessary for a future revolution in the 1873 Constitution, creating the foundations for a strategy of protracted national political and military resistance.[91] It attempted to adopt new technologies and rejected tactics that weakened their legitimacy – terrorism in particular. The low profile of the IRB, the marginalisation of the physical force approach for two decades and the prominence of active and former IRB members in Irish society created new opportunities for the advancement of IRB interests in the early twentieth century.

Most importantly, the IRB proved resilient. It overcame defeat in 1867 and adversity in the 1880s by maintaining its commitment to its goal – an independent Irish republic – while adapting its policy and its form and recognising the need for strategic retreat and renewed efforts at mobilisation. The IRB perpetuated a radical political tradition in an era where constitutionalism and moderation were both popular and effective in securing benefits for the Irish people. The IRB and Clan weathered dangerous splits, leadership turnover, informers in key positions (on both sides of the Atlantic), and government repression, all factors common in the defeat of other terrorist groups and revolutionary organisations throughout history.[92]

During the Irish Revolution (1912–24), the IRB adopted yet another form – a revolutionary elite, operating for its own (republican) ends, cooperating within (but distinct from) a broader nationalist movement that eventually became Sinn Féin and the First and Second Dáil Éireann. It became, in effect, a secret vanguard party, with Sinn Féin resembling the kind of popular/national liberation front favoured by Communist movements after the Russian Revolution as a means of gaining wider political support. The IRB determined to keep the military under its control and the physical force republican tradition alive, even if political leaders made compromises with Britain. This policy led to civil and military tensions in the last months of Ireland's War of Independence, increasing militarism on both pro- and anti-Treaty sides in the civil war (where major leaders were ex-IRB), and contributed to an army mutiny in 1924 that led to the disbandment of the IRB as an organisation.

The combination of persistence, adaptability and resilience allowed the IRB to move from one period of revolution (the nineteenth century, with its character of war) to a new one (the twentieth century and the emergence of protracted nationalist resistance). This allows us to compare it favourably to

91 Again, nineteenth-century military theory focused on guerrilla warfare as a problematic tactic. Col. Callwell's *Small wars* failed to detect the potential synergy of guerrilla tactics with national political resistance, despite Britain's experience in America (1775–83) and South Africa (1898–1902). This unusual blind spot continued in British small wars manuals in the 1930s, which did not try to take lessons from the recent Irish example.

92 Cronin, *How terrorism ends*, p. 201.

many of the other nationalist movements that followed it – an organisation that survived, adapted and eventually proved partially victorious over a sixty-five-year struggle with one of history's great empires. However, perhaps the most interesting aspect of the IRB and the Clan is how they both faded with a whimper rather than a bang, dissolving rapidly after the Treaty and the Irish Civil War.[93] The cause for which they fought, however, remains an element of Irish politics today, both in the constitutional realm in the form of Sinn Féin, and in the physical force dimension in the form of the remaining traditionalist or dissident republican paramilitary groups.[94]

93 The Clan continued to exist, headed by Joseph McGarrity, but shrank to a mere shadow of its former influence in both Ireland and the US after the establishment of the Irish Free State.

94 The views contained here are those of the author alone, and not those of the U.S. Naval War College, the U.S. Navy or any other branch of the U.S. Government. The author would like to thank two anonymous reviewers who exhibited great insight and kindness in examining an earlier draft of this chapter – it is much stronger because of their review.

Index